Great Lakes Steelhead

Great Lakes Steelhead

A Guided Tour for Fly-Anglers

A Steve Pensinger Book

Bob Linsenman & Steve Nevala

Foreword by Carl Richards

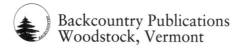 Backcountry Publications
Woodstock, Vermont

An Invitation to the Reader

With time, access points may change, and road numbers, signs, and landmarks referred to in this book may be altered. If you find that such changes have occurred near streams described in this book, please let the author and publisher know, so that corrections can be made in future editions. Other comments and suggestions are also welcome. Address all correspondence to: Fishing Editor, Backcountry Publications, PO Box 175, Woodstock, VT 05091-0175.

Library of Congress Cataloging-in-Publication Data

Linsenman, Bob.
   Great Lakes steelhead : a guided tour for fly-anglers / Bob Linsenman and Steve Nevala ; foreword by Carl Richards.
      p.   cm.
   "A Steve Pensinger book."
   Includes bibliographical references (p. 293) and index.
   ISBN 0-88150-312-6
   1. Steelhead fishing—Great Lakes Region—Guidebooks.   2. Fly-fishing—Great Lakes Region—Guidebooks.   3. Great Lakes Region—Guidebooks
   I. Nevala, Steve. III. Title.
   SH687.7.L55   1995
   799.1'755—dc20   95-30537
                                       CIP

Published by Backcountry Publications
A Division of The Countryman Press, Inc.
Woodstock, Vermont 05091-0175

Cover design by Julie Gray
Text design by Rachel Kahn
Photographs in color plates by Bob Braendle
Black-and-white photographs by the authors, except where otherwise noted
Maps by Mapping Specialists, Ltd., Madison, Wisconsin © 1995 The Countryman Press, Inc.

Printed in Canada

10 9 8 7 6 5 4 3 2 1

DEDICATION

*This book is dedicated
to those individuals who take an active role
in protecting steelhead and their environment,
to those who contribute advocacy,
time, energy, and resources
to the future of the sport.
To those of you who make a difference,
this book is for you.*

ACKNOWLEDGMENTS

We specifically thank the following individuals for their enthusiastic support and tireless energy in support of this project.

Canada: Jeff Black, Bill Boote, Joe Cain, Eric DiCarlo, Ray Ebertt, David Evans, Pat Furlong, Jon George, Larry Halyk, Judy Hammond, Bud Hoffman, Tim Horton, Jock Imhoff, Mike Jones, Trevor Kellar, Dawn Kemp, Steve Lebel, Ian McMillan, Bruce Miller, Lester Ridgeway, Jock Simpson, Scott Smith, Les Stanfield, Bruce Thacker, R.T. Thomson, Karl Vogel.

United States: Bear Andrews, Glen Blackwood, Bob Blumreich, Bob Braendle, Miles Chance, Doug Decker, John Dembeck, Jim Dexter, Dan Donarski, Jim DuFresne, Jac Ford, Kelly Galloup, John Hunter, Jim Johnson, John Kluesing, Rick Kustich, Fred Lee, Deb Lindner, Marc Linsenman, Ron Manz, Dennis Nevala, Tom Pero, Dave Peterson, Jerry Pytlik, John Ramsay, Bruce Richards, Carl Richards, Ray Schmidt, Dorothy Schramm, Jim Scott, Paul Seelbach, Jerry Senecal, John Skrobot, Glenn Snook, Steve Snook, Fred Vargas, Bob Willacker, Mike Yarnot.

And Countryman Press: Everyone, but especially Steve Pensinger and Carl Taylor.

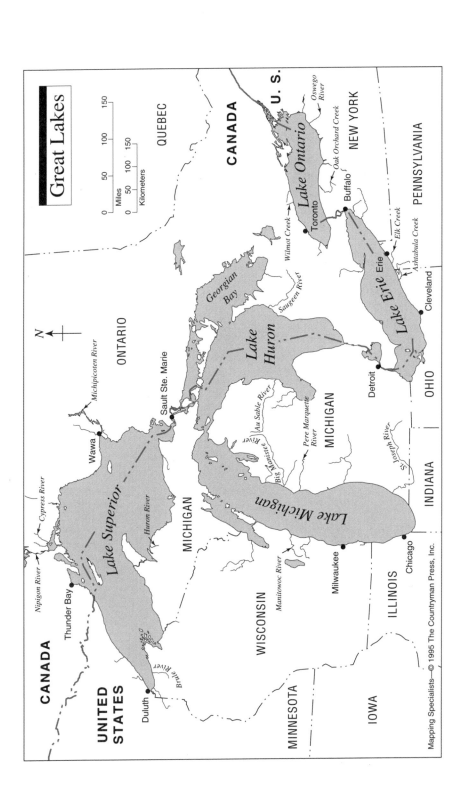

Great Lakes

Contents

Foreword

The Great Lakes Basin is a huge area with thousands of rivers, streams, and creeks emptying into the Lakes. Most of these waterways contain steelhead at various times, and some, like the Rogue River in southwestern lower Michigan, have very large runs. This little stream is only 3 miles long from its mouth to a blocking dam, but a few years ago more steelhead were taken in it during a 3-week period than were taken in all the rivers of the entire West Coast combined—during that *year*. Because the fishing is so good now, interest in Great Lakes steelhead is exploding, which makes this a much-needed book.

Some rivers emptying into the basin, such as the Big Manistee and the St. Joe (with the recent introduction of summer-run Skamania), enjoy runs most of the year. The Big Manistee is a wide, brawling river where steelhead fishing is like it should be. The summer runs are very good, and the fish take dry flies and wet flies just under the surface. No need for heavy lead, but long casts are necessary and the best casters take the most fish.

In this book Ray Schmidt, a guide on the Big Manistee, explains to the authors the techniques he developed for it. One of the most respected guides, conservationists, and fly-tiers in the entire region, Ray has created deadly fly patterns for his river. These, along with many other tiers' innovations, are beautifully illustrated in this book. The photographer who took the shots of the flies in the color plates is Bob Braendle. I consider him the best. He also took the color photos of the imitations for my books *Prey* and *Backcountry Flyfishing,* and his shots seem to leap off the pages. This book is fully illustrated with 4 color plates, 30 black-and-white photos, 13 line drawings—of stream habitat, casting techniques, and tackle—and 22 maps of the basin and its rivers.

The authors do a magnificent job of exploring and explaining the large and complex Great Lakes system, which has more fishing possibilities than any one person could master in a lifetime. They have created new methods of fishing for steelhead and ferreted out others created by some of the best guides and anglers in the region. All are clearly explained. Each significant geographic area is discussed fully, with detailed descriptions and maps.

With the introduction of summer-run fish, and the late spawning of fish in the St. Mary's, it is now possible for knowledgeable steelhead anglers to successfully practice their sport all year long. The operative word here is *knowledgeable,* and this book provides all the information needed for successful angling. For the beginner it contains information on steelhead life cycles, the biology of these magnificent fish, and the necessary equipment and most effective methods of fly-fishing for them. For the experienced steelheader it details many innovative techniques developed by expert guides, some of which allow an angler to eliminate the use of annoying heavy split shot and the chuck 'n' duck technique.

I know some of the guides in this book personally and can attest to their ability and knowledge. In the chapter on the Pere Marquette River, John Kluesing, a superb fisherman and fly innovator with whom I've fished, explains that you don't need to use the most effective (albeit offensive) method—egg fly with a heavy sinker—if you don't wish to. You can opt for several other methods that allow you to actually fly-cast and not lob lead. You may not hook quite as many fish, but you'll have a lot more fun both casting to and fighting them.

The chapter on the St. Mary's rapids is especially interesting to me. This is a beautiful stretch of classic pools and riffles that contains steelhead from early spring far into the summer. It also has a summer run of Atlantic salmon, and a fall run of pink and king salmon. If this river were in Quebec it would cost you three or four thousand dollars a week just to get on it. Here it is free. Dan Donarski, another very knowledgeable angler who has been my guide in the past, knows this water like the back of his hand and does a great job of explaining how to fish it. Last year my friend George Germain and I fished the rapids in July for Atlantics. We were using dry caddis imitations, and George hooked a fish in a pool on the Canadian side. We naturally thought it was an Atlantic salmon, so I grabbed my camera and got some shots of George landing it. The fish turned out to be a female steelhead dripping roe. An incredible feat: a hen steelhead on an active bed taken with a dry fly. This is a piece of water where anything can and often does happen.

There are chapters on other guides whom I know by reputation, and they present an abundance of information we all can learn from.

I used to believe the Atlantic salmon was the hottest fly-fishing target anywhere, but about 15 years ago I discovered the fall-run steelhead in Michigan. These are bright chrome, fresh-run fish that show up in late September on the Pere Marquette—earlier on some rivers. These fish follow the king salmon run in the fall, feeding behind their redds on the stray eggs, caddis worms, stonefly larvae, and mayfly nymphs that the salmon kick loose with their nest building. The steelhead actively feed, often gorging themselves. I have taken them when they were so full they regurgitated food when landed. This is a time when it's not necessary to place the fly right in front of the fish's nose. They are looking for a meal, and they will often charge clear across the river for one. I have seen them jump on a strike, land on the bank, flap back into the river, and dash three bends downstream, all in the blink of an eye. Nothing on the planet will outfight a fall steelhead—although summer-run fish can be just as exciting. Both varieties of this great fish are well covered in this book.

This important work has been thoroughly researched and very well written and is a must-have book for anyone with any interest in the mighty steelhead. It will not be read and then put on the shelf: It will be read, reread, and used many times as a reference by Great Lakes steelheaders.

—Carl Richards

Introduction

Steelhead (*Onchorhynchus mykiss*) debuted in the Great Lakes in 1876, hatched from fertilized eggs of Pacific Coast stock. That initial planting provided the base genetic pool for what is today one of the most alluring game fish in the world.

If you ask any serious fly-angler to list his or her "top five," you can be almost certain that the steelhead will make the list. Tarpon, salmon, permit, bonefish, bass, billfish, musky, and others will be popular, but the steelhead will likely be the dominant consistent choice.

Fly-fishing for steelhead has both its roots and its shrines in the Pacific Northwest. Pioneers of the sport struggled with the unknown and over time developed benchmarks in tackle, techniques, and fly patterns. The rules of the game as dictated by nature, the chilling, awesome splendor of wild rivers in raw valleys, and the untamed essence of the quarry inspired a body of excellent literature, art, and photography, still growing, that is both captivating and enlightening. Anglers' appetites for this sport have grown beyond the capacity of the Northwest fishery, and from around the globe they are turning to Great Lakes tributaries in pursuit of chrome.

This quest is undertaken virtually year-round in the Great Lakes Basin. The traditionally most dominant upstream runs occur in the spring, beginning in March and going into June (depending on latitude, weather, and species adaptation). Steelhead hit the tributaries again in the fall, staging in the lower reaches as early as September, with October, November, and December seeing peak angling action up in the rivers. Many of these fall fish hold over into spring. Summer strains provide a late June, July, and early August fishery.

Local television stations often highlight the steelhead fishing, and a northern Michigan station recently featured "man on the stream" interviews with three groups of touring fly-rodders. The first group, three men from Germany, stated that this was their first visit to the United States, and it was the Little Manistee and Pere Marquette

Rivers that lured them. A husband and wife from Reno, Nevada, made the journey by motor home (for 8 years running) to fish the flies-only stretch of the Pere Marquette, and a pair from Bozeman, Montana, admitted that they could chase steelhead closer to home, "but the fishing is much better here."

The success story of the Great Lakes steelhead is largely due to the dedication and cooperation of fisheries professionals in Minnesota, Wisconsin, Michigan, Illinois, Indiana, New York, Pennsylvania, Ohio, and the Province of Ontario. Thankfully the creature itself has proven to be wonderfully adaptable and, in relatively few breeding generations, has become "native." From the rugged coastline and brutal winters of Thunder Bay, Ontario, to the more temperate conditions near Chicago, Illinois, and Pulaski, New York, the steelhead has become accessible glamour.

This accessibility has had an interesting and welcome tangential benefit, a measurable increase in the sensitivity to and appreciation for the true elements of angling sport. Fair-chase, flies-only, catch-and-release, and concern for the environment and the beauty of the surroundings are more widely embraced each season. River "stewards" in the US and Canada are looking hard at fixing streams, rather than relying mostly on stocking. We also doff our drizzle-soaked caps to those who pause to pick up streamside litter and who financially support the efforts of the sport's conservation organizations.

We wrote this book with two hopeful intentions foremost. First, we wished to condense and present our experiences and observations from over 30 seasons (each) of gleeful pursuit with the long rod. This may help others, if just a little, in preparation, execution, and enjoyment of the chase. Second, and more importantly, we long ago realized that the Great Lakes fishery is so immense and geographically diverse that it is beyond the scope of two anglers to fairly present the breadth and depth of acquired, detailed knowledge in fly patterns, river profiles, run-timing, and effective methods. Because there is a lot of ground and thousands of rivers between Thunder Bay and Pulaski, hopeful intention number two was to chronicle and then condense the knowledge, personal philosophies, and technical approaches of some of the top fly-fishing guides and experts from representative rivers throughout this vast region into a format useful to both novice and advanced devotee.

We emphasize a practical, "how-to" approach, particularly so in the treatment of fundamentals in part I. This presentation is based largely on our personal experiences spanning four decades, often punctuated by learning (and relearning) the hard way.

In the face of climatic extremes that push the limit of human endurance and the physical properties of rods, reels, lines, and other tools of the sport, it seems appropriate to offer a base point on equipment suited to those conditions. The comfort zone at the frontier of fly-fishing is reached not just by the application of a large bank account to unexplored territory; it is also achieved at the thin line of nature's tolerance, and nature is never more whimsical than she is in the Great Lakes Basin.

Equipment, clothing, and safety are most appropriate topics for this volume; so are suggestions that might help you detect a subtle take, make a specific cast, read and understand holding water, and safely land, photograph, and release that steelhead of your dreams. Waders and clothing must protect when the thermometer is well below freezing, yet still allow ease of movement and provide comfort throughout a long day. Our discussions of techniques and tackle are, to reiterate, based largely on what has worked, and what continues to work for us. We want to provide the basics that will assist you in making the necessary cast to deliver the right fly in a likely hold at the right depth. We hope the steelhead takes your fly. If it does, maybe we have spared you some agony, no small part of which could be the stomach roll of buyer's remorse.

Flies and their recipes have been carefully sifted and represent favorites from throughout the region. Each has proven to be seductive over repeated seasons and has earned its designation. Within each pattern type—nymph, Spey, et cetera—there are entries from simple to complex that are most productive under specific conditions or in certain watersheds. We have made notations on use that should assist in the selection of a manageable assortment for an anticipated set of conditions in a given locale. As an example, a viable selection for a May visit to Ontario and Lake Superior's Cypress River will be distinct from a November assortment keyed to the Oswego River in New York.

Part II is the heart of this book. We worked (fished) with some of the top fly-fishing guides in the region with the hope of learning from them, sharing philosophies on the sport, and fairly reporting the special tips, techniques, and nuances each brings to the endeavor of attaching oneself, however tenuously, to the wild steelhead via the artificial fly.

It is a long way from the northwest coast of Lake Superior to the southeast shore of Lake Ontario. Scores of rivers enter this, the world's largest interconnected pool of fresh water, and each is different from the other. Each lake, each area of each lake, and each of the thousands of streams that feed the lakes is distinct. Not only have they forced genetic evolution such that wild steelhead are specifically adapted to each watershed in the Great Lakes, but they have also forced the evolution of method. The fly-fishing steelhead guides of the Great Lakes are top notch. They are, as a group and individually, as good as any you will find in the profession, and they have developed approaches to the sport that are productive in the specific requirements of their areas.

Obviously we could not work with all of the guides or local experts in this vast region, and, of course, we missed some who are absolutely first class (perhaps your favorite), but be assured that those represented in these pages are knowledgeable, hardworking, and dedicated. They are congenial, willing teachers totally committed to fair play and the preservation of the resource. Hopefully our anecdotal accounts of these trips will be helpful in your planning and fishing success.

Part III is a listing, biased though it may be, of a few of the more productive rivers (some covered in part II) best suited to fly-fishing in each geographic section. Our own experience and preferences, and input from guides, local experts, and fisheries professionals are represented. In addition, we have included a catalogue of information sources that will aid in preparing excursions to other rivers in the Great Lakes Basin.

How can the essence of this sport be fairly represented by simple words and a few photographs? What drives us to stand waist-deep in a heavy flow of 33-degree F (1-degree C) water with frozen rod guides and fingers numbed by a chilling fog? The fish and its environment dictate the rules, and our own natures draw us to the game. Melville's Ahab touched on this, albeit allegorically, when he spoke of what drove him to pursue his chosen leviathan: "He tasks me; he heaps me; I see in him outrageous strength . . . That inscrutable thing . . . "

The steelhead often sulks in deep cold and requires repeated accurate deliveries with slow, natural drifts and sixth-sense detection for success. This same animal ascends rivers in the full blaze of glorious autumn and heartily smacks a delicate Spey on a sweeping downstream arc.

And the steelhead brings out extremes, both the best and the worst of the human species. Poachers slither through deep cover and the mask of darkness with weighted treble hook and spear, while anglers invest heavily in the sport and treat the fragile resource with care and respect.

Great heartening strides have been made in cleaning up this, the world's largest freshwater system, but there are still threats to the fish, to the environment that supports it, and to the pleasure of sport derived from the combination. While DDT and PCB levels have fallen dramatically in the Great Lakes, we still need to be concerned about other dangers such as airborne pollution, storm drain runoff, and new chemicals. Animal-rights organizations have filed legal protests to steelhead fishing, and poachers, meat hogs, and slobs are real factors in the future of the fishery.

We urge you to patronize establishments that promote clean water and conservation, to support the national and local organizations that work for the future of our sport, to subscribe to and read the publications that feature steelhead, and most importantly, to become involved. Volunteer for stream cleanup, educate youngsters in sporting ethics. Make a difference.

PART I

THE FUNDAMENTALS

We intend in this first section to provide a basic understanding of, and a sense of perspective on, the sport of fly-fishing for steelhead throughout the basin.

Anglers should know some of the history behind the adaptation of the western steelhead to the fertile expanses of the Great Lakes and their tributaries, as well as the evolution of genetically distinct populations for specific watersheds. They should be familiar, as well, with the life cycle of the fish, its feeding habits, fighting capabilities, and what lies down the road in terms of better management. The thrust of chapter 1 is to capsulize this broad range of information.

Proper equipment allows all of us a wider and more complete enjoyment of the sport. Chapter 2 presents a *base* set of personal recommendations derived from decades of trial and error. Sport has few moments more miserable than those that present themselves to a poorly outfitted fly-fisher in pursuit of large, spirited game fish in cold rivers under climatic extremes.

We hope that chapter 3 increases your effectiveness in regularly finding, fooling, playing, and releasing fish. It presents a bit more than the pure fundamental elements of technique because our objective is to take readers beyond the level of novice. The information in this chapter, combined with practice and patience, should take you to a skill level that produces consistent results.

Chapter 4 is an overview of productive fly patterns currently in widespread use, either throughout the basin or within specific regions. *Overview* is the key word. Each fly pattern type has numerous specific dressings with countless variations, and it would be impossible to list them all, even in a dedicated volume. Local fly shops and particularly guides in an area know what the fish are eating and will be happy to share the information.

1
The Fish

Short of going to the sonnets of an Elizabethan or to the impassioned lines of a Cavalier poet, each trying to portray (and win) the love of a fair lady, you are not likely to find a tapestry of words richer than those penned by angler/writers describing steelhead. Every synonym for silver, every verb denoting explosive movement, every adjective for terrain and weather that means harsh—they weave colorfully into their tellings. Tattered thesauri abound; it is wonderful fun. And may these crimson-flushed writing shards of ethereal mercury slash their shimmering paths through our angling literature for decades to come. Steelhead *are* the stuff of piscatorial poetry, and they deserve our veneration.

Just what is this fish we pursue, protect, and describe with such avidity in the Great Lakes watershed today? Discussion of the species per se is a complex, lengthy, ever-changing story worthy of scientific treatises, one we will condense into a utilitarian overview. But whenever that "just what is it?" query comes up and thoughts are gathered to answer, an old remembrance recurs; it is that of two clueless, ill-equipped youths asking this very question after their first close encounter with this addiction-inducing creature.

Thirty years ago some forgotten saint idly remarked to Bob that if he liked stream trout so much (he did), he ought to test his skills on "those really big rainbows they call steelhead," that he had heard of a guy who had recently caught one in the Platte River near Honor, Michigan.

A few days later, in the lower reaches of that scenic river, Bob played a leaping, dashing form for many exciting minutes. Slow current and lack of snags enabled him eventually to bring the fish into the shallows on his little trout rod. I chased it around with the net for a couple more heart-stopping, advice-shouting minutes, and finally managed to fumble it into the meshes. Then we stood and stared, little realizing how this was to impact our lives.

"Is that a steelhead?" I asked. She had an iridescent blue back, a silver underside, and a head that seemed small for her 6-pound body.

"I think so," Bob answered, unsure because he had envisioned a red-striped side, of which there wasn't a sign. "Whatever it is, I want more." It was the most beautiful trout either of us had seen outside of magazine covers, and regardless of genetic strain, we haven't stopped wanting more to this moment.

In spite of greater publicity and the highly increased popularity of the species, today the name "steelhead" still provokes debate regarding its exact taxonomy. For our purposes when we say "steelhead," we refer to *Onchorhynchus mykiss* (formerly *Salmo gairdneri*), the migratory, or anadromous, rainbow trout. If we ever say "rainbow," we mean the permanent nonmigratory inhabitant of a river.

It is difficult to offer an "average size" estimate for a mature Great Lakes steelhead since varied strains (smaller wild Lake Superior fish, larger planted Skamania) skew the statistics, but on a "cut-me-some-slack" scale, naturalized mature steelhead caught in most tributaries average 5 to 14 pounds, with corresponding lengths of 24 to 36 inches.

Physical appearance varies from fish to fish, even among those of the same strain. One can be long and lean, another stocky with considerable girth. Coloration is not constant either, though mature steelhead of either sex fresh from a lake will be mostly whitish silver. Some will have backs of a bluish, gunmetal hue; others sport a more olive or gray-green back. The dark speckles of the salmonids dot their upper halves and tails. The classic rainbow red stripe becomes more apparent, particularly in males, as spawning time approaches, and gleaming red patches mark the gill covers of many. Those that remain in the rivers for extended periods will darken considerably, becoming charcoal gray and even black.

Today's steelhead have evolved from stock brought into the Great Lakes system in the late 1800s (most sources agree on 1876 in Michigan's Au Sable River), and have adapted well—with some peaks and valleys. The McCloud River (California) strain was Michigan's original fish of choice, and most other "Big Lake" states (and Ontario) got involved bringing in additional West Coast strains with varying degrees of success; what we have now in the Great Lakes are naturalized strains that don't have just one genetic link. They are an evolutionary product adapted through the "survival of the fittest" process to meet the differing demands of the varied watersheds.

This self-sustaining "wild" population is believed to be the major source of adult steelhead that spawn in most tributaries of the Lakes. Fish management emphasis is turning to better handling of wild stock, which, when allowed to, reproduce better and are a hardier breed. The increased use in hatchery experiments of returning brood stock from home streams to enhance wild steelhead runs is likely to continue to be supplemented with hatchery-reared fish where the need is seen.

There have been some recent marked successes with hatchery strains, the "domestic chickens" of the steelhead world, as the Michigan Department of Natural Resources fisheries biologist Dr. Paul Seelbach refers to them, with no disparagement intended. One of these "chickens" is becoming increasingly popular throughout the Great Lakes and merits some attention here.

SKAMANIA

In the late 1960s the State of Indiana brought the Skamania strain from Washington to provide a summer fishery. Other states experimented with various strains of summer steelhead, but the Skamania has proven to be the front-runner, and it is now stocked in each of the Great Lakes. The strain provides bigger fish, better returns, and fewer hatchery problems than other strains tested. Nor does it appear to jeopardize separate genetic stocks.

They were originally brought in to provide a viable nearshore fishery—and the bulk of them are taken in the lakes and river mouths—but they will run some streams and rivers of favorable quality and temperatures. Skamania can tolerate higher water temperatures and will remain active even at high 60-degree F (16-degree C) levels. Skamania *prefer* cooler temperatures and will slow down and hold in the coolest spots they can find if water temperatures go much above 70 degrees F (21 degrees C).

They come into spawning streams in June and early July seeking the cooler water temperatures found in deep pools and at the mouths of feeder streams. They eat little as they wait for their January–February spawning time, but will hit anglers' offerings. The Skamania are long and lean, very silvery, and often exceed 20 pounds. This and the fact that they fight exceedingly well, leaping and tearing about with wild abandon, have already made them popular trophies.

So far there has been no significant natural reproduction, except some reportedly in the State of Michigan, so it is more of a put-and-take fishery. Catch-and-release fishermen should be aware that released Skamania show a high mortality rate when caught in waters with temperatures in the high 60s F (high teens C).

BRULE RIVER STRAIN

Of the various wild stock being managed in the Lakes, the Brule River strain of Lake Superior steelhead is a noteworthy breed, one of those unique strains adapted to one certain river. Studies have shown that this fish, which runs in Wisconsin's storied Brule River, differs genetically from other naturalized steelhead in Lake Superior. If a Brule River steelie lives its full life span, it can reportedly reach 10 years of age, weigh 12 pounds or more, and spawn up to seven times.

Adult steelhead of any wild, self-reproducing strain in Lake Superior generally run smaller than those in the lower lakes. *Cold* Superior has only a couple of months when its surface temperature reaches the mid-50-degree F (13-degree C) mark, and its forage base is not as rich as that of the other Lakes, so a 4- to 6-pound steelhead is more the average. But the harsh environment allows only the fittest to survive, and the Brule River strain has stood the test of time and nature.

It is a beautiful, hard-fighting fish, and Wisconsin is working hard to maintain it in the face of such dangers as severe winters, predation, and overharvest. The latter threat is something the Brule River steelhead is especially susceptible to since, according to Wisconsin's Department of Natural Resources (DNR), around 80 percent of a year's run enters the river in autumn, making it vulnerable to anglers for several months (unlike most other Lake Superior tributaries which have comparatively brief spring runs). More restrictive seasons and a one-fish-over-26-inches size limit are steps recently taken to provide a stable future for this unique, hardy strain.

We mention the Skamania and the Brule River strains here to illustrate marked successes with both hatchery and wild fish management. Many other strains of steelhead wander the basin, since each state and province bordering the Great Lakes has planted countless thousands of fish in past years. Some of these governments continue to plant heavily and to experiment with new breeds. Michigan, for instance, while pretty happy with its proven Little Manistee strain, has tested many others over the years, among them the West Coast summer-run Rogue, Umpqua, and Siletz strains. How much, if any, of this and other experimental stock remain in the soup and/or have "hybridized" with other state/provincial planters like Londons, Arlees,

A typical slender Lake Superior steelhead

Kamloops Ganaraskas, Chambers Creeks, and so on is anybody's guess. And the coming years will undoubtedly see new varieties added to the immense Great Lakes "lab situation" available to our concerned fisheries biologists.

Regardless of genetic background, the Great Lakes "naturalized" steelhead all go through a similar growth process. Knowing this is helpful in understanding any strain and can ultimately be a big factor in taking steelhead on a fly.

A fertilized egg somewhere in a gravel riffle develops for some weeks (time contingent on spring water temperatures) until it "hatches" into a yolk-sac-carrying "sac fry." It absorbs the sac for nourishment and becomes a free-swimming fry, feeding and growing for the next few weeks to reach fingerling size. It winters in deeper water, and by spring is considered a yearling or parr. It feeds through the summer, and by fall is 6 to 8 inches long, but destined to winter once again in the river. The next spring at age two it "smolts" (turns silver), and hormonal urges send it downstream to whichever Great Lake receives that river's flow. But the smolt has been imprinted on that river.

It spends its third summer roaming the lake, feeding mainly on invertebrates and insects, and in its fourth year adds small forage fish to the menu. In the fall of that fourth year, the young steelhead may enter its natal stream or a stream in the same drainage, resplendent in chrome colors, much larger, and very robust. Once in the river, the "early-runner" feeds, then finds a wintering-over hole, darkens, and waits for spring. It doesn't spawn in the fall, but waits for the warming waters of spring. Joined by spring arrivals from the lake, it seeks the gravel to begin spawning when temperatures warm enough to trigger the urge.

Selecting a site her instinct tells her is right, then using her tail in a fanning motion, the female digs a depression, called a redd, in the gravel. Males queue up behind and beside her, jousting and sparring for favored positions. As she moves into position on the nest, a male moves up beside and a bit downstream of her. When she quivers and releases the eggs, the male releases his milt and the fertilized eggs fall to the rear of the redd. Gravel from the repeated activity covers the eggs, and the configuration of the nest prevents silt from smothering them.

Done with spawning, the steelhead rest, then migrate downstream. Referred to as "drop-backs" in many areas, they regain appetites and, eventually, the lake, where the fish school and feed throughout the summer.

The process of returning to spawn is repeated for the next 3 years, so that if all goes well, the steelhead's life span can be around 7 years. Unfortunately, the rigors of spawning make this "ideal" a rarity. The majority do not survive the repeated weakening of their body reserves and assorted other trauma, and it is an exceptional fish that lives to a ripe old age, spawning more than a couple of times.

You used to hear it more than you do now: "Steelhead don't feed while in the rivers. They strike out of instinct and/or aggressiveness." There is a large measure of truth to the second statement, but it's no secret anymore that they *do* feed in the rivers, particularly in the fall. We know *what* they eat and *where* they find it, but *when* they eat is still something of a guessing game—which adds to the fun and frustration of it all.

The fall fish come to the tributaries looking for food as well as a place to winter over and be in proximity to spring spawning areas. They feed heavily on the eggs of spawning salmon and trout (hence the popularity of egg fly patterns), and they pick up nymphs kicked loose by mating activity. In many Michigan rivers, for instance, caddis larvae (the green rock worm) are the preference of these fall feeders. In fact, a survey showed 30 to 40 percent of steelhead stomach samples contained caddis through January, February, and March.

*Steve Nevala caught this Lake Ontario male
during a warm spring rain.*

The bug of choice in the St. Mary's River rapids, for further example, is the green caddis—well into spring.

Mayfly nymphs are eaten also, especially those of the *Hexagenia limbata.* This nymph becomes active in the spring, but if there is a midwinter snowmelt, the steelhead show a marked taste for the "spring wiggler."

Winter fish tend to be off their feed more often than not, the natural result of lethargy due to slowed metabolism. Water temperature becomes a more critical factor in triggering feeding activity. Gener-

ally (this varies somewhat from region to region), if water temperatures are below 35 degrees F (1 degree C), you are in for a tough day;
35 to 38 degrees F (1 to 3 degrees C), worth the effort; 38 to 60
degrees F (3 to 16 degrees C), be there.

Later in winter and into spring, early black stone fly nymphs are
targeted, and once spring spawning begins, steelhead will, for whatever reason, pick up their own eggs. They also nab minnows and
other predators that stray near spawning gravel, more likely out of a
protective instinct than a desire for food. Occasionally spawners will
take a break, go off the redds, feed on nymphs, fry, invertebrates, or
the odd terrestrial, then resume mating.

This unpredictability in feeding habits drives anglers to distraction. You have in front of you a river full of fish who for 2 hours eat
nothing. Then, for no apparent reason, a switch somewhere is flipped,
and they eat—almost anything. Be it a minute change in temperature,
barometric pressure, solunar influence, water level, angle of the sun,
or myriad other possibilities, who can say with certainty? But you
may say with certainty that they will shut down again, leaving you
plenty of time to practice casting, change flies, or contemplate taking
up golf.

Since fly-fishers are primarily concerned with what steelhead eat
while in the rivers where they generally angle for them, that has been
our focus. But we would be remiss in not reminding you that while
prowling the Great Lakes proper, steelhead feed heavily on whatever
forage fish are available—herring, alewives, smelt—and as veteran
steelheaders remind us, "They do remember those baitfish, they do
remember . . . " And so should the fly-angler.

Once in a while we do remember. It just takes longer now. Even
years ago we used to go brain-dead for periods of time: On Michigan's
White River we once spent a good 2 hours working the only fish we
could locate. Every nymph, streamer, and egg pattern from every fly
box got a turn. It wasn't until we presented a Mylar-bodied baitfish
pattern that a take occurred—on the first pass. The fish had to move
6 feet to hit it. Did that fish remember its halcyon days in Lake Michigan where silver-sided alewives were easy prey? Maybe. We asked it,
but it wouldn't say, and that is probably the only way a totally definitive answer to the feeding propensities of a steelhead will ever be
obtained.

Since chapter 4 deals with specific fly patterns, as do goodly por-
tions of the "guided tour" section, we won't here go into patterns

that best imitate food items that bring about desired hook-ups. However they come about—probably through proper presentation of a reasonable facsimile rather than a perfect match of the food item—now comes the real test.

FIGHTING CAPABILITIES

The streamlined, muscular shape of the steelhead enables it to swim countless miles in search of food in vast expanses of open water, facilitates long journeys up spawning rivers through rapids and heavy current, and allows it to leap obstacles 5 or 6 feet high and then dash through shallows at 20-mph speeds. A fish so designed and so tested by nature and so avidly sought by so many sportspeople obviously has superior fighting capabilities—and these can all come into play, with an additional burst of adrenaline, when a steelhead takes your fly.

These inherent capacities for speed, power, and endurance, coupled with the fact that fighting tactics chosen by individual fish can vary considerably, result in encounters that are most often gloriously unpredictable. Regardless of where in the Great Lakes Basin you hook the fish or from which genetic strain it evolved, rarely will two steelhead, similar in all outward respects, behave the same as they endeavor to rid themselves of you.

One fish may take your fly so subtly you will set more out of curiosity. When hooked, it will bore to the bottom of the pool and hold stubbornly in place. No matter the wizardry you perform with graphite wand, the battle becomes a test of stamina and endurance. If the steelhead tires sufficiently before your tippet parts or your wrist gives out, it may come to the top, wallow a bit on the surface, and be yours to net or beach. *More* likely (same initial scenario), it will come to the top, take one look at you, and depart the general environs with some considerable haste, taking you into your backing and leaving you to stumble along in its wake.

Another fish from the same spot may smack your fly so aggressively you don't even have to set, and then immediately take to the air, tail-dancing in your face for a time or two before high-balling its way toward some safer haven. In smaller rivers we have had them rocket up into and back down through overhanging brush—two, three times—leaving fly line festooned crazily about as if some demented spider had been at work.

JAC FORD PHOTO

A stocky male in dark spawning hues

The next fish could be a head-shaker or a twister, making you hold your breath as you feel, almost hear, your tippet grating and scraping on its jaws and head as it rolls and contorts below the surface.

Steelhead are capable of numerous other maneuvers, plus variations on those just mentioned. It is not a dull sport when hook-up takes place. Nor is body size and weight a predictable indicator of the type of fight you can expect. A 5-pound fresh fish may stay subsurface during the entire battle, making you think you have something twice that size, while a 20-pounder with the girth of a tree trunk can cavort about in the stratosphere as might a 2-pound resident rainbow. This past November we witnessed the awesome performance of a Pere Marquette River 40-incher, well over 20 pounds, that came fully out of the water nine times.

While it is capable of the wildest, most unrestrained runs imaginable at the first sting of the hook, like a petulant child given a caress and soft words rather than a whack on the butt, the steelhead can sometimes be lulled by gentle treatment. On one stretch of the Little Manistee there used to be a bank-to-bank logjam with good holding water immediately above it, so close to trouble that the end of a drift would flirt with the snarls. Countless fish were hooked here, fought for frantic moments, and nine times out of ten lost when the fish bolted into the security of the jam. But one angler we watched landed nearly every fish he hooked in this spot by babying them. After a take above the jam, he would apply the gentlest pressure, trying never to alarm the fish into a panic dash to cover. Ever so patiently he would coax them with constant light rod pressure, eventually leading them to his net. If he missed out on the tail-walking, white-clouds-of-spray kind of fight of which the quarry is so capable, he gained a lot of personal satisfaction in outsmarting a wily adversary where others could not.

Be the fish a leaper, deep-borer, dasher, shaker, long-runner, in-close slugger—whatever form the battle takes, anyone who has fought a steelhead will own up to having had an exhilarating experience. But friendly arguments sometimes arise over the fighting merits of one strain versus another. Some anglers and/or writers contrast the Pacific Coast steelhead with the Great Lakes variety. The latter gets points for a greater weight-to-length ratio due to better diet, but the seagoing steelhead is touted as leaner, meaner, and faster due to its greater struggle to survive in the immensity of the dangerous ocean. The coastal steelhead, a proponent will say, may have to run hundreds of miles upriver to spawn, while the tributaries to the Great Lakes are generally shorter and tamer, therefore . . .

Similar debates are even heard over one Great Lakes strain versus another. A North Shore Lake Superior angler will likely claim that one of his smaller, hardened fish, say a 5-pounder, will dramatically outperform a 5-pound Little Manistee strain steelhead from Lake Michigan. For spectacular acrobatics, a Skamania will put others to shame, its backers will contend.

And so it goes. A challenging fish as geographically diversified as the steelhead is bound to inspire differences of opinion. We shan't enter into it here—except to offer a few lines Ernest Schwiebert once wrote: "I've caught Northwestern steelhead and also those in some Great Lakes tributaries. I've caught salmon in the Northeast and in Europe. Some trips have been better than others. Some fish have fought harder than others. But there has been no generalization possible, and I think I'll quite happily continue fishing for both."

Amen. We will be quite happy fishing for and battling any strain of steelhead, since each one that takes a fly has a unique gameness that makes it supreme among fighting fish.

We have lauded the steelhead for its beauty, challenge, unpredictability, fighting capabilities, and everything else with a round turn to it. But once one comes to know the fish, there is that which inspires even further reverential regard. It is a survivor. Look what it has gone through.

When steelhead were introduced to the Great Lakes region, lumber barons were ripping apart the ecosystem. The slash left from their indiscriminate timber cutting dried out and burned. Whole towns like Peshtigo, Wisconsin, and Seney, Michigan, were destroyed by resulting firestorms—with considerable loss of life. And while the lumbermen couldn't burn down the rivers, they did manage to heat them up. They took the trees; the loss of shade caused warming; the loss of root systems allowed runoff and silting, and much of what didn't silt over was dynamited to break jams. The huge logs then scoured river beds as they rumbled and scraped their bark-shedding way to the lakes. How do you like your new home so far, *mykiss?*

Progress continued into the mid-1900s and saw the construction of dams that blocked upstream spawning areas. Turbines and intakes at power plants chewed up cruising steelhead. The opening of the Welland Canal permitted the sea lamprey access to all the Great Lakes. This parasitic eel took a huge toll on mature fish capable of spawning, and alewives (eaters of fry and eggs) proliferated as the larger predator fish declined.

Winters can be severe all over the basin. During particularly cold ones, parr and smolt numbers decline due to hypothermia, low fat reserves leading to starvation, and injuries from anchor and crystal ice. Lake ice can block streams well into spawning time, and when it goes out, the grinding chunks, waves, and winds can shift sands at river mouths and further impede the passage of anadromous fish.

Chemical contaminants, animal predation, human predation (legal and illegal), zebra mussels—it all makes one wonder how any steelhead survive. It certainly should engender healthy respect for those that do.

This appears to be happening where it counts, at management level—and none too soon. There are a number of factors that are making fisheries personnel view steelhead as the fair-haired child of the Great Lakes sport fishery.

Studies have shown the contaminant body burden of steelhead to be less than in other commonly stocked salmonids: They consume a greater diversity of prey fish, they supplement their diets with invertebrates and zooplankton (thus reducing impact on prey fish stocks), the smolts enter the Lakes too large to be eaten by alewives, and due to the steelhead's life history variability, fishing pressure is distributed more equitably.

In view of these and many other pluses, anglers' associations and fisheries managers are showing increased interest in the species and are considering innovative strategies to better its management. Michigan, for instance, is turning to computer modeling and has employed geneticists and anadromous-fish specialists for a more scientific approach to steelhead research. "We're starting to lay a much better foundation for the future," says Michigan Department of Natural Resources fisheries biologist Dr. Paul Seelbach, who has high hopes for this aggressive new PERM (Partnership for Ecosystem Research) program.

Whether we end up fixing streams rather than increasing stocking, or managing "types" of streams rather than individual streams as separate entities—whatever the studies show as the best course(s) of action—it is heartening to see decision making based on modern science. And it is even more heartening to see the Great Lakes steelhead become the focus of such concern.

2
Equipment and Safety

Many of us look at the popularity explosion of fly-fishing with mixed emotions. On the down side, our rivers see much more angler traffic, which makes steelhead nervous, which, in turn, forces us to be smarter. But a truly objective view of this phenomenon also gives evidence to heightened concern by this growing body, and thusly, our rivers have more friends—individual and corporate.

The corporate friends have vested interests (as do we all) in the preservation and rejuvenation of the resource because many of them manufacture, distribute, or retail the toys—rods, reels, waders, lines, clothing, and endless gear—we love and covet so intensely, our passion fueled by technological advances, artistic refinement, and precise, strategic marketing.

In this chapter we endeavor to present a fair analysis and a set of basic recommendations based on our personal, hands-on experiences over the past 30 years. You will see we don't always agree with the preferences of the guides profiled later in the book. But differing opinions are part of what makes fly-fishing for steelhead the ultimate sport. Opinion and preference foster competition, which develops better products, which, in turn, promotes more discussion. It is all great fun and a vital element in the larger game.

Another significant factor that affects our enjoyment of the sport is safety—which translates to peace of mind. Ours can be a game of risk involving real hazards in wading and exposure. In the Great Lakes Basin we do not push the envelope of sport by throwing a heavy wallet at the costly exploration of exotic destinations, but we definitely push the outer limits of human endurance in climatic extremes.

Common sense is the key to minimizing personal danger, and later in this chapter we add to that element some of our observations and suggestions based on diverse encounters with heavy, frigid current, unsure footing, and biting winds.

FLY RODS

Steelhead anglers are beneficiaries of considerable study by rod manufacturers and custom crafters as well. May this recognition and close attention long continue. So far, the results are impressive, with a proliferation of quality merchandise designed for the special demands of the sport and consumers' whims.

The *basic, all-around* steelhead fly rod needs the power to deliver weight to distance with control, but not so much as to require exceptionally high line speeds for efficient and accurate casting. It needs the strength and backbone to subdue large fish quickly. Further, the rod must have sufficient length to facilitate mending and line control. It should be comfortable to fish for several hours, and lastly, it should be durable. Currently, graphite is the material of choice for most anglers.

The translation of all this into specifications reads as follows: The rod should be at least 9 feet in length, with 9½ or even 10 feet preferred. It should accommodate a 7- or 8-weight line.

Beyond this minimalist approach it is comforting to have a heavier rod—say a 9- or 10-weight of 9 or 9½ feet for throwing large streamers in the wind tunnels so common on our largest rivers. And you may well succumb to the siren song of Spey rods. They are fantastic tools for controlling line on complex drifts and for throwing precise, lengthy roll casts, and they are pleasant to use. A lighter tool, perhaps a multipiece travel rod for a 6-weight line, can deliver *most* of what the sport demands (and can be a real advantage in forced marches through the heavy bush near wilderness streams), but it is a disservice to the sport to use anything with less power.

"Noodle rods" (named for their longer length and very soft action) are effective in presenting a fly on gossamer tippets. And that soft, spongy action protects the tippet somewhat in any contest between fish and angler, but this results in an encounter so prolonged that the fish often dies. Additionally, the time it takes for a noodle rod user to subdue a large fish unfairly monopolizes a stretch of water and frequently irritates fellow anglers. It is more sporting to use a rod suited to steelhead and their environment.

Quality production rods designed to meet the rigorous demands of the sport are widely available in North America. Today's rods are vastly superior to those held in high esteem just 10 years ago; improvements are likely to continue as producers recognize and address the growth segments of the larger industry.

Your local fly shops have a selection of brand names in various models; we suggest you take advantage of these opportunities to take several in hand and discuss their features with knowledgeable and objective professionals. Buy the best rod you can afford from someone whose opinion you respect.

We have fished, and continue to, a number of rods bearing different brand names. They are all reliable performers, but we have developed some strong preferences. The rod I reach for most often is a Graphite-USA, 9½-foot, 8-weight. It is reasonably priced, handsome, and nearly bulletproof. Steve fishes a 10-foot, 8-weight Winston and a 9-foot, 9-weight Graphite-USA in fairly equal proportion. Both suit his casting style and sense of touch.

Spey rods become more popular each season and are now available in varying lengths for different line weights. Sage, Winston, Gold 'N West, Scott, and Graphite-USA make superb rods that reflect design and engineering considerations of Great Lakes conditions as well as a commitment to quality. As with our "standard" steelhead rods, Graphite-USA Spey models have emerged as favorites due, in part, to their incredible strength and durability.

Custom fly-rod crafters offer anglers more than cosmetic variations in appearance. They can specifically adapt the total configuration and performance of the end product to meet precise requirements. They can make a travel rod with saltwater components to serve dual purposes. They will utilize oversized guides to facilitate longer casts or to delay freeze-ups in subzero temperatures, and they can and will work with customers to accommodate special, human physical conditions.

Dorothy Schramm of Pentwater, Michigan, has been crafting special-order rods for many years, and her customer base continues to grow. She pays special attention to both the primary intended use (example—steelhead on large rivers) and any possible secondary application (example—bonefish on the flats). She concerns herself with the comfort of the angler with the rod and addresses physical characteristics such as hand size most carefully.

Jerry Pytlik of Bay City, Michigan, agrees with Dorothy's approach and has gone so far as to design a special cork grip for cold-weather fly rods that accommodates the gloves that the angler will often be wearing. He has built special jigs to control the shaping of his design, but hand finishes each grip to the customer's casting hand.

Dave Peterson of Richfield, Minnesota, produces stunning, functional rods for a wide range of fly-fishing applications. He has followed the boom in the market closely and pays strict attention to the special quality attributes required in fly rods for steelhead in northern rivers.

There are many custom rodbuilders throughout the basin who can create that "perfect" rod for you. We highlight Dorothy, Jerry, and Dave because we have fished their rods hard, and we have found them to be excellent. A rodmaker in your home area will be interested in your special needs or wants; if you feel a custom rod is the way to go, pick up the phone.

REELS

Here are our two absolute requirements for a reliable steelhead fly reel: It must be able to carry *at least* 100 yards of 20-pound-test backing behind a 7-weight, weight-forward line; it must have a strong, adjustable drag with smooth start-up and transition to high RPMs.

Now to the fun part (let the debates begin): The reel should really be a little heftier; it should have more line capacity so that with an extra spool, different rods and conditions can be serviced; it should be of proper weight (fully loaded) to balance your *primary* fly rod; it should be black or a dark color to minimize reflected glare; it should resist freezing or lock-up under winter conditions; it should be pretty and maybe even affordable.

With fuel heaped on the fire, we now reach for the gasoline. Many of the golden-hued beauties oft pictured against the backdrop of a straining permit or leaping tarpon are best left on the saltwater flats. Although their drags are superb, they seem to freeze solid at the mere mention of cold water. This is not a positive feature in a fly reel for the Great Lakes region.

As with fly rods, Steve and I have used and abused a number of reels over the years, and some favorites have surfaced. The following recommendations are made because we know these reels do the job; they have performed reliably for us, but in no way do we suggest these recommendations comprise the complete list of quality products.

The Abel reel is the spendiest on our list. It is a professional's tool, not a toy. The Abel's drag is near perfect, with fluid and uniform start-up and wobble-free, undeviating revolutions at high speed. Its frame strength is without peer; its finish, impregnable.

While fishing the St. Mary's rapids, I broke a fall from a 4-foot berm onto a pile of rocks with my outstretched hands, one of which held rod and reel. The Abel #1 met the largest boulder straight-on, driven by 200 pounds of clumsy angler. No broken bones here, and not a scratch on the reel's finish. And even the Russian judge gave me a 9.2.

Like the Abel, the Heron fly reel has a silent disk drag. It is a smooth operator with generous line capacity that has proven its dependability over time and under severe stress. It is moderately priced and freeze-resistant.

The Ross Gunnison and Cimarron models are efficient and cost-effective tools for both the committed and the casual steelheader. Both have reliable drags (the Gunnison seems to be a tad smoother) with an outgoing click and nonglare, matte finish. The G-4 and C-4 sizes have more than enough backing and line capacity and rarely freeze—even after complete immersion and retrieval in very cold air.

Scientific Anglers markets System II reels that have proven over the years through two product generations to be one of the "higher-value-per-dollar" items available. They meet all the requirements straight-on, with fully adjustable drags, rim-control spools, hard finishes, enormous line capacities, and affordable price tags. They are impervious to weather and are Butkus-tough, as is the new Harris Solitude.

We fish these reels day after day. They have not failed us. You will, of course, select the reel that you like, and there are a great many good ones to choose from. Just be sure it meets all of the "absolutes" and most of the "should haves" discussed earlier.

LINES AND LEADERS

Like most offerings in a competitive growth market, fly lines and leader materials get better every year. Scientific Anglers, Cortland, Teeny, Air Flow, and others pay attention to and manufacture quality lines for steelheaders. Specialized steelhead tapers, Spey tapers, floaters, full sinkers, sink tips, and shooting heads of high, weather-resistant quality are available in suitable weights.

These line types serve well under a variety of stream conditions, but each is best suited for a primary fishing application. A quick overview may therefore be helpful for planning purposes. The steelhead tapers are specialized weight-forward floaters with elongated, more gradual reductions in diameter, and stiffer cores. These features are most helpful in achieving long casts and in maintaining line control and mending over distance. Floating lines with standard tapers can be and often are put to good use by steelhead anglers. Both double-taper and weight-forward configurations see service, but the weight-forward is more useful over a wider range. A full-sinking line carries a uniform density throughout its length. The *entire* line sinks at a prescribed rate, and although these are the most troublesome lines to use (they are difficult to mend and to pick up cleanly for the next cast), they serve well in the deepest, longest runs and holes of larger rivers. Sink tips are the most popular type of sinking line. They feature a sinking front section (usually 10–15 feet) hinged to floating line in the front end of a weight-forward taper. These lines are versatile and easy to use. They are available in sink rates, or densities, that range from class I (sink rate of 1.5 to 2.75 inches per second) to class V (sink rate of 5.5 to 6.5 inches per second). Shooting heads are 30-foot lines that are attached to running lines and are capable of extremely long casts. They can be purchased (or made at home) in both floating and sinking densities. Teeny lines are specifically designed for steelhead fishing and feature 24-foot sinking tips hinged to 58 feet of floating running line. They sink quickly, offer good line control, and function well in very cold water.

To meet most river conditions without a hurried trip to the fly shop, one should have a varied selection on hand. We carry spools with floating weight-forwards and also use class III or IV sink tips as standard procedure. If we are going to fish bigger, deeper water, we load up with a Teeny 300 or 400, or perhaps a high-density shooting head.

Everyone has a favorite brand name in fly lines, and they are all pretty good. For whatever it's worth, we prefer Scientific Anglers.

Chemists and engineers seem to be working overtime in the leader material field. They are creating new synthetic chains as well as braided filaments that have (supposedly) increased our capacity to enjoy the sport by producing nearly invisible and nearly unbreakable leaders. It naturally follows that we will fool more fish, and, with the incredible strength of the new materials, rarely break off. But this stuff is really expensive and what do you do when your fly gets hung up on a rock or log? How do you break loose without risking a fractured rod, cut hands, or ruptured connector loop/knot to your fly line?

Our philosophy (by necessity) is simple. If it works, don't fix it. There is too much other stuff to worry about. With that consideration at the forefront, we recommend Maxima and Rio steelhead material for leaders and tippets. Both brands are abrasion-resistant, uniform, and retain their strength in cold water; they are cheap, so we can reserve our cosigners for larger items. (See chapter 3 for specific leader formulas.)

WADERS

Many years ago Steve and I stood on the bank of the lower Pentwater River. The afternoon shadows lengthened and the temperatures dropped. My partner shifted his weight, jiggled his feet, and exclaimed, "They're leaking! I bought these yesterday and the *@!* things are already leaking!"

"You should have bought the pair that were marked '100% waterproof.'" My comment to the effect that "100% waterproof" seemed to be the desirable number on a pair of waders was met with a cold, mirthless glare.

Today's waders, both boot- and stocking-foot, are vastly improved, and that is a very good thing because waders are the foremost, critical component for ensuring comfort and safety.

All of the guides who worked with us on this book and nine out of ten experienced steelhead anglers have made neoprene their fabric of choice. Neoprene is warm, durable, and relatively buoyant, and it remains flexible in cold weather.

Depending on weather conditions and hiking requirements, a choice can be made between stocking-foot and boot-foot models. Generally speaking, the boot-foot type is warmer while the stocking-foot, with separate wading boots, is more comfortable for walking.

Felt soles, while not required everywhere on every river, are highly recommended around rocks and gravel to secure and hold safe footing. For the most part, rubber lug soles are fine on sand-based streams, but you might want to try the St. Mary's rapids some day, and in that river rubber soles will likely introduce you to your long-departed ancestors. Felt soles are a pain in the neck in snow. Wet felt holds and condenses snow into uneven blocks that make walking clumsy and uncomfortable. Consider using strap-on cleats or chains under these conditions. Felt soles wear out and need to be replaced, but they remain the best all-around bet among current options.

Before buying a pair of waders, try them on. Make sure they provide enough fabric and stretch in the crotch and legs to allow you to step *comfortably* over a stump or to crawl out on a steep bank. Be sure they have sufficient room for layers of clothing, particularly in the seat-to-chest area. Remember that you will most often be wearing more layers of heavier material than what you wore into the store, and you will want to be able to bend and breathe as well as cast and wade. Also, neoprene's elasticity compresses heavy clothing against your stomach, and a tight fit can produce discomfort.

Prices vary widely and are generally reflective of overall quality. Pick a brand name you trust and try on a few pairs. We have found Red Ball, James Scott, and Glacier Glove waders to be comfortable, warm, moderately priced, and best of all, 100 percent waterproof.

CLOTHING

Steelhead angling in the Great Lakes Basin is frequently done in frigid temperatures. Don't worry about appearing in *GQ* or *Vogue*—go for warm and dry over style.

A layered, systematic approach to clothing will provide the most flexibility in meeting variable weather conditions. An underlayer of fabric like polypropylene that retains body heat but allows moisture to escape is the first critical selection.

For the feet, we have found that thin sock liners (silk works well) and wool or fleece socks make a good combination. There are now several quality brands on the market: We have discovered the excellent silk liners available from Winter Silks and a very warm and tough-wearing fleece sock from Acorn.

On the legs, hips, and waist use the aforementioned breathable underwear and a pair of light wool or light-to-medium fleece pants. Stirrups are nice as they will hold the pants in place rather than allow them to ride up when waders are pulled on. Or you can stuff stirrupless pants into stockings and get the same effect.

For the upper body—shoulders, arms, and neck—remember that freedom of movement needs to be accommodated. Start with the "wicking" undershirt; over this follow a light turtleneck with a light fleece (the "200" weight is about right) pullover with elastic or otherwise snug cuffs. Depending on the weather forecast, another layer of fleece or wool can be added.

A short, hooded rain jacket (*always* in the back of your vest) or a wind/rainproof wading jacket will provide the last layer of protection from the elements.

Although not always weather-induced, a lot of our problems come from the neck up. A turtleneck or neck gaiter is helpful in retaining

Winter steelheading requires careful layering of proper clothing.

warmth, and a head covering that will also insulate the ears is most desirable. Some kind of a bill is necessary to cut glare and eyestrain, and a baseball cap–stocking cap combination can be made to work. On a recent trip to the Great Lakes Fly Fishing Company in Rockford, Michigan, I found a new fleece product that is a complete head covering and Velcro-closing scarf all in one. It is very reasonably priced and I bought several of these "Handihoods" as gifts for shivering friends.

Eye protection is vital, even on dark, cloudy days. *Always* wear a good pair of polarizing glasses. And keep a soft, cotton handkerchief available to wipe water drops from the lenses.

We wear gloves more often now than we used to, and we both like to think that it is because the weather has turned colder as we have aged. Perhaps. But whatever the reason, gloves are vital to cold-weather comfort. A pair of silk liners will be much appreciated under wool or fleece outer gloves (for their quick-dry properties), and for *really* cold weather we have found liners under neoprene gloves to be an excellent choice. Among neoprene gloves you will discover a significant price range. Remember to try them on before you purchase them; be sure that there is a tight fit above the wrist. Glacier Glove neoprenes have Velcro closures and they come with effective liners.

We have found them to be a superior product. Any glove in any fabric will affect your ability to handle line, tie knots, and change flies. Bear this in mind.

Chemical hand warmers are marvelous inventions. They are cheap, long-lasting, and small. Carry a few in your vest. Once activated and slipped into pockets or gloves or wader boots, they produce a comfort zone for several hours.

You have probably noticed that there is no mention here of down clothing. This is by design. Down vests, jackets, underwear—you name it—are light and effective insulators, but they become worse than useless when wet. Fleece and wool, by comparison, can be "dried" by hand-wringing and swirling through the air; when damp they retain body heat, a distinct advantage over down.

VESTS AND TOYS

A steelhead vest needs to be short enough to allow deep wading, big enough (with numerous roomy pockets) to hold substantial gear, and comfortable enough to wear for long periods. In order to be comfortable, its design must accommodate weight suspension by even distribution and provide for freedom of movement over bulky clothing. And, it should be made of a dark, tough, water-repellent fabric.

Pick the vest that has the necessary features and that feels comfortable. Try on a few samples *over* your jacket. Reach in the pockets. Bend over forward and to the sides. If you like the pocket arrangement, if it feels good and seems to have too much room—buy it. Steve wears a shorty model made by Columbia and I have a Wheatley. It's a matter of personal preference; there are many models available to choose from that are carefully thought out and very well made.

How much room do you need in a vest? Or perhaps the better question is "How much room do you *want* in a vest?" Be your own judge, but here is a list of the contents of my vest (inventory taken in mid-December, one day *after* fishing the Rifle River)—one small plastic box (2½ by 3½ inches) containing assorted strike indicators, one pair of glove liners and one pair of gloves, extra set of keys for my Suburban, extra set of keys for Steve's pickup (He carries the same extras. This precludes callous, self-serving remarks like, "If you must cross here, give me the car keys"), pair of reading glasses, extra pair (mangled) of light-framed Polaroid sunglasses, small pocket knife, extra boot lace, kitchen matches in film canister, stream thermometer, hook hone, extra reel spool with a sink-tip line, folding tippet wallet with 12-, 10-, 8-, and 6-pound test spools and three mini–sink tips, fishing licenses in plastic zip bag, tape measure, pair of Abel pliers, two granola bars, two packages of split shot, one large (3½-by-7-inch) folding fly book for nymph patterns, one fly book for Spey flies, one fly book with Egg-Sucking Leeches, Woolly Buggers, and streamers, one small box with Micro-Egg patterns, compass, one extra roll of color film, partial roll of toilet paper in plastic zip bag, lightweight shorty rain jacket, four candy wrappers, piece of Styrofoam cup, and a litter bag. *On* the vest I see a retractor with nippers, a hemostat, a pewter steelhead pin, and a foam fly patch.

A vest cannot hold all of the gear one needs for fishing; it only carries the vital, the essential. For the rest of life's necessities one must have a *bag*—a big, tough bag with pockets and a padded shoulder strap. You will need enough pockets so that you can temporarily *lose* stuff right in the bag. Steve recently found his missing fly-tying vise in one of the pockets of his Abel "holds-everything" bag. He had been looking for that vise since returning from Montana several months earlier. I told him that he should never mix stream-trout gear with steelhead gear or fly-tying paraphernalia with fishing tackle. He agreed, and I'm sure he went right out and bought two more Abel bags.

So what *should* be in the bag? Who knows. Here is what I discovered in mine: System II 8/9 reel and extra spool, Harris Solitude reel, three large (7-by-11-inch) plastic fly boxes with "back-up" flies, wader repair kit, line cleaner, plastic folding cup, pair of Glacier Gloves and liners, neck gaiter, extra spool for Harris Solitude, three rolls of film, three pens, two flashlights, one butane lighter, one note pad, three bandannas, extra spools of Maxima and Rio tippet material, one HiD shooting head, one floating WF line, one class IV sink tip, folding knife, three packs of matches, two bags of split shot, extra stream thermometer, needlenose pliers, two hemostats, two small plastic fly boxes (empty), four chemical heater packs, one Croakie, small first aid kit, pair of cotton gloves, pair of boot laces, a dog whistle, a wool stocking cap, an Ontario road map, and a Mounds bar.

Strapped *to* the bag is another, smaller, zippered nylon bag that holds a Minolta underwater camera, several rolls of film, and two extra batteries. It is worth noting that this camera is only waterproof to a depth of 3 meters, but I reason that if I and the camera are together at or near that depth, a major error is involved and photography will be a secondary concern.

SAFETY

The only way to be completely safe and enjoy fly-fishing for steelhead is to pop a videotape into the VCR and snuggle into the couch. Total safety is a cozy lie in the northern outdoors, but *relative* safety is a sensible objective that is easily reached with just a little forethought and planning.

The tributaries of the Great Lakes do not typically feature the severe hydraulic gradients and spooky, freestone flows associated with western waters. *Our* rivers, for the most part, are more gentle in the discharge of their volume and *seem* safer. And there is the rub. They can lull an angler into a false sense of security, cause him or her to stay too deep too long, and then, when the overtired fisher turns to gain the shallows, they can topple and sweep and soak and kill.

Wading safety is a matter of common sense and caution. If the water looks too deep to wade, it is. If the current feels too heavy, it is—get out of there. When fishing unfamiliar water you should have a companion close by. Be prepared to lock arms and double-team any questionable crossing. Wear felt soles (maybe even chains or studs) where required, and carry, or cut, and use a wading staff in heavy flow and/or on slippery bottoms. Avoid walking on exposed clay or in deep muck and silt. Move slowly. Carry an *entire* change of clothing in your vehicle.

If an accident does occur, two deadly situations can develop quickly. If a victim has been underwater for any length of time, death by drowning is a real possibility. If the person is still breathing he or she will need to be treated for hypothermia, but if he or she is not breathing, emergency CPR is required. Take a class in CPR/Rescue Breathing. It could save a life.

Hypothermia can develop without warning. Symptoms include: uncontrollable shivering; vague, slurred, and thick speech; blueness or puffiness of the skin; stumbling walk; drowsiness/exhaustion; and, in the late stages, rigid or tense muscles.

Hypothermia is a serious situation and it *must* be treated immediately. If it is not possible to get the victim quickly to the safety of warm shelter for whatever reason, take emergency action. First, yell for help. Next, take steps to minimize heat loss: Keep the individual as *inactive* as possible; protect from the cold; insulate from the ground; remove wet clothing; wrap in dry clothing/blankets. Then take action to increase body temperature by giving warm liquids and using

JIM DuFRESNE PHOTO

In high water, stay close to a companion.

heat packs. Yell for help continually, and when it arrives, get the victim to safety/hospital as soon as possible.

Frostbite is painful, and it can carry long-lasting aftereffects. Symptoms include crystals forming on skin, pale gray or white skin, pain or blisters, and itching or numbness. Part of the treatment calls for immersion in warm (100–105 degrees F; 38–41 degrees C) water, but this is not likely to be readily available on a river. If warm water is not handy, wrap the affected area in clothing or blankets. If possible, exercise the affected area after normal color reappears and drink warm liquids. *Do not* smoke or drink alcohol. *Do not* break blisters if they appear. Get medical attention quickly.

Always, always wear eye protection. Not only do stout polarized lenses help you find fish, but they will shield your eyes from unseen twigs, branches, and speeding, feathered hooks. If an accident occurs, do not attempt to remove a fly that is embedded in or near the eye. Get to a doctor or hospital in a hurry.

Some of our best fishing weather and action occur in the fall. Often a fresh run of aggressive steelhead will show right around opening day of the firearms deer season. Be smart. Wear a blaze orange jacket or hat.

Our dementia leads us to proximity with other hazards: Determined anglers can find hornets and bees during the summer, maybe even a poisonous snake if they work hard enough, but the majority of safety issues arise during cold weather and in the water. To catch steelhead, anglers put themselves in harm's way to *some* degree. The trick is to use common sense and minimize the risk or retreat to the VCR.

3
Essential Techniques

There are methods, both simple and complex, fundamental and advanced, to our madness. In this chapter we want to present a mix of method and tactical strategy that will increase your rate of success in locating, fooling, landing, and safely releasing steelhead.

As in the development of fly patterns, there has been a continuing evolution of techniques over the past 30 years; it continues today. Specialized casts have been perfected and applied to distinct situations. A better understanding of the animals' behavior has widened our perspective on where they are likely to hold and so sharpened our ability to locate them. New knots and advanced chemical engineering have greatly improved the actual strength and abrasion resistance of our connection to the quarry and thus influenced our ability to apply extreme, calculated pressure, shorten the battle, and release vigorous fish with little harm done.

Our earliest attempts to catch steelhead on flies were painful—not just from the cold. Our understanding of the fish was lacking—we reasoned that since they are just big trout, they would act/react like other stream trout. The tackle we used was woefully inadequate; the few pioneer fish we managed to hook broke tippets and smoked a few reels. Thirty years ago we did not fully understand or appreciate the differences (sometimes subtle) in how this specialized game needs to be played.

Many failures, countless frustrations, and a few meager triumphs served to stir that early pot. Over the years our success rate improved significantly in direct correspondence to growing experience. The most important lesson we learned (and relearned) over the long haul is that the fish is adapting; there can be no rule cast in stone. The game can take an indirect shift, so our strategic approach should be fluid.

READING THE WATER

Coming from security (the protective deeps of the Great Lakes), steelhead ascend rivers in nervous moods. Instinctively they know they are more vulnerable in this skinny water, and they seek out the relative comfort of depth and structure.

They spend the first few hours after entry traveling rapidly. The urge to close in on their natal gravel drives them hard, and the fish stop infrequently unless they are slowed and tired by abnormally heavy currents or made even more timid by the obvious danger of low water. They make most of their rapid transit by night or in the low-light conditions of early dawn and late evening. Sunrise presents a series of pools and runs full of fresh fish holding in water that was totally barren the previous day.

Where should you look for steelhead? How can you narrow down the *possible* holding areas to the manageable few that are the most likely to harbor fish?

Remember that spawning gravel is the attractor and the paramount reason the fish are in the river. They did not leave the comfort of the lake and expend energy reserves in a dangerous environment just to munch a few stone fly or caddis nymphs. This is particularly true in the spring as ideal conditions for spawning converge, but even fall-run fish that will overstay the brutal winter want to be close to their ultimate target. Locate the gravel areas, and center your attention there and in the nearby *up- and downstream* reaches.

Steelhead harbor in specific kinds of cover, or water types, within a given river. Staging locations, rest stops, feeding and holding areas, and actual spawning sites are often representative of a wide range of such cover. Deep riffles, heavy runs (particularly those with broken, current-deflecting bottom structure), long sweeping holes, and diminutive, protected pockets are all utilized, but some are much more attractive to the fish and more productive for the angler than others.

Climatic conditions—cloud cover, temperature, barometric pressure, and so on—angler pressure, and boat traffic impact relative population densities in various cover types within a given area of your chosen river, but experience, logic, and consideration will enable you to find fish if they are present in reasonable numbers.

RIFFLES AND RUNS

Depth, bottom characteristics, and proximity to gravel are key elements that attract steelhead to runs and riffles. Flows 2 feet deep or less will more likely hold fish under low-light conditions when there is spawning gravel immediately under them or nearby. At depths beyond 2 feet all but the most crystalline rivers begin to afford some

Fig. 3.1 Pocket Riffles and Runs

Gravel

Gravel

Sand

Flow

veil and sense of cover and security to steelhead, and the fish will make more use of this water throughout the day.

Pocket riffles scattered through a gravel flat often host extraordinary numbers of active, eager fish. Look for smooth gravel spreads interlaced with small areas of lively, dark water (see Fig. 3.1).

These pockets will usually be small, perhaps as narrow as 4 or 5 feet and only as long as your car, but often they widen as they drop, and if you find an undisturbed pocket riffle that appears to reach depths of 3 feet with a width of 10 feet or more over a 40- to 50-foot length, you may have struck pure gold.

Fish these pockets thoroughly from as far off as you can with repeated, drag-free drifts. Steelhead that are most anxious to rush the redds will often station themselves near the heads of pocket riffles; it is a good practice to drop a few casts upstream so that your fly reaches proper depth and washes downstream as the current drops over the pocket's lip.

Cover the entire spread of a pocket riffle or run by starting at the head and fishing the water closest to you first (two or three good drifts are sufficient for the closest water), then lengthen your casts to cover the breadth of the run before making two steps downstream and repeating the process.

You will often be standing in fairly shallow water, which produces a very high angler profile and shadow. Remember to keep low, wade quietly and slowly, and keep your rod movements to a minimum. If the fish don't see you or your rod, if you deliver a decent fly on a drag-free drift, if you did not scrunch the gravel, and if you did not burn an orphanage before breakfast—you may strike a fish.

HOLES AND POOLS

We are not exactly clear on the precise distinctions that separate the terms "hole" and "pool" when applied to moving pieces of water (see Fig. 3.2). The words seem to be freely interchangeable among a high percentage of steelhead anglers. We think of a hole as a deep, dark bend in a river or as a sudden plunge into a black roil at midstream. Pools, in our personal lexicon, are classified as such because they are more subtle. They have more length, and although they may hold considerable depth, they seem more friendly with a gentle slope near one bank and a gradual tail-out. Holes are deeper and scarier. Their ominous churn insists on careful wading and suggests that something may lurk beneath the surface that you might not want to touch.

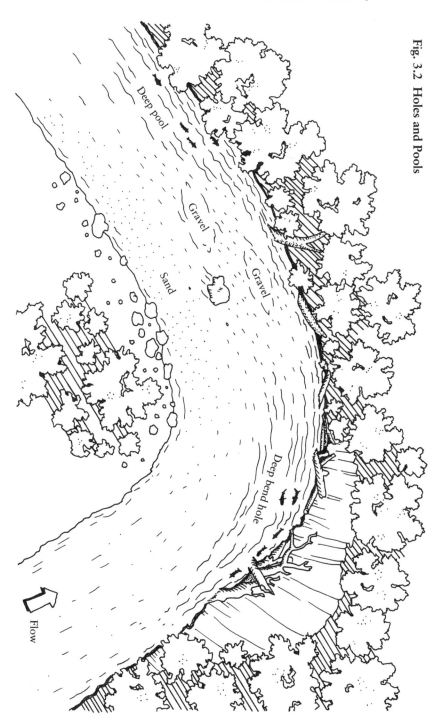

Fig. 3.2 Holes and Pools

Regardless of name, "Geezer Hole" or "Old Timer's Pool," these deepest sections of rivers often hold the most steelhead and need to be studied and fished thoroughly.

Cold temperatures, bright skies, fishing pressure, or simply the need to rest will move steelhead from other covers into concentrations in the deepest water. If the bottom of the pool/hole is broken by boulders, rocks, or submerged logs, so much the better. If the pool/hole is edged with a tangle of brush, or overhung by trees with penetrating roots, better yet. And if the bottom supports concentrations of large nymphs, you will likely find your quarry agreeable to your offerings. The "ideal" spot is deep with an irregular bottom but not so snag-infested as to grab all of your flies. (Guides who work for fly shops call such spots "retail holes.") They are edged with wood—either logjams, or tangles of roots and brush—and their silt banks support *Hexagenia limbata* nymphs. Least favorable situations present holes of moderate depth with clean, light sand bottoms and little or no wood structure at the outside bends. These look good, but their sterility is unattractive to fish.

A variety of methods can be applied to fishing these spots. Summer- and fall-run fish often chase and pounce on swinging, multicolored Woolly Buggers or shimmering Spey flies. As long as water temperatures hold above 45 degrees F (7 degrees C), a sink-tip line and an across and down swing with a "high-action" fly that breathes (example—marabou Spey) can be productive. At colder temperatures, particularly during the winter, or if the water has recently cooled a few degrees, slow, drag-free drifts with nymphs or nymph-and-egg tandems are more likely to pay off.

Always fish the water closest to you first, and it is a good idea to scrutinize the edge of the dark water very closely before casting or entering a pool because fish often hold near the *seam* of light penetration and visibility. A careless step or wayward cast might spook the fish you could have hooked.

The "hot zone" of any given pool or hole will vary, but it will almost always be near the deepest water and the heaviest cover. All pools and holes have discernible centers of flow where the current, however slowed by increasing depth and width, is visible. This is often near or roughly centered in the outside bend. If the main flow is in the center of the hole or pool, you will notice slower water on both sides, and very likely you will find a back-flow or miniature whirlpool near the outside bank. These slower side currents should be fished thoroughly, but most likely you will find the heaviest concentration of fish in the very heart of the main current and at the seams on both sides.

Fish these areas slowly and methodically. Maintain a dead drift and watch your leader/line connection or strike indicator closely. The take in slow water is often very delicate, with only a slight twitch as the signal of success. Mending your line to achieve a longer dead drift is critical, and often it is advantageous to employ several small mends rather than two or three larger efforts. Smaller mends are less likely to jerk your fly or otherwise disturb the drift, *and* they actually serve to slow the whole presentation down and, in effect, swim the fly in front of the steelhead for a longer period of time.

POCKET WATER

The "Tear Drop" is among our favorite pockets on one of the most heavily fished steelhead rivers in the entire Great Lakes Basin (see Fig. 3.3). It is narrow and short, but deep, with heavy brush on one bank. It is approximately 60 yards upstream from a deep hole at the confluence of the main flow and a substantial tributary. Surrounding the Tear Drop pocket is an expanse of rough gravel and cobble in a moderate run with depths ranging from 2 to 3 feet.

This pocket always seems to hold fish despite its diminutive dimensions. The "sweet spot" is about 8 feet wide and 18 feet long and is heavily edged by an overhanging tree with submerged roots.

Why do steelhead shelter in such small spaces?

Proximity to gravel is one reason, but the main attraction of small pockets like the Tear Drop is a sense of relative security. When low, clear water conditions combine with cloudless skies and significant angling pressure (any warm, sunny weekend), the fish first leave the riffles and runs and congregate in deeper pools and holes. If boat and wading traffic continues at a high level, the steelhead soon enough feel compelled to leave all but the deepest, most snag-infested depths (remember the "retail holes") for the sense of peace afforded by smaller, sheltered pockets. Here the fish are not pestered and will shortly mellow enough to eat a nymph or egg pattern.

Under these conditions steelhead sometimes stack up in small pockets in incredible densities. Often bypassed by drift boats and wading anglers in favor of deeper, more obvious holes, even a small pocket like the Tear Drop can easily host a dozen fish.

Small, dark flies such as Gold-Ribbed Hare's Ears, Sparrows, Black

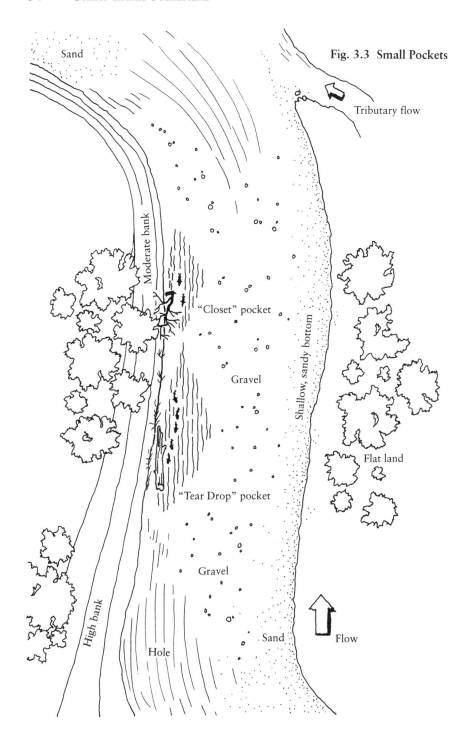

Sand

Fig. 3.3 Small Pockets

Tributary flow

Moderate bank

"Closet" pocket

Gravel

Shallow, sandy bottom

Flat land

"Tear Drop" pocket

Gravel

High bank

Hole

Sand

Flow

Stones, and Olive Caddis are usually the best first choices for pocket fishing. The steelhead have been harassed; they are probably still a bit nervous, and a subdued offering is often more effective than a larger, more flamboyant pattern.

As is frequently the case, dead drift is key to success. Drop your fly above the "lip" of the pocket so that the downward rush of water carries it to the proper depth quickly; you should be able to drift the entire length of the "sweet spot" with only one or two small upstream mends.

SPOTTING FISH

With all due respect to bonefish on the flats, it is widely held among well-traveled and experienced anglers that "bright" steelhead are the most difficult to spot of all the world's top fly-rod game fish. A steelhead fresh from the big water is a wavering filament of pewter-edged silver. It is an ethereal shimmer that shows its ghostly being more as shadow and reflection than form and substance. In addition to the neutral physical coloration of the animal, its preferred riverine habitat presents a mix of hues and shades, a jumble of irregular shapes and shadows, a blend of light and depth, and a broken, reflective, moving surface. Damn, they're hard to see.

Fish that have wintered over or that have been in the river for more than a few days absorb the impact of the environment and darken. They show the red stripe and black spots of a stream dweller, and males develop a noticeable kype and menacing appearance. These darker fish are easier to spot than new arrivals, but they still present a solid argument for concentration and Polaroid glasses.

Many rivers that host runs of anadromous trout exhibit, over their courses to their lakes, varieties of bottom configurations and water clarities that complicate already problematic issues. Other rivers maintain a set of dominant features or characteristics of flow that, when understood and accommodated, present some sense of consistency to the task of spotting fish.

CLEAR WATER

The St. Mary's River separates Canada and the United States at Sault Ste. Marie. The Michigan side of this international waterway boasts the Soo Locks and supports the vast commercial tonnage of the upper lakes. The east bank of the river is in Ontario and there the crystalline rapids host aggressive steelhead for many months of the year.

Here the steelhead up from Lake Huron shelter in invisible depressions, in the buffered drift of rocks and boulders, and in the scattered shade patterns of drifting clouds. They are the most difficult fish to spot we have encountered; this is due to a combination of the camouflage of bright steelhead and the shifting picture presented by the heavy flow of ultraclear, reflective water over a multihued, jumbled bottom. Seeing and identifying fish under such conditions requires a serious effort—a combination of stealth, patience, and deep concentration.

We learned to focus even more intently on the subtle shadows in wavering shards of light and dark by closely following the exemplary performances of Dan Donarski and Karl Vogel (see chapters 8 and 9). We honed our vigilance and concentrated on locating just part of a fish—tail, jaw, or telltale movement—lateral shift, side sweep of tail.

Above all we learned to look for shadows that run parallel to the current. Those that appeared to be between 2 and 3 feet in length were studied with the greatest rigor, particularly if they harbored near large rocks or boulders or happened to keep company with several other vague forms.

In addition to the value of forced, deep concentration, we learned that sometimes it's helpful to "memorize" the features or pattern of the bottom in a likely, manageable section of river. We now look for a nebulous form, puzzling feature, or unintelligible shadow that was not noted earlier. That "form" is then the recipient of dedicated scrutiny up to the point of its identification as mirage or steelhead.

Concentration is key. It is the only way consistently to differentiate among logs, rocks, shadows, and bright steelhead over a multihued, broken bottom. Concentrate and be patient. That shadow, if it is a fish, will move a pectoral fin, jaw, or tail. Keep at it. Clean the spots from your polarized lenses; adjust the bill of your cap to minimize frontal glare; cup your hands over the forward sides of your face to form a "light tunnel" with the brim of your cap. Look *through* the water to the bottom. If you think you noticed a slight drift of the shadow or the quiver of a fin, you most probably did. You have found a steelhead.

TURBID WATER

Roily or cloudy water gives steelhead a higher degree of perceived security. They are less concerned with imminent danger from above and are more likely to hold in open areas than under clear water conditions. That's the good news. The bad news is that the same turbidity that provides a sense of protective cover to the fish does, in fact, do just that—it makes them harder to see.

The protective screen of colored water takes on various tones and features in the Great Lakes Basin. The spate, fast-fall rivers of Lake Superior often carry the tea stain of cedar swamps or the hue of copper ore. The cobbled rivers of Lake Ontario take on a milky quality reminiscent of Alaska's glacial silt, while the meandering, ground-spring rivers (like the Little Manistee in Michigan) often show a mix of attributes dependent on the dominant ground features of the surrounding countryside.

The Oswego River in New York after a rain gives the impression of glacial melt. Even in shallow water the fish rarely show except as a sidewise, low-angle flash. The dark, tea-stained waters of the Jackpine and Cypress of Ontario's Lake Superior coast hide fish effectively under almost all water levels. Rivers like the Pere Marquette and the Au Sable in Michigan, and to a lesser extent the Brule in Wisconsin, ride giant aquifers through a gentle gradient. With a heavy sand base and stretches of silt and gravel through much of their course, they present a variety of conditions for the angler's study.

Spotting fish when the water *has* color remains a matter of patience and consideration, but since the fish are decidedly less timid, they are much more apt to congregate closer to the gravel shallows and are less likely to notice your approach or subsequent arm and rod motion. Look most closely on the gravel spreads and at the edge of the gravel near undercut banks and at the upstream rim of riffles and runs. Mentally draw a border around a manageable section of river and watch for movements of fins, tails, mouths within that area—before you move on to frame and analyze another. Remember to check closely around the edges of brush tangles and logjams. Often enough you will spot the tail of a fish that thinks it is hidden. That steelhead might be in an inaccessible lie for the moment, but it will probably move out to a fishable position later in the day.

A "spotter" can provide tremendous advantage. If you are fishing with a partner and you suspect there *may* be fish in a particular lie but cannot make positive identification, consider a team approach. One angler remains on station and the other crosses the stream, maybe even climbs partway up a tree to change the visual perspective and, perhaps, to direct exact placement of a cast.

Steve and I have often put this approach to productive use, and one of our favorite sections of the Pere Marquette was renamed "Dog Run" after a vociferous, swaggering yellow Labrador stumbled into a silent, staring spotter named Bob. The brief, unexpected encounter terrorized both players, and it was punctuated with a roaring bark, a scream, and the awkward, clownlike launch of the spotter from the bank into the stream.

You won't always be able to see your quarry, but that does not mean that steelhead are not in the area. If they are not visible, they will be near bottom in the deep runs, pools, and holes, and your efforts should be directed there. By *not* showing themselves they tell you their whereabouts almost as surely as if they were in plain view over a washed gravel bar in 2 feet of clear water.

Catching and releasing a fish that you spotted from a distance is a special thrill; it has all the elements of a successful big game hunt—analysis of cover, sighting, stalk, cast, with the added bonus of live release.

SOME BASIC CASTS AND MENDS

For most of our steelhead fishing the fly or flies must be at or near the bottom to maximize chances for success. In order for the fly to achieve proper depth, some dense form of weight is required. This weight can be in a sink-tip or full-sinking fly line, weighted fly or leader, or a combination. Regardless of form, adaptations in casting technique are required by this weight.

We must appreciate that high line speed is not an advantage. In fact, for most action in the Great Lakes Basin, high line speed is a distinct, sometimes dangerous, disadvantage. Imagine a weighted Stone Fly nymph, perhaps with a split shot a foot or so up the tippet, screaming past your ear. Hear the blowing leaves and the moving air as the wind rushes through the river valley. Feel the thud, see the stars. You have been "skulled." The wind pushed your rapidly accelerating forward cast just a bit off kilter and now you are on hands and knees trying to remember your name. Take heart. If the split shot and fly had not bounced off your head, they may have caught your rod under full stress, and you would now be holding a four-hundred-dollar splinter. Forget all the marketing hype about speed and distance. Slow everything down; maintain control and accuracy.

THE REACH CAST

This cast is a *basic* tool for steelhead angling. It significantly aids the rapid attainment of drag-free drift, and this is its greatest value. Most simply stated, the reach cast is achieved by an uncomplicated shift in direction of casting arm and rod through the power stroke of the forward cast.

Visualize the standard forward cast: Pick up with power between 10 o'clock and 12 o'clock, drift to 2 o'clock, slight pause, forward power stroke from 2 o'clock to 12 o'clock (O.K.—11 o'clock), then drift. Remember to slow everything down to accommodate added weight, if it is being used. Then all you have to add to the standard forward cast to achieve the reach cast is a shift in rod and arm direction.

Let us simulate a stream situation. Say the current in front of you is moving from right to left. There is a deep pocket that looks promising about 25 feet in front and 5 feet downstream from your position. You want to drop your nymph slightly above the upstream edge of the pocket so that it sinks to the bottom quickly. A drag-free drift on the first cast is critical.

Because a reach cast produces an exaggerated upstream belly—like a huge mend—in the line, it shortens the effective distance of your cast: 35 feet of line and leader will accommodate a fishing distance of 25 to 27 feet as an example.

So now that it is show time, you need to throw 35 feet of line/leader to fish that pocket. On your forward power stroke you will need to shift the direction of your rod-arm lever approximately 45 degrees upstream. Your rod has prescribed an arc to this point and pushed a loop into the line that falls on the water in an upstream curve. This upstream curve uses up about 10 feet of line and effectively aids the desired drag-free drift. The reach cast throws a large upstream mend while the line is still in the air.

Current flow often dictates that a reach cast be made with an across-the-body delivery to the angler's offhand side. This reach cast is slightly more difficult in that it demands making an awkward, unnatural casting stroke with timing and control. The shift in arm and rod direction to prescribe the 45-degree arc to your offhand side necessitates moving the rod arm across and in front of your chest in an exaggerated downward sweep from about 12 o'clock to 5 o'clock on the forward power stroke. The cast works best when the 45-degree downward arc starts from a high, extended arm position and is pushed with power down and across the body, with the rod-arm wrist locked and pointed to the target. The downward across-the-body arm sweep should bring your bicep very close to your face. Practice this a few times and you will find the motion, while clumsy feeling at first, delivers an effective loop in the fly line right about where you want it.

That is *all* there is to it. Practice this cast. You will find it highly useful in most of your future fly-fishing (see Fig. 3.4).

The downstream reach cast, although less frequently used than the upstream version, is occasionally required to effectively fish a side eddy, or to *accelerate* the fly's movement and raise its swimming angle through a shallow pool. The base instructions are the same as for the upstream reach. A 180-degree arc, either large or small, is prescribed by rod-arm movement in the proper direction—in this case, down-

Fig. 3.4 Upstream Reach Cast

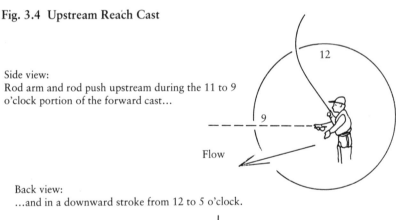

Side view:
Rod arm and rod push upstream during the 11 to 9 o'clock portion of the forward cast...

Back view:
...and in a downward stroke from 12 to 5 o'clock.

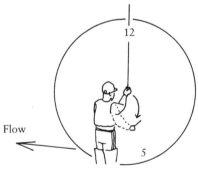

stream. We would caution that the downstream reach cast can impart greater speed to your drift and therefore suggest that a few trial casts be made with smaller arcs (which result in smaller loops/mends) so as to measure the acceleration and make proper adjustments.

THE ROLL CAST

Quite often in steelhead fly-fishing the leader is encumbered by one or more weighty and less-than-aerodynamic attachments. Strike indicators, slinky weights, split shot, and droppers complicate any cast and seem to affect the roll cast most negatively of all.

The theme needs repeating: Every part of the motion of the early part of the roll cast needs to be in slow motion. You are raising your terminal rig from depth. Your leader probably carries a strike indicator, a split shot or two, and perhaps a weighted dropper fly. You cannot raise this mess into a smooth forward roll without following this procedure:

With the line and leader under the water in front of you, take up the slack with your free hand, secure the line against the grip with your rod hand, and *slowly* raise the rod until the entire leader, with all ornaments and flies, is on *top* of the water. The fly line should form a *moving* loop that extends from the top of the rod down *behind* the rod and out to the fly. As the fly breaks the water's surface, continue the pull toward you by accelerating and extending the rod in the backward motion. The forward power stroke should start between 2 and 3 o'clock and be applied with smooth but exaggerated power through the 10 and 9 o'clock positions. There. You've done it without breaking the rod or denting your scalp (see Fig. 3.5).

With our backs frequently against a wall of brush, a roll cast is quite often the only way to deliver a fly to a likely position in the river. Practice until you can deliver a 35-foot cast with accuracy 90 percent of the time. That distance will cover most of your needs, and frankly, is about the effective limit for a weighted terminal rig on a 9½-foot, 7- or 8-weight rod.

THE TUCK CAST

The primary application of this cast is in pocket fishing. As we say elsewhere, steelhead often lie near the upstream edge of small pockets or depressions, and there is rarely enough water space to allow your fly to settle to the appropriate depth with a standard delivery. The tuck cast throws a weighted fly straight down, with speed, into

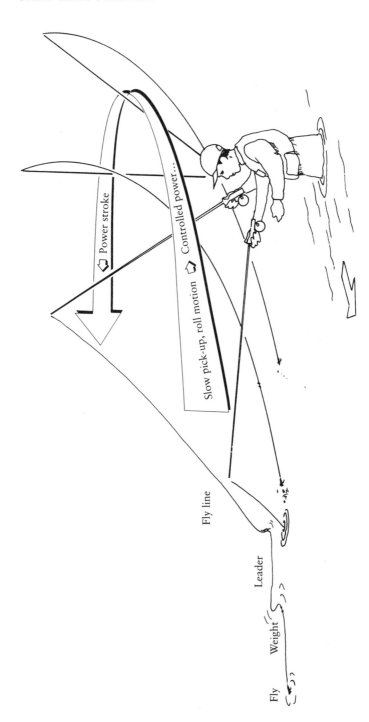

Power stroke

Controlled power...

Slow pick-up, roll motion

Fly line

Leader

Weight

Fly

Fig. 3.5 Roll Cast

the water. The fly (and extra weight if used) and leader precede the fly line in this plunge and the fly settles to depth quickly.

The tuck cast is made by applying additional power on the forward cast and making a hard, abrupt stop to the forward stroke at the 11-o'clock position. This abrupt stop shocks the rod, causing a violent, fast, forward-backward thrust. This *stops* the forward movement of line and leader, pulls it back toward the angler slightly, and then pushes the weighted fly straight downward. The heaviest weight—fly or split shot—will enter the water first, pulling the leader straight in behind it.

The effect is a near instantaneous delivery of the terminal gear—tippet and fly—to significant depth. The advantage is clear. In small, short pockets the tuck cast allows the entire area to be fished from head to tail, while a standard cast might require a drift through a major portion of the pocket before the proper depth is reached (see Fig. 3.6).

THE CHUCK 'N' DUCK

This is a controversial technique that employs a weighted leader rather than a heavy fly line as the propellant of a cast. Controversial or not, there are certain conditions that call for deviation from traditional methodology. Here in the great, frozen North we often fish in subfreezing temperatures. Frequently we are midthigh in 36-degree F (2-degree C) water, the air temperature is about 30 degrees F (-1 degree C), and the river is making ice—all day. The ice slowly builds on the roots and stumps at the banks, in the slow edges of deep holes, and most significantly in the guides of our fly rods. As often as not we are in a narrow slot with little or no room for a standard cast. The small hole in front of us is dark and *very* deep. If we are not shivering, either we have reached the second level of hypothermia, or we are properly clothed with layers of fleece and wool and warmly gloved. In either case, casting is difficult.

Under these extreme conditions the "chuck 'n' duck" delivery was developed, and here it finds the widest base of appreciative practitioners. Detractors of the chuck 'n' duck state bluntly that it is not fly-fishing. Some people say that angling with added weight is not fly-fishing. Others contend that fishing "dry" is the "One True Way," and some British folks adhere to the principle that the One True Way is with the *dry fly, upstream cast, only to rising trout.*

We have our opinions (and strong ones), of course, but it is not

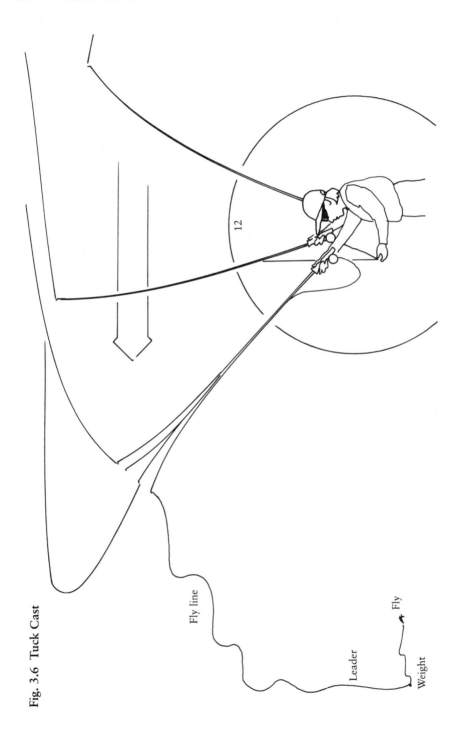

Fig. 3.6 Tuck Cast

Fly line

Leader

Fly

Weight

12

our purpose here to foment argument on proper fly-fishing—except to say that you need a fly rod, a fly reel, and a fly.

The point of controversy surrounding the chuck 'n' duck approach centers on the line itself. In most cases, a memory-free monofilament—like Amnesia—or a fine-diameter floating, running line—such as a level fly line of 1 or 2 weight—is used instead of a standard, tapered fly line. Since there is very little weight in the line, the weight attached to the leader carries the fly to the desired location.

So picture this. You have 60 feet of running line attached to the backing on your reel. Knotted to the end of the running line is a 6-foot section of 10- or 12-pound-test stiff leader material. A barrel swivel connects the butt section of 12-pound-test to a 2-foot tippet and your fly. A *significant* weight is attached to this rig, ahead of the fly, at or near the barrel swivel. This weight pulls the running line through the guides and propels the whole mess into the water.

The trick now is to get everything moving under some sense of control so that an accurate cast can be made. With your rod in the 10 o'clock position, let the leader and about 2 feet of running line out through the tip guide. Hold about 15 feet of running line in three or four large coils in your free hand. Now raise the rod past 12 o'clock slowly to 2 o'clock and back from 2 o'clock, slowly, to 10 o'clock. You have now created a moving pendulum with the weight as the pulling force. Take care to keep the weight of the pendulum and its arc to the outside of your rod to minimize the potential for graphite tragedy. When the weight swings forward through 8 o'clock (remember the arc and pendulum are at the bottom of the clock face) release the line in your free hand and the moving weight will pull the cast outward, hopefully to a point somewhere near the target (see Fig. 3.7).

This takes some practice. Take care not to overpower the delivery and firmly entangle your intricate rig in the trees on the far bank. When the fly and weight enter the flow, take up slack immediately to control the drift. Strike indicators are commonly used and should be positioned properly, depending on depth, on the butt section between the running line and the tippet. If you are using an indicator, lift the rod to clear enough line to raise the indicator to a visible position.

Some anglers, possessed of great daring and good insurance, advocate overhand delivery of this assembly, but we have found effective control a dicey proposition when this is attempted. Unless you like headaches, tying knots, and fumbling for more flies, work on a sidearm "chuck," both backhand and forehand.

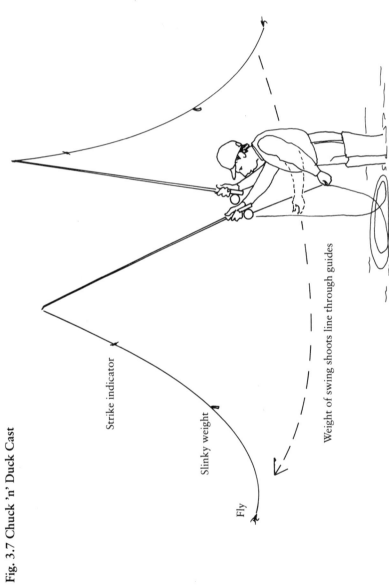

Fig. 3.7 Chuck 'n' Duck Cast

Strike indicator

Slinky weight

Fly

Weight of swing shoots line through guides

SIMPLE MENDS

Precise, artful mending is the best answer to twisting, conflicting currents, both those that are obvious on the surface and those, less so, hidden beneath, that cause drag. A reach cast will start the drift properly, but it must be nursed through to the end.

Mending line is a simple action, one that should be taken on nearly every cast and drift. An upstream mend throws a curve of line upstream, or *behind* the leader. This allows the fly and leader to precede the line in its downstream drift, ideally making the fly the *first* thing a fish sees. And by preceding the thick fly line, the leader and fly are less likely to be influenced by drag. Conversely, a downstream mend throws a curve of fly line *ahead* of the fly and leader, which serves to pull the fly more quickly through its drift. This is rarely a good move, but is necessary on occasion to move your fly into a chosen drift line when currents conflict.

To "throw a mend" in your line you need only to move your rod in an overhand 180-degree arc. This arc can be large, throwing a large curve, a "heavy" mend, or small curve, a "mini" mend. To throw a heavy mend you need to move your rod arm through the 180-degree arc: the bigger the arc, the bigger the mend. A mini mend is accomplished with little more than a flip of the rod tip in the form of the 180-degree arc (see Fig. 3.8).

A series of smaller mends, as stated earlier, is usually more effective than one or two larger efforts. Smaller mends allow continuous control of the drift and closer contact with the fly. Throwing larger mends often results in the fly actually being jerked out of its drift by the upstream energy of the line curve.

TERMINAL RIGGING

Opinions conflict vigorously when discussions turn to effective methods of presenting feathered hooks to steelhead. Advocates of full-sinking or sink-tip lines prefer short leaders—6 feet or less—and they often swim unweighted flies. Floating lines usually connect to longer leaders—as long as 14 feet with weight added near the tippet; weighted or unweighted flies are employed as preferences and conditions dictate. Running lines, either lightweight fly line or stiff mono, are tipped similarly to the floating-line rigs.

Regardless of delivery vehicle, the desired result is the same—de-

Fig. 3.8 Mending Line

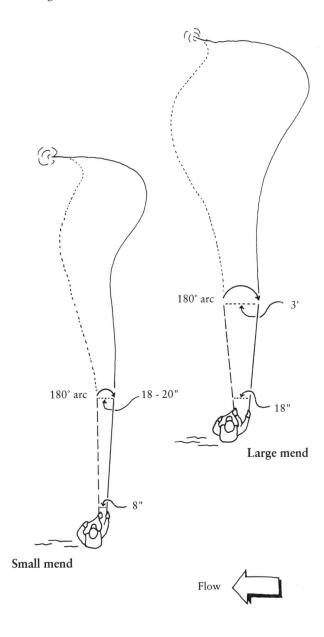

180° arc   3'

180° arc   18 - 20"

18"

Large mend

8"

Small mend

Flow

liver the package to the fish drag-free at the proper level. This package must present the illusion of life: something good to eat drifting or swimming naturally in the current.

LEADERS

Cold water, strength, abrasion resistance, and invisibility are key elements in selecting leader and tippet material for Great Lakes steelhead. At water temperatures below 42 degrees F (6 degrees C), many of the "ultrafine/ultrastrong" products lose durability. Knot strength noticeably decreases and the material seems to break (just about anywhere) at about 50 percent of advertised limits. Abrasion resistance is critical. Your leader, particularly the tippet, will be scraping and bouncing through rough cover. Rocks, gravel, stumps, log pilings, and even coarse sand quickly take their toll. The ultrafine stuff is great for normal trout fishing, but it does not stand up to the rigors of this game.

Effective leader construction is as important as the material; although there are several quality, prepackaged, brand name products available, most experienced anglers and most of the guides we know build their own.

Several alternatives for construction of simple, workable leaders follow. Specific brand name suggestions are given in the Equipment chapter, and because there are so many good knot recommendations and diagrams elsewhere, we won't replicate them here.

- *Leader of 4–6 feet for use with full-sinking lines, sinking shooting heads, or sink-tip lines (see Fig. 3.9).* Shorter leaders are fished with sinking lines in order to keep the (usually) unweighted fly at about the same depth as the point of the line. A long leader allows the fly to wander and "float" away and up from the desired depth.

- *Leader of 8–10 feet for use with floating fly line, or running line (see Fig. 3.10).* This is a good average length for much of the fishing in the Great Lakes area. The leader is long enough for most applications in that it will penetrate to fishing depth without bringing the fly line too close to the fish.

- *Leader of 12–14 feet for use with floating fly line, or running line (see Fig. 3.11).* This greater length is required when the fish are nervous due to bright sun, clear skies, low water, angler traffic, et cetera. It keeps the fly line and indicator, if one is used, away from the quarry.

Fig. 3.9   4 - 6' Leader

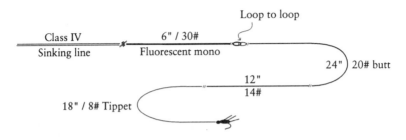

Fig. 3.10   8 - 10' Leaders

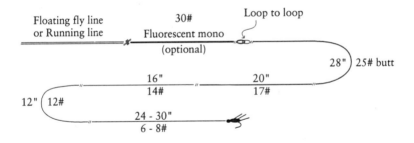

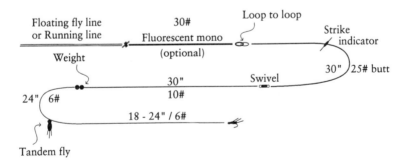

Using barrel swivel and tandem flies, strike indicator, and weight.

Fig. 3.11   12 - 14' Leaders

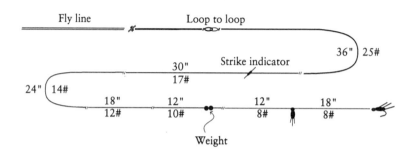

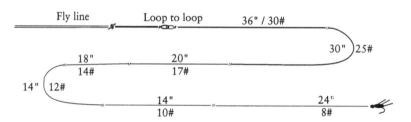

This leader is often used with two-handed rods. It performs well with Spey and roll casts and will allow an unweighted Spey fly (heavy hook) to sink to fishing depth.

TANDEM FLIES

Fly-angling for steelhead is a complicated game. It seems foolish, therefore, to throw another potentially aggravating ingredient into the soup, but many of us do. I like to fish two flies at once, most often contrasting, complementary patterns. Steve is more pragmatic; he occasionally fishes tandem rigs, but generally prefers the single presentation. The pros and cons of fishing a tandem fly setup always seem to sink heavily to the cons side of the scale. The pros are

Fig. 3.12 Tandem Fly Options

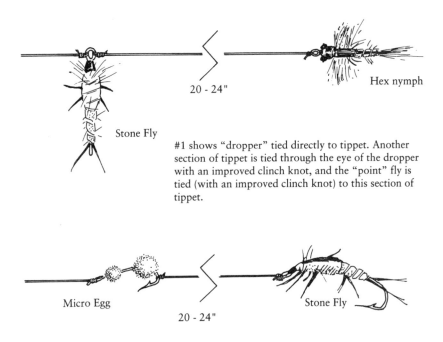

20 - 24"

Hex nymph

Stone Fly

#1 shows "dropper" tied directly to tippet. Another section of tippet is tied through the eye of the dropper with an improved clinch knot, and the "point" fly is tied (with an improved clinch knot) to this section of tippet.

Micro Egg

Stone Fly

20 - 24"

#2 shows the leader tippet coming off the bend of the hook of the "dropper." Both the dropper and and the "point" fly are secured by improved clinch knots.

few and capricious; the cons are many and *serious*.

The singular advantage to fishing more than one fly is that it provides an element of choice—both to the fish and to the angler. Those of us who have difficulty in making life's critical decisions are calmed by tying on, say, a Micro-Egg (two-colored) *and* a Stone Fly nymph. The steelhead is now forced to make the decision for us. Great! But, sadly, I have often observed that the fish will alternate and waver; one fish gobbles the Micro-Egg and the next take is on the Stone Fly. What to do? Stay with the tandem. Meanwhile, Steve is hammering them with a single Hex nymph.

The disadvantages are legion. After you scrape the rocks long enough, you sit down and hone two hook points. When you snag on the bottom or overpower a cast into the woods, you lose two flies at once. When it is *really* cold, tying on that extra fly is maddening. It always sinks into the back of your glove or into the tip of a finger or falls into the water—unattached.

The biggest problem with tandem fly rigs, however, is reserved for the big scramble after a fish takes and you set the hook. "Which fly did it take?" your buddy asks.

"I dunno." The fish is surging deep in a dark hole and gains access to a logjam. The line goes slack. *Both* flies are always missing.

During a float with Jerry Pytlik on the Au Sable, I managed to lose two bright fish that scraped along the (seemingly) clean bottom and found something on which to hook the trailing fly and pop the whole system. In the St. Mary's the fish often power straight out into the rapids, then make a hard 90-degree turn up- or downstream around a large boulder. My extra fly usually snags up on a rock during this maneuver. But the worst feeling sinks in after I've weathered a few of these storms, and it feels as though I might be gaining control of the contest. The big male wallows. The point fly, a Hex nymph, shows clearly in his jaw and the Micro-Egg is straight-lined above his head. He turns to gain deep water and dives. The sensation of the rod and the pull of the fish seem very different now. I cannot lift or lead. He is sideways in the current and smashes through the tail-out with the Micro-Egg embedded firmly in the dorsal fin, my only point of contact. He is now snagged and surely lost. So it goes with tandem flies.

If you decide to occasionally or regularly fish two flies for steelhead, forget about all the old techniques and knots for attaching a "dropper." These aggravate an already complicated formula and serve no purpose other than weakening your leader, causing extra tangles, and raising anxieties.

Here are two strong and easy-to-tie connections for fishing a pair of flies. Both are in-line systems that do not cause tangles or weaken your terminal rig (see Fig. 3.12).

Lastly, if you make it your practice to fish two flies on a consistent basis, your pals down at the fly shop will send you the "good" Christmas card.

PARAPHERNALIA

Cork, foam, fluorescent leader material, and yarn strike indicators in various colors and sizes are in wide use on our rivers. Whether you like them or not, or call them "indicator" or "bobber," the fact is that they are aids in detecting the subtle take of nymph or egg patterns.

Strategically placed on the leader, they tend to rivet the angler's concentration on the drift. A slight, momentary pause of the fly telegraphs up the leader and translates into a twitch or perhaps a faint downward dip of the indicator. This could mean that the fly or weight has bumped the bottom. It can also tell you that a hungry fish has entered the game. If the indicator stops, then rushes upstream or to the side a few inches, there will be no doubt—you have ignition and will soon see lift-off.

Regardless of size, color, material, or method of attachment to the leader, an indicator must be seen and easily tracked to be effective. It needs to be positioned high enough on the leader to float on or near the surface for visibility, but not so far from the fly that it causes a "belly" in the leader. This belly or sag between the indicator and fly delays and softens the transmission of a take signal and can actually cause unseen, crosscurrent drag.

Indicators can be moved up and down the leader with ease, and this flexibility, combined with adjustments in leader and tippet length, makes the entire terminal setup adaptable to most conditions. Figure 3.10 shows a strike indicator/toothpick float placed at a reasonable starting point on a 9-foot leader.

Swivel snaps and barrel swivels, although not generally regarded as acceptable fly-fishing tackle, find ready, useful application and warm reception among cold-weather steelhead guides and anglers. The swivel snap is most often engaged in securing a "slinky weight" to the leader's butt, and the barrel swivel is God's answer to our prayers for deliverance from the need to knot two pieces of vastly different-sized leader sections together in a howling wind with numb, wet fingers. A small bead between the snap swivel and the barrel swivel will hold the weight away from the barrel and eliminate friction on the knot. Figure 3.13 shows a sample arrangement.

WEIGHT

Various dense alloys are rapidly replacing lead as the material of choice for the manufacture of split shot, tube, rubber core, and other weights. Federal regulations, along with an environmentally concerned population, will likely accelerate the conversion and improve the product.

Weight, added to the leader by a variety of means, is a staple throughout the basin. It is clumsy to cast and inelegant in the extreme, but it is certainly effective. It is the most expeditious way to sink a fly to fishing depth.

Fig. 3.13 Sample Weights

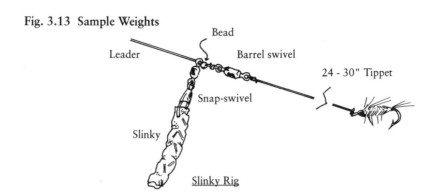

Bead

Leader

Barrel swivel

24 - 30" Tippet

Snap-swivel

Slinky

Slinky Rig

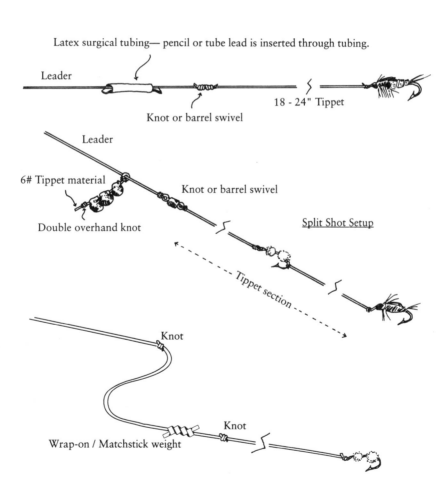

Latex surgical tubing— pencil or tube lead is inserted through tubing.

Leader

Knot or barrel swivel

18 - 24" Tippet

Leader

6# Tippet material

Knot or barrel swivel

Double overhand knot

Split Shot Setup

Tippet section

Knot

Wrap-on / Matchstick weight

Knot

Tube lead or pencil lead is available in long pieces or coils. The lead, which is fairly soft, is between ¼ inch and ⅜ inch in diameter and can be cut to desired length easily. A short piece of latex surgical tubing (¾ inch is a good length) slips over the leader/tippet, and the pencil weight is wedged into the tubing. This makes a pretty nifty rig as the tubing is restrictive enough to hold everything in place, yet flexible enough to allow easy adjustments by sliding the tubing and weight up or down the leader.

Slinky rigs are popular and available in commercial packaging. They are also extremely easy to make. Cut a length of parachute cord, remove the inner core, and melt one end of the hollow "rope" with a match or lighter. This seals that end and allows split shot to be packed into the hollow core. After a suitable number of shot have been packed to achieve the desired weight, the open end is melted and sealed, and the slinky rig is ready to use.

This kind of weight is attached to the butt section of the leader with a snap swivel. The snap pierces the tip of the sealed cord and is closed. The swivel rides the butt section of the leader and is held away from the fly by a bead and the barrel swivel that connects tippet to butt.

The old standby is, of course, split shot. Relatively cheap, easy to use, and infinitely adjustable, split shot can be affixed directly to the leader/tippet; they are more wisely and more often attached to a separate length of mono looped behind a leader connection knot or barrel swivel. A double knot in the tag end of the mono holds the shot in place but allows passage under stress if your weight hangs up on a snag. This often saves the better part of your terminal setup from loss. Figure 3.13 shows this assembly along with examples of pencil lead and slinky-type arrangements.

ACTION!

With some knowledge of preferred habitat and shelter areas, a sense of what to look for when trying to actually see the fish, reasonable skill in making the basic casts, and decently assembled terminal setup, we are ready to turn to the heart of the matter. To come to a satisfactory result after accurate casts, we must develop and maintain an effective, lifelike presentation of the fly. The take of the fly needs to be recognized and the hook instantly set. Now the steelhead must be *quickly* beaten and safely released.

DRIFT AND STRIKE DETECTION

To paraphrase and consolidate the sentiments of most professional steelhead guides, "manipulation of the fly for 'action' and steelhead fishing rarely mix." The fly or flies should drift naturally in the current without jerks or twitches imparted by rod or line manipulations. Motion of the *materials* that make up patterns enhances the illusion of something edible, however, and is desirable. A drag-free dead drift with a seductive fly is a first priority.

Proficiency in recognizing the movement when a steelhead takes a nymph or fly pattern is a bit like being able to spot fish: It is an acquired skill composed of concentration and practice. Conversely, when a large buck sails out to intercept a writhing Marabou Spey or ambushes an invading streamer on a downstream swing, there is no doubt about what has happened. A counterstrike is rarely required. But soft and gentle pauses, sometimes nearly imperceptible movements, represent the majority of takes by steelhead in this region.

Strike indicators, as discussed earlier, provide advantage to the angler. They serve to focus attention, and, when properly placed and tended, they amplify the slightest signal sent up the leader. Whether you elect to use a floating indicator, a section of fluorescent monofilament, or nothing other than the knot that connects your line and leader, you must select a focal point and follow it closely through each drift. Watch for anything, any *sense* of unnatural movement that might mean a trout has eaten your fly. Your focal point might seem to slow a bit; it might pause slightly or dip a fraction of an inch. Each and every questionable movement should be answered with positive action—a quick, sharp, controlled response to plant the fly in the fish's jaw.

STRIKING THE FISH

One of the most critical factors affecting productive sets is hook sharpness. It is a reasonable bet that fewer than 30 percent of the flies in any given box or fly book are sharp enough to penetrate quickly and deeply.

Many of the new hooks available to fly-tiers are of the highest quality, with improved tensile strength and chemically or laser-sharpened points, but these will dull and blunt with the repeated ticks of rocks and gravel. Diamond stones with built-in grooves for sharpening hooks are well worth the few dollars' investment. If these are not available at your local fly shop, purchase an alternative product, place it strategically in your vest so that you must touch it/move it to change flies, and use it often.

Control of slack line is another key element to effective striking. Excess coils of line drifting near your feet or snaking between your rod tip and the line of your drift make it impossible to react quickly enough to remove the slack and plant the hook.

Retrieved line should not be allowed to hang loose between the stripping guide and your reel. The line should be held firmly between the rod grip and your hand so that there is a straight connection through the rod to the drift. Slack line should then be kept between your rod hand and the reel. Keep as much slack line as possible *behind* your rod hand by carefully mending and pulling the slack off the water and back through the rod.

The actual motion involved in striking a fish varies among anglers. Some folks obviously believe in the literal reality of the name steelhead and strike with a reckless ferocity that results in broken tippets and severe muscle cramps.

With needle-sharp hook points and slack line under control, there is no need for violent, moon-shot reactions. Simple, sharp upward pops of the rod tip will firmly set nymph or egg patterns. A good way to accomplish this is as follows: With your rod tip pointing at and following the drift (remember—no slack), place your free hand behind your rod hand so that the free hand is palm *down* on *top* of the reel; simultaneously push the reel sharply with your free hand and raise the rod grip with your rod hand. This will immediately raise your rod tip about 1 foot, which will jerk the fly upward 3 to 4 inches. If it was a fish that caused you to strike, you have hooked it. Now that you know it's a fish, you can bang him harder to ensure a good set—though that is usually unnecessary. If it was a false alarm, you have only moved your fly a few inches. It is still in the proper zone at the right depth, and you have not destroyed your entire drift.

Practice this method of striking. When you become accustomed to the placement of your free hand and the up-down reflex motion, they will become second nature; you will no longer stare with embarrassed bemusement at the launch of a horrified 6-inch brookie into the alders.

PLAYING AND RELEASING THE FISH

Hooked steelhead display a range of characteristics, almost like personality traits, when confronted with the imminent danger of capture.

Some fish seem to explode from within, displaying an electrically charged panic that erupts into a helter-skelter series of cartwheels, vaults, and high-speed dashes. Others take a more studied, controlled approach to escape. Like boxers moving slowly around a ring, they size you up while organizing a plan, then sail into the wood pile or into deep pools to slug it out near rocks and tangles.

Regardless of the game plan employed by a specific fish, your objective is to keep it off balance and yourself in firm control, so that the fish reacts to your attack rather than vice versa.

Most fly-rodders, particularly novices, tend to apply vertical, upward rod pressure in hope of gaining the advantage. This rarely works. The more effective use of that long graphite lever lies in the application of sideways, lateral pressure that pulls the fish away from its line of escape. Repeated changes in the direction of lateral pressure disorient and confuse the fish, and force it to quickly and repeatedly alter its avenue of flight. This tires the fish much more rapidly than a steady upward pull. Never let a steelhead rest, not for a moment (unless it is necessary for the angler to gain a better fighting position). The aching wrist and tennis elbow can be babied *after* the fish has been mugged, hugged, and released.

Steelhead should always be played directly from the reel. The reel's drag, set properly, will prove to be a much more reliable control mechanism than the frantic stripping and releasing of line by hand. Sometimes a fish will rush toward the angler and it will be necessary to strip line very quickly with the free hand to regain direct contact, but the immediate goal thereafter is to take up the slack onto the reel and to get back on the offensive.

There are some behavioral tendencies of the steelhead to bear in mind that may help you during a fight, but they are only tendencies. Don't bet your Wheatley fly box.

- A steelhead hooked in a large, deep pool will often elect to remain there and fight it out if you don't pry it away. If the pool is snag-free, maybe it's the place to stay.
- One hooked in the shallows, say off spawning gravel, is apt to leave quickly, seeking cover. Note the terrain for best wading avenues. (Occasionally a hooked fish really intent on spawning will try to stay near the redds. Go figure.)
- A lot of steelhead escape near the end of the fight. The sight of you or the net, or the feel of sand on belly, often brings a final surge. Stay awake and lighten your drag.

- Rod pressure applied from an upstream angle usually causes the fish to go downstream and vice versa.

There is an exception to this latter tendency that may help you. We have used it on more than one occasion, but the best illustrative example coming to mind is below a bend on Michigan's Little Manistee River. For years a mess of downed trees provided a wonderfully productive deep hold immediately above the tangle. One has the usual two ways to go with a fish, downstream into the "can of worms and malaria germs" setting, or upstream into a sweeping, gentle, snag-free bend that extends for 200 feet. The angler, of course, prefers upstream, but how to get his recalcitrant dance partner to cooperate is the dilemma.

We have found, particularly in this stretch, that many fish will allow themselves to be *led* upstream if you can keep them relatively calm in the first few seconds after hook-up. If the steelhead holds steady after the initial flurry, you may, with rod held low to the water, walk upstream applying a steady, gentle pulling—more of a "towing" motion—and the fish will often come along. The pressure is from above, but we have walked fresh fish 15, 20, 30 yards before changing the rod angle and "putting the boots to 'em." Of course, having no other choice tends to make things work.

When the steelhead is tired, it is time to remove the hook, perhaps snap a photograph of the release, and head off in search of a fresh playmate.

There are three basic methods of gaining final, absolute control of a tired fish so that a practical release can be made. Netting, beaching, and tailing are all effective and are frequently used interchangeably by anglers on any given day, based on prevailing circumstances.

A wide-mouthed, long-handled net is perhaps the best tool and surest approach to effecting final capture. The "net person" (hopefully a calm and patient soul) should be stationed several yards downstream from the tired, wallowing prize. The net should be braced in a forward, upstream direction, *submerged* at a 45-degree angle downward, and held firmly with *both* hands. The fish should be held on a tight line (be ready to give line quickly in case the fish marshals an extra ounce of energy) and walked to a point just upstream from the net. Raise the fish's head and it will turn to the right or left (beware of Barry Sanders–like feints) and move downstream into the net. Of course, the net person needs to be ready to adjust the net's center right or left to intercept the fish and then to lift. The prize is yours.

JAC FORD PHOTO

Maintaining a low angle and side-to-side pressure

Remove the hook quickly, while the fish is still in the net, with the net bag and the fish in the water.

Beaching a steelhead successfully is very much dependent on the available real estate—you need a beach. Sand-, gravel-, silt-, or ledge rock–bottomed beaches and bars, even tiny coves, can be adequate spots to slide a tired fish to capture.

A reliable mode of swimming a steelhead onto damp ground is to pull in a steady, accelerating curve from the fish to the shore. The rod is held at approximately 30 to 40 degrees and prescribes an arc from stream to bank. The acceleration of your pull will cause the fish to react and swim faster; in *most* cases it will follow the arc of your rod and swim up the shallows to a point where it flounders.

Here "tailing" comes into play. The flopping fish can injure itself on rocks and gravel or by passing coarse sand through its gills. With a soft and *wet* cotton or wool glove, grab the slender "wrist" just ahead of the tail and grip tightly. It is not necessary to apply mountain-man handshake pressure; a firm hold suffices. The game has now ended except for hook removal and release.

Barbless hooks facilitate fly removal and timely resuscitation and release of any fish. They have other benefits as well. As with removal from a steelhead's jaw, they are much easier to pick out of a sweater

A St. Mary's River hen is gently revived.

or glove or dislodge from an ear or the small of your back. Removal of barbed hooks is made much easier by a backward, quarter-twist pull with a pair of angler's pliers. This hurts my ears.

If you want to photograph your triumph, do it *before* resuscitation. Hold the fish in the water by grasping it at the "wrist." Support its head and forebody gently with an open, upward-facing palm. Before you lift the fish, even slightly, position the photographer and make sure all is ready (background is acceptable, film is advanced, et cetera). Now, lift the fish smoothly, take the picture, lower, revive, and release. Photographs can evoke stunning memories of great moments. The pictures we like best are those that reflect the release of a healthy, vibrant trophy. Steelhead held out of the water for more than a few seconds suffer drastic mortality rates. Take your photo of tired fish quickly, revive patiently, and be assured that you did it the right way.

WEATHER NOTES

We all talk about it, but not even the professional Doppler radar jockeys can forecast it with any prideful measure of accuracy here in the Great Lakes Basin. Millions of acres of water complicate matters of accurate weather prediction.

Weather and its attendant mystery play a major role in steelhead angling. Barometric pressure, precipitation, cloud cover, moon phases, and most of all, fluctuations in temperature, have a direct and dramatic impact on steelhead behavior.

An *ideal* set of conditions includes a slightly rising or steady barometer, a layer of cloud cover, a new moon, a slightly off-color flow caused by a warm, mild rain, and water temperature that has risen from the high 30s to the high 40s. Did we forget wind? Let's not have any wind, maybe just a faint westerly breeze.

Under these conditions fish should be fresh and active during the day. Tinted, higher water gives them a sense of security and ease of mobility. A full moon and clear sky did not light up the night, so they will not be resting and lethargic after being hyperactive during the nighttime hours. The cloud cover strengthens their calm and provides a mask to our flailing, bumbling efforts. And most importantly, the rising water temperature has triggered the movement of thousands and thousands of stone fly nymphs, caddis larvae, as well as the emergence and molt of countless *Hexagenia limbata* nymphs.

Conversely, Steve and I often find ourselves sheltering next to a swaying, leafless birch. The cursed east wind howls across the cloudless blue, pushing the wind-chill factor to a level of pressing concern. The water is low and clear and its temperature has fallen to 32 degrees F (0 degrees C) from the previous evening's high in the 40s F (single digits C). Even my stripping guide is frozen solid. We look at each other, shrug, stand, and resume casting. The weather clowns fooled us again, but you fish when you can.

4

Fly Patterns for the Great Lakes Basin

The evolution of fly patterns in our region has been dramatic. In 1965, many of us believed that Great Lakes steelhead would not take flies. By 1970, layers of that myth were peeling away through the efforts and successes of persistent, innovative anglers. New patterns were developed, new techniques applied, and as the success rate of fly-anglers soared (in many cases eclipsing that of bait and hardware devotees), the myth died.

Bright, large, and gaudy would be fair terms to apply to the most popular patterns in use during the 70s. Heavily weighted, garish streamers of fluorescent marabou, chenille, and hackle were in wide-spread use. Yarn flies, simply a hunk of yarn looped, or snelled, to a bait hook were (and are) effective, as were magnum Glo-Bugs, some the diameter of a quarter. Nymphs were not widely used during this period, but the more inquisitive among us fished "wiggler" patterns in sizes 4 or 6, or large western-style wets like the Bitch Creek, Black Stone, and Girdle Bug with mixed results.

The high end on the success chart for these flies seemed always to coincide with slightly high or discolored water and low-light conditions. Clear water and bright skies, with very few exceptions, produced mediocre to poor results. "The fish are too spooky today," was the common lament.

The popularity of fly-fishing for steelhead grew geometrically in the 1980s. Improvements in tackle, waders, and clothing, combined with a growing understanding of steelhead behavior, raised anglers' comfort levels in the ofttimes gruesome weather and significantly increased levels of confidence in being able to hook and land such demanding and powerful fish.

Concurrent to this increase in popularity (translate to pressure) came a rapid series of trends in the development of more effective fly patterns. The ever-curious and speculative angler/tiers experimented with ways to seduce fish under pressure and otherwise more difficult conditions. The resultant success was keyed directly to imitative nymphs and to hook size. Patterns were developed to represent common prey items of the steelhead more faithfully, and they were tied in the proper sizes, which meant there was a significant downsizing of the fly. Finer tippets and smaller, more lifelike artificials produced a dramatic improvement in overall success—even under the most demanding, difficult conditions.

This evolution continues in the 90s. Twenty-five years ago we carried flies in hook sizes 2, 4, and 6. They were flamboyant featherduster streamers, concussive nymphs, and huge (by today's standards) egg patterns. If the sun was high, or the water low, we would take a nap, pick mushrooms, or adjourn to a game of euchre. Today we carry nymphs on size-16 hooks, Micro-Eggs, and diminutive softhackles. And we catch a lot more fish.

Steelhead *do* feed in the rivers. Before and after spawning, they key on mayfly, caddis, and stone fly nymphs, drifting trout and salmon eggs, and baitfish. When they are actively spawning and holding on the redds, they are least interested in food items (although they will take a fly, particularly the more aggressive males). When they are on the gravel, steelhead are most likely to be foul-hooked and should perhaps be left to their private tasks.

When they leave the security of a big lake and enter rivers, steelhead are intent on rapid travel. In the rush to reach home gravel, they cover long distances in a surprisingly short time span. During this upstream surge, they will stop and rest briefly in selected holes and deep runs and are then vulnerable to dead-drifted nymphs or egg patterns.

Upon arrival at chosen spawning areas, Great Lakes steelhead seem to go on a feeding binge for approximately 48 to 72 hours. They are usually open in their selection of items from the menu during this brief period and will take most well-presented offerings.

A recent example of this behavior comes immediately to mind. Steve and I had been fishing a favorite stretch of the Little Manistee River in mid-April. There were a few fish in the runs and pools, but these were mostly overwinter steelhead at the edge of their nerves due to a combination of low, clear water, cloudless skies, and the quickening urge to spawn in the warming flow. We decided to take a break and drive a few miles downstream to the Department of Natural Resources egg-taking station and inquire about when their quota would be reached and the weir opened to allow the steelhead passage to the upper river. Soon, we hoped.

We chatted with a grizzled veteran who kindly informed us that the fishing was off, that he'd been fishing spawn since noon and had not had a touch, and after looking at our vests and flies stuck in the patches, he said "They won't take those dinky things anyway. They only eat spawn and real wigglers." Right. We thanked him and decided to head back toward the village of Irons for a sandwich and a game of pool.

As we neared the area we had been fishing earlier, a wader-clad teenage boy with a rod in one hand and a large male steelhead in the other stepped onto the road, making strange and frantic motions with both burdened arms. He clearly wanted us to stop. He was lost, he thought. Camped near Phillip's Landing with his brother and a friend, he had been fishing in a downstream meander for several hours with no luck until about an hour before he saw us in the Suburban. "They came in waves," he said. "I only landed this one." The young man was delivered quickly to the bosom of his friends, and we checked the water near their campsite. The fish had not yet reached the runs and gravel that far upstream, which meant that they *should* be in the stretch we had been fishing earlier in the day.

It did not take long to drive back to the area we had been trying in the morning. One look from the high bank into the clear water of the Little Manistee had us scrambling for waders, rods, and cameras. Several large steelhead were in plain view in shallow riffles near log-jams, and we saw more bright fish sliding in and out of the dark runs by stretches of gravel.

Steve waded into position near a deep slot next to a timbered bank and downstream from a gravel flat. I took up station just below a narrow chute that spread over a sand flat and funneled into two distinct midriver runs. We were both quickly into fish. The low, clear flow dictated fine tippets and small flies, and we each made a few "long-line releases." We quit at dusk after 2 hours of nearly constant excitement. Fourteen fish had been hooked, six landed and released. They had taken small Green Caddis Larvae, Black Stone Fly and tan *Hexagenia* nymphs, and Olive Hare's Ears, as well as Micro-Eggs.

The next morning found us in the same general vicinity, and again we enjoyed fabulous action, but only for about an hour. That evening and the next day saw a return to business as usual. The fish were still in the area in good numbers, electing to stay rather than move farther upstream, but they had settled into the behavior pattern typical of steelhead waiting for ideal spawning conditions. They would still take a fly, but the quicksilver span of reckless abandon had passed.

The most aggressive feeding, independent of climatic influences, is often undertaken by fish that have completed spawning and are resting, or beginning the arduous return journey to the big lake. These fish are hungry and overeager to ingest any reasonable chunk of protein. Nymphs, egg patterns, crayfish imitations, streamers, and the classic Woolly Bugger all spell survival to these spent steelhead.

A note of caution: They will not perform as well in battle as a fresh fish and should be landed as quickly as possible, then released with the utmost care to avoid mortal stress.

Our selection of fly patterns for Great Lakes steelhead is divided into two main categories. Those that mimic specific foods are classified as Imitative, and within this grouping are subdivisions for nymphs, eggs, and baitfish. The Attractor classification could probably be split into listings for flies that *seem* to be either stimulants or irritants, but since no one we know professes clear knowledge of this topic, we decided it was probably an unnecessary (perhaps artificial) delineation and left the Attractor class bundled.

The following listings are not meant to be all-inclusive of successful steelhead flies. Rather, they are presented as a sampling of highly productive, time-tested patterns from many of the prime areas of the Great Lakes.

The selection process involved the evaluation of our own notes and experiences, as well as the input of friends, fly-shop professionals, and of course, the guides we worked with in putting this book together.

We debated the wisdom of suggesting hook styles for each of the patterns that follow and decided that the combination of dressing specifications and photography should be sufficient to direct the reader to his/her favorite hooks for a given fly type. We tie most of our flies (and especially nymphs and streamers) on a variety of hook styles manufactured by several different companies. As an example, we often tie Stone Fly and Hex nymphs on the radical bend L141 by Eagle Claw, the moderate bend 200 by Tiemco, or the venerable straight-shank 9672 by Mustad. The choice is made by perceived need, whim, or availability.

IMITATIVE FLIES

This grouping is split into pattern types that have proven most effective in representing actual foods ingested while steelhead are in the rivers or staging near the mouths of rivers, and while they are most easily reached by fly-rod anglers. Although steelhead will eat mice, frogs, and so on, on occasion, nymphs, eggs, and baitfish pretty well cover the majority of fly types you will need to entice feeding fish.

NYMPHS

In the upper section of the "flies-only" stretch of the Pere Marquette River, there is a long, deep run that drains a large dark hole at the foot of a curving gravel bank. About 90 yards downstream the run flattens, then floods a bouldered hole near an iron footbridge. Between these two prominent holding locales, the run itself harbors fish near less obvious shelter.

We were tired and cold. The mid-March weather was the breath of the lion, not the lamb. The water temperature read 39 degrees F (4 degrees C) and the air was colder. Rain turned to sleet, and then (thankfully) to snow. Ice locked the guides tight every third or fourth cast. To top it off, we had an encounter with "Yosemite Sam," the blustery "git off my property, you neoprene-clad varmints!" caretaker for one of the private clubs on the Pere Marquette. Sam, as we fondly refer to him, did not seem to care that we were in the river and definitely *not* trespassing. His swagger diminished, however, when his Rottweiler began shaking with joy and anticipation to our shout, "Hi, Puppy—atta boy—how ya doin' big ol' pupper—wanna treat?" Sam noticed that we had been picking up bankside refuse—beer cans, tennis shoes, and the like, stuffing same into carryout trash bags. "Come on, Killer," he said. "You guys stay in the river." Killer looked longingly in our direction, then dutifully trudged off with Sam to harass some other frozen anglers.

Steve decided to try a few more casts with a small Glo-Bug, but I thought I'd change from the Micro-Egg and try a small Stone Fly nymph. This was more for an excuse to warm my hands and back out of the deep chill than from any real attempt at scientific method.

The water was clear, so I elected to stay with a 3X tippet and tied on a size-10 Black (in honor of our new pal, Killer) Stone Fly nymph. "Let's go warm up," Steve called from 30 yards upstream.

"In 10 casts," I answered. On the fourth cast I noticed the frozen guides and freed the ice by plunging the rod into the water and pulling the line back, hard, through the guides. The fifth cast went where I wanted it to; the fly dropped 6 feet upstream from a small, dark depression about the size of a tabletop. As the drift passed under an ice-encrusted bush, the indicator blinked, just the slightest quiver, and I lifted the rod tip to the heavy, slow pulse of a good fish. "Here son, is a steelhead," I notified Steve, who reeled up with a sigh of relief and came down to watch.

We did not land this fish, but we did see it. It was in the 30-inch range, as wide, bright, and wild as a creature can ever be. He played a bit, made a short, fast run upstream about 30 yards and wallowed. Just enough to stop the heart. Then he sailed back in our direction, jumped once, and tore through a tangle of roots and small logs on the far bank. Somewhere between the jump and the tangle, the tippet gave up and the fish and I were disengaged. "Whew," said Bob. "Cool," said Steve.

Stone fly nymphs were active on that trip, and the fish keyed on them for the remaining 2 days we fished the Pere Marquette and the Little Manistee. Nymphs are always on the steelhead menu, but particularly so before active widespread spawning introduces large numbers of eggs into the flow.

Three of the most important stone flies in Great Lakes tributaries are the early black stone fly (*Capnia vernalis*), the great black stone fly (*Pteronarcys dorsata*), and the great brown stone fly (*Acroneuria lycoris*). The nymphs of these flies are important food items throughout the year, and they are particularly meaningful to steelhead anglers from late February through mid-April.

These are substantial morsels. The Early Black is best tied on size 10 and 12 hooks. The Giant Black seems to work best on a curved hook, like the Eagle Claw L141 in size 6; the Great Brown fishes best on a similar hook in sizes 8 and 10.

Remember, when tying or buying nymphs for steelhead, that nymphs of all stone flies, mayflies, and caddis do not hatch from the egg at full size. They are present in the river in a wide range of sizes for all species at all times. Only near the period of emergence is a nymph at the full size we see depicted in photos, drawings, and tying instructions. We do not know, nor will we ever, if a steelhead grabbing a size 12 Black Stone Fly nymph thinks it's eating an adult early black, or an immature giant black. The fact is, the fish doesn't care, and neither should we. Our considered opinion is this: If you err in size selection, it is better to be on the small side of the scale.

The following recipes cover a range of current stone fly nymph patterns in wide and productive use throughout the region. Some are precise while others are suggestive, reflecting the preferences of the tier more so than the fish. Steelhead seem to like them all.

Bear's Flashback Stone
Hook size: 4–10
Thread: Black
Tail: Black hen saddle
Rib: Blue copper wire
Back: Peacock Krystal Flash
Body: Black Mohlon
Hackle: Black hen saddle
Eyes: Bead chain
Comment: Bear Andrews developed this one. It is very effective.

Bear's Stone
Hook size: 6–10
Thread: Black
Tail: Goose biots
Rib: Silver wire
Back: Turkey tail
Body: Black squirrel dubbing
Hackle: Black speckled hen saddle
Eyes: Black mono
Comment: This pattern mimics several species. Another Bear
    Andrews development.

Strawful Stone
Hook size: 6–10
Thread: To match
Tail: Goose biots—or fine rubber
Antennae: Same
Back: Black or dark brown Swiss straw—folded twice for wing case
Body: Black or dark brown dubbing (chenille may also be used)
Hackle: Color to match hen saddle
Eyes: Bead chain or mono
Comment: One of the most effective Stone Fly nymphs, but a bit
    fragile. The wing case is often torn by teeth.

Mike's Stone
Hook size: 6–10
Thread: Black
Tail: Black goose biots
Rib: Thin rubber strip cut from black balloon

Wing case: Lacquered turkey quill
Body: Brown dubbing
Thorax: Brown dubbing or ostrich herl
Hackle: Grouse or brown hen saddle tied *over* the thorax
Comment: Developed by Mike Seward and Scott Smith, this pattern is in wide use on the North Shore of Lake Superior.

Spring Stone
Hook size: Long shank 6–10
Thread: Black
Tail: Red or fox squirrel fibers
Rib: Gold oval tinsel
Body: Black chenille
Thorax: Black chenille
Wing case: Lacquered squirrel tail
Hackle: Brown hen saddle
Antennae: Trimmed tips of squirrel-tail wing case
Comment: A Scott Smith fly that is easy to tie and very durable.

P.M. Stone
Hook size: 6–12
Tail: Black hen saddle fibers
Abdomen: Black dubbing
Rib: Gold wire
Wing case: Pheasant tail treated with Flex-Seal
Thorax: Peacock herl
Hackle: Hen saddle
Comment: This Bear Andrews tie is also very effective in olive and dark olive shades.

Brown Stone
Hook size: 6–10
Thread: Dark brown
Tail & antennae: Brown goose biots or fine brown rubber legs, as you prefer
Rib: Copper wire (optional)
Abdomen: Tyvek paper strip tinted with waterproof marker, or tinted latex over dubbed body
Wing case: Tyvek or latex, cut to shape and tinted
Thorax: Dark tan chenille or dubbing

Legs: Brown partridge hackle or substitute
Eyes: Plastic bead chain
Comment: A complex tie, but valuable in most Michigan, Wisconsin, and Ontario rivers.

Peacock Stone
Hook size: 8–12
Thread: Black
Tail & antennae: Fine black rubber
Rib: Copper wire
Abdomen: Black Swiss straw over black dubbing
Wing case: Black Swiss straw
Thorax: Peacock herl
Legs: Black hackle
Comment: Productive in early spring.

Mayfly nymphs are desirable food items; certain large species are so vital to the trout's diet that reasonable imitations will take steelhead in sections of rivers that provide less than optimum habitat for the particular insect.

Northern Wisconsin's Brule River, for example, flows generally south to north into Lake Superior. North of the tiny town of Brule on US 2, the river picks up speed as the gradient increases on the final rush to Lake Superior. This is the prime stretch of the Brule for steelhead anglers, and although prime brown drake (*Ephemera simulans*) and *Hexagenia limbata* habitat is far upstream, lifelike patterns that mimic these two nymphs are effective on the lower river.

Similar circumstances occur on many rivers throughout the Great Lakes fishery. The Pere Marquette's prime Hex water is downstream from the "flies-only" stretch, but Hex and Brown Drake nymphs are very productive under the right conditions in the upper reaches. A "better-safe-than-sorry" rule to follow is that if a stream has *Hexagenia limbata* and/or *Ephemera simulans* populations, carry a representative assortment of nymph patterns for these insects.

Other mayfly larvae are consumed by steelhead as well, but in the interest of both honesty and practicality, it is rarely necessary to tie specific patterns for them. A selection of Gold-Ribbed Hare's Ears, Squirrel Nymphs, and Pheasant Tails in various hues and shades will adequately cover additional requirements.

In addition to dressings for specific mayfly nymphs, the following group includes some all-purpose suggestive patterns like the Hare's Ear variations and the Sparrow.

Bear's Hex
Hook size: 6
Tail: Pheasant body feather marabou or three natural gray ostrich herls
Body: Dirty yellow dubbing—a mix of yellow Antron and fox squirrel works well
Rib: Fine gold wire
Gills: Natural pheasant filoplume
Back: Pheasant tail, treated with Flex-Seal
Wing case: Same as back
Legs: Hen saddle, folded and palmered
Eyes: Black mono
Comment: Another wonder by Bear Andrews. This is certainly one of the very best flies for the Great Lakes tributaries.

Sparrow Nymph
Hook size: 4–8
Tail: Pheasant body marabou
Body: Olive dubbing
Rib: Gold wire (optional)
Hackle: Pheasant rump
Head: Filoplume—collared
Comment: Created by Jack Gartside, this has become a "must have" standard.

Dusty's Fuzz Buster
Hook size: 8
Tail: Marabou from the same hen feather used to collar the fly
Body: Ostrich herl
Rib: Gold wire
Back: Pheasant tail treated with Flex-Seal
Wing case: Same as back
Eyes: Black mono
Hackle: Grizzly hen saddle, dyed to match body color
Comment: Tie with any color ostrich herl and use hen saddle to match.

Pheasant Tail
Hook size: 6–12
Tail: Pheasant tail fibers
Rib: Gold wire
Body: Wound pheasant tail fibers
Wing case: Pheasant tail, treated with Flex-Seal
Thorax: Peacock herl
Hackle: Pheasant rump
Comment: Try olive-dyed as well as natural pheasant tail.

Soft-Hackle Hare's Ear
Hook size: 6–12
Tail: Hare's mask fibers or partridge fibers
Body: Dubbed hare's mask or hare's ear blend
Rib: Gold wire
Hackle: Partridge
Comment: Tie in natural, cream, olive, and dark olive shades.

Oscar's Hex
Hook size: 6–8
Thread: Orange
Tail: Brown pheasant rump fibers
Body: Cream sparkle yarn
Rib: Gold wire
Back: Lacquered pheasant tail
Gills: Gray filoplume
Thorax: Orange sparkle yarn
Hackle: Brown, palmered and trimmed flat on bottom
Wing case: Lacquered pheasant
Eyes: Black mono
Comment: Oscar Feliu originated this pattern, which has now been
   widely adapted. It is most effective.

Latex Wiggler
Hook size: 8–12
Tail: Squirrel, pheasant, or partridge feathers
Underbody: Cream or yellow yarn
Body: Narrow strip of cream latex
Back: Fox squirrel (optional)

Hackle: Brown, palmered to eye and clipped flat on back
Comment: This pattern is also productive in areas that support
  good populations of brown drakes (*E. simulans*).

Spring's Wiggler
Hook size: 6–10
Thread: Brown
Tail: Fox squirrel fibers
Back: Fox squirrel
Body: Pale yellow yarn, dubbing, or chenille
Hackle: Brown, palmered
Comment: This "older" pattern, adapted by Ron Spring, is still in
  widespread use. It can (and should) be tied in a variety of color
  combinations.

Prolific is the proper word to describe the populations of caddis
species throughout the Great Lakes region. Net builders, case builders, and free swimmers in all sizes, hues, and tints are abundant from
Lake Superior's North Shore streams to the tributaries at the eastern
edge of Lake Ontario.

The fact that caddis are found as a substantial share (up to 40
percent) of the stomach contents of fish is a fair indication of their
importance as a food source. They are readily available throughout
the year and throughout the length of most, if not all, tributaries that
host anadromous rainbows.

There are many effective pattern types and specific species for imitating both the larval and pupal stages of caddis, but (thankfully) for
the purpose of duping steelhead, the process of selection is simplified.
Pick a pattern *type*—latex or dubbing with heads of fur, peacock herl,
or ostrich herl—and tie shades of green, cream, tan, and brown in sizes
10 to 16. Generally speaking, you are well armed for the entire region.

The patterns that follow represent basic styles, in various shades
and colors, that work well throughout the basin.

P.M. Caddis
Hook size: 8–10
Body: Chartreuse Larva Lace
Hackle: Hen saddle
Head: Dubbed hare's ear or squirrel blend

Comment: Other body colors may be used but only if body is dubbed.

Schmidt's Caddis
Hook size: 8–10
Body: Grannon green dubbing
Rib: Gold wire (optional)
Head: Peacock herl
Comment: As simple as it gets. Easy to tie and fish like it.

Vogel's Caddis
Hook size: 8–12
Tail: Hackle fibers—dark dun
Body: Gray or dark olive dubbing
Hackle: Dark dun, palmered
Back: Pheasant tail or turkey
Head: Peacock herl or black thread
Comment: Karl Vogel fishes this pattern with excellent results in the rapids of the St. Mary's River.

EGGS

Trout and salmon eggs are present in our rivers throughout the year. Stream trout and steelhead feed on them whenever the opportunity arises. Long after active spawning ceases, the eggs are occasionally dislodged from the gravel and drift free—for a time. When steelhead (and brown trout) and salmon are on the redds, thousands and thousands of eggs that did not find the security of the gravel drift in the current and become a preferred food source for every predator in the system.

The female's act of cleaning the gravel for spawning casts stone fly, mayfly, and caddis larvae into the flow. The undulations that release her eggs for fertilization by an attentive male accomplish the same feat. This mix of foods, both nymphs and eggs, drifts free at a time when, typically, the water temperature has risen to an optimum point, and the fish respond enthusiastically to this combination of stimuli.

It is our opinion that many of the "egg flies," and specifically the Glo-Bug-type patterns in use today, are far too large to be consistently effective. Trout and salmon eggs are really quite small, 3 mm to 5 mm in diameter, and the more productive copies (for us) closely approximate the size of the natural product.

A Selection of Great Lakes Steelhead Flies

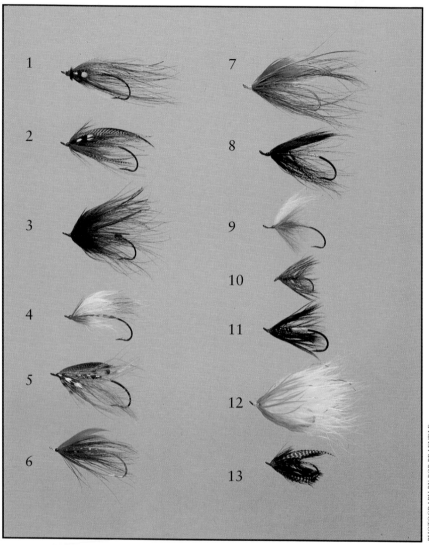

PHOTOGRAPH BY BOB BRAENDLE

1. ST. MARY'S SPEY
2. CLARET STEELHEAD SPEY
3. THUGMEISTER SPEY
4. BOREDOM
5. LEGAL EAGLE
6. PURPLE AND ORANGE SPEY

7. GOLDDIGGER SPEY
8. GREEN STREAK SPEY
9. STEELHEAD STINGER
10. CRYSTAL WOOLLY SPEY
11. GREEN BUTT WOOLLY SPEY
12. MARABOU SPEY
13. BUSH WEASEL

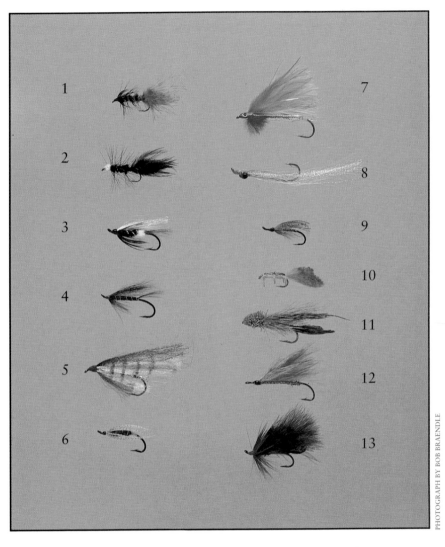

1. MULTI-BUGGER
2. EGG-SUCKING LEECH
3. GREEN BUTT SKUNK
4. PURPLE PERIL
5. ANTRON TIGER
6. WET SPYDER

7. OSWEGO SMELT
8. CLOUSER DEEP MINNOW
9. BLUEBERG
10. STRIP NYMPH
11. MUDDLER MINNOW
12. MARABOU MICKEY FINN
13. MARABOU SPRUCE

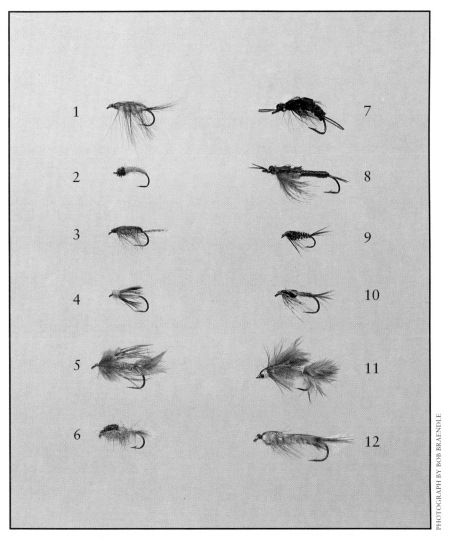

PHOTOGRAPH BY BOB BRAENDLE

1. WIGGLER	7. STRAWFUL STONE
2. SCHMIDT'S CADDIS	8. BROWN STONE
3. VOGEL'S CADDIS	9. P. M. STONE
4. P. M. CADDIS	10. PHEASANT TAIL
5. SPARROW NYMPH	11. BEAR'S HEX
6. GOLD-RIBBED HARE'S EAR	12. OSCAR'S HEX

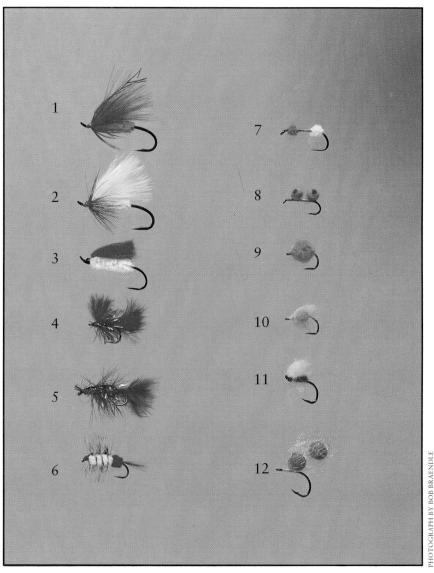

1. CHERRY BLOSSOM   7. MICRO-EGG
2. LEMON DROP   8. CHEERLEADER
3. FRAMMUS   9. GLO-BUG
4. CACTUS FLY   10. YARN EGG
5. CACTUS WIGGLER   11. NUKE BUG
6. WOOLLY WORM   12. HAMMOU EGGS

The patterns pictured in the color plates run the gamut from small to quite large, from subtle and lifelike with natural colors to loud and brash with a high visibility advantage. Following here is a list of dressings for some of the best patterns of this type currently in widespread use throughout the Great Lakes.

Glo-Bug
Hook size: Wildly variable
Body: Glo-Bug yarn in single or mixed colors pulled tight and cut to general egg shape
Comment: The most widely used egg fly.

Cheerleader
Hook size: 10–12
Body: Two 5-mm pom-poms, threaded on clear mono and tied to hook
Eyes: "Paint" dark spot on each pom-pom with waterproof marker
Comment: Extremely easy to tie. Thread several pom-poms on mono at one time and tie multiples.

Micro-Egg
Hook size: 10–14
Thread: White
Body: Fine-diameter chenille, two colors; wrap in shape of egg
Comment: Chartreuse and flame orange are a good combination. A sparse wrap of pearl Krystal Flash between two eggs is optional.

Lemon Drop
Hook size: 6–10
Body: Fluorescent yellow chenille
Wing: Fluorescent chartreuse
Hackle: Bright red, collar
Head: Fluorescent red thread
Comment: John Dembeck of Oswego, New York, feels this is one of the best flies for Lake Ontario streams.

Cherry Blossom
Hook size: 6–10
Body: Fluorescent *light* pink chenille
Wing: Fluorescent pink marabou

Hackle: Two turns of cerise hen saddle, collar style
Head: Fluorescent cerise thread
Comment: Another of Dembeck's favorites for eastern Lake
   Ontario tributaries.

Nuke Bug
Hook size: 6–10 egg style
Thread: White
Body: White spot or "dab" of pink, chartreuse, or orange glo-yarn
"Wing": Partial strand of lighter, egg-colored glo-yarn
Comment: The "wing" should cover the body spot, yet allow it to
   show through for a translucent, natural effect.

Cactus Fly
Hook size: 6–10 egg style
Thread: White, orange, red
Tail: Tuft of fluorescent marabou
Body: Two tight wraps of Sparkle Chenille or Estaz
Wing: Tuft of fluorescent marabou
Comment: A Scott Smith pattern effective in stained water.

Frammus
This is a larger version of the Nuke Bug. The primary differences
   are hook size (6–8 2X long), and the fact that the body is
   wrapped, or wound, chenille.
Comment: Easy to tie and very productive.

Cactus Wiggler
Hook size: 6–10
Tail: Tuft of fluorescent marabou
Body: Sparkle Chenille or Estaz
Back: Fox squirrel tail fibers
Hackle: Palmered red, orange, or chartreuse
Comment: This high-tech version of the Spring's Wiggler is produc-
   tive in the tea-colored flows entering Lake Superior.

STREAMERS

Baitfish are the primary food source for steelhead while they are in
the lakes. Alewife, smelt, herring, whitefish, immature game fish—
the list goes on—are all nutritious, fattening forage that produces

dramatic growth rates. Once the spawning urge pulls the steelhead far upriver, baitfish imitations, although still important and productive at times, become less effective as baitfish decline in percentage among available prey items.

There are exceptions to this loose hypothesis and some are quite notable. When fish first stage in the lowest reaches of a river or at the mouth, baitfish are still the predominant prey, and a reasonable artificial is likely to "fire the synapse," to trigger the reflex that brings a strike.

The sudden or continuous appearance of large numbers of a specific food fish often triggers selective predatory action even when steelhead are far upstream and on or near spawning gravel.

John Dembeck showed us how to fish shad and smelt patterns with excellent results below the dam on the Oswego River. Baitfish were stunned or dizzied by a sudden drop in water temperature, and the game fish (both steelhead and large browns) actively hunted them.

John Kluesing showed us the quickfire reaction steelhead make to emerging salmon fly. His lesson on the upper Pere Marquette was revealing, and his Blueberg fly, tied to represent the tiny kings as they leave the safety of the gravel, was taken aggressively.

Male steelhead often chase and whack large marabou streamers, perhaps because of territorial instincts, and a deftly fished sculpin pattern can be deadly in many situations. And like the Egg-Sucking Leech, a streamer with an egg at the eye of the hook can be irresistible to the preferred quarry, an aggressive buck.

Egg-Sucking Leech
Hook size: 4–8
Tail: Black marabou
Body: Black chenille
Hackle: Black, palmered
Egg: Small wrap of fluorescent chartreuse or orange chenille at the head
Comment: Black and chartreuse seem to be the best of all the combinations we have tried.

Blueberg
Hook size: 6–10
Tail: 2–3 strands of blue Flashabou or Krystal Flash (optional)
Body: Blue Flashabou, Krystal Flash, or Diamond Braid

Underwing: 3–4 strands of blue Krystal Flash or Flashabou
Wing: Mallard or wood duck flank
Throat: Red hackle fiber
Comment: Deadly in rivers that have runs of king salmon.

Strip Nymph
Hook size: 6–10
Tail, abdomen, gills: A strip of tanned hide; Australian opossum
    works well
Thorax: Tan or creamy white dubbing
Back: Peacock Krystal Flash
Legs: Tan vernille, shaped with heated needle
Comment: Is it a streamer or a nymph? Originated by Gary Borger,
    the pattern has been adapted by noted Michigan tier Fred Vargas.

Oswego Smelt
Hook size: 2–4
Body: Medium pearl Mylar
Wing: 50% white marabou, 25% fluorescent blue marabou, 25%
    dark green marabou; four strands of pearl Flashabou on each side
Head: Green with painted eyes
Comment: Developed by John Dembek for eastern Lake Ontario
    rivers, but effective everywhere.

Clouser Deep Minnow
Hook size: 2 with 1/36- or 1/50-oz eyes
Wing: Bucktail or synthetic hair with 8–12 strands of Krystal Flash
    or Flashabou to complement wing colors
Comment: Favored color combinations are chartreuse/white, gray/
    white, dark brown/pale orange, and red/white.

Muddler Minnow
Hook size: 2–10
Tail: Turkey wing quill
Body: Gold tinsel
Underwing: Brown kip tail
Wing: Turkey quill
Head: Deer, antelope, or caribou hair; spun, packed, and clipped to
    shape
Comment: Any good sculpin imitation works as well.

Marabou Mickey Finn
Hook size: 4–8
Thread: Black
Body: Gold tinsel or Diamond Braid
Wing: Underwing of yellow marabou, center wing of red marabou, overwing of yellow marabou
Throat: Red hackle fibers (optional)
Comment: This fly agitates males and is most effective at dawn and dusk.

ATTRACTOR FLIES

We do not know why a steelhead rushes to take a classic Spey, a shimmering Marabou Spider, or a Green Butt Skunk, but they do. We do not usually dead-drift these flies in front of the fish's nose, but instead we swim them with or across the current, and steelhead may decide to chase and eat them. This makes the game even more exciting.

One of the most incredible fish I ever hooked came recently to a yellow and fluorescent orange Marabou Spey of the type originated by George Cook. Steve and I were fishing Oak Orchard Creek with Rick Kustich and I decided to try this quivering, snaky invention on a heavy sink tip across a wide gravel flat.

To make this as short and sweet as possible, I'll simply state that she hit *very* hard as the downstream swing passed the three-quarter point. The fish was instantly in the air, then again—but way over there, and yet again—*way* over there. And so it went. Back and forth, in and out. It was raining and cold, my hands were shaking, and when we landed her, the tape measure stuck at 32 inches. She was a bit beyond that; I released her and sank to my haunches as Rick wiped the camera lens. "What a fish! What fly did she take?" he asked. "Spey—Marabou Spey," I croaked.

There is a lot of room for maneuvering within the attractor category, and it is possible to make a case that any fly that does not mimic a *specific* food is an attractor. In that case a Gold-Ribbed Hare's Ear would be an attractor, as would a Clouser Minnow, but we decided those, and similar patterns, should be left in more typical (acceptable to us) classifications.

Dry flies, such as Bombers, large caddis, and *Hexagenia* imitations, account for a few Great Lakes steelhead each year. Usually these are summer-run or late holdover fish present when a major emergence takes place. This is not to say that steelhead do not eat surface foods, but is strongly suggestive that dry-fly fishing for Great Lakes fish is underdeveloped. Neither we nor the guides we worked with have enjoyed great success to date. We will, however, keep trying.

Green Butt Skunk
Hook size: 4–10
Thread: Black
Tag: Fluorescent chartreuse chenille or dubbing
Tail: Red hackle fibers (optional)
Wing: White calf tail
Hackle: Black
Comment: An old, proven standby.

Multi-Bugger
Hook size: 6–10
Thread: Black
Tail: A mix of brown, gold, and olive marabou
Body: Olive chenille
Rib: Gold wire or Krystal Flash
Hackle: Brown palmered over rear half of body, black over front half
Comment: Steelhead seem to prefer this variation to the classic tie.

Marabou Spruce
Hook size: 4, 6, 8 Atlantic salmon
Thread: Red 6/0
Tail: Peacock swords
Body: Rear half—fluorescent red Antron; front half—peacock herl
Wing: Brown grizzly marabou
Collar: Brown hackle
Comment: Accomplished angler Fred Lee of Kalamazoo considers this one of the very best spring patterns.

Antron Tiger
Hook size: 4, 6 4X long streamer
Thread: Red 6/0
Body: Pearl Mylar tubing over lead wrap
Underwing: White Antron over which red is placed
Overwing:

1st: White fluorescent Antron
2nd: Orange Antron
3rd: Fluorescent chartreuse Antron
4th: Olive Antron
5th: Green Krystal Flash
6th: Dark brown Antron
Tease all fibers to blend
Comment: This is an adaptation of the tiger streamer that was developed by one of the region's top guides, Walt Grau. Fred Lee gives Grau's original and this variation very high marks.

Purple Peril
Hook size: 4–10 up-eye
Thread: Red or black
Tag: Silver tinsel
Tail: Purple hackle barbs
Body: Purple chenille
Rib: Silver tinsel
Hackle: Purple, collared
Wing: Fox squirrel tail
Comment: A classic West Coast pattern that serves very well in the Great Lakes Basin.

Wet Spyder
Hook size: 6–10
Butt: Floss of desired color
Body: Peacock herl
Rib: Oval tinsel
Collar: Mallard body flank feather
Comment: Originated by Al Knudson, this fly is effective on shy or pressured fish.

St. Mary's Spey
Hook size: 6–1
Body: Burnt orange angora goat
Rib: Gold tinsel
Hackle: One large blue-eared pheasant, half stripped and turkey butt, half stripped very sparse
Wings: Lemon wood duck or orange-dyed mallard flank
Throat: Orange guinea hen

Cheeks: Jungle cock
Head: Black ostrich herl
Comment: A clear-water beauty developed by Steve Sallard.

Claret Steelhead Spey
Hook size: 6–1
Tag: Gold oval French tinsel medium
Body: Claret silk
Rib: Gold oval French
Thorax: Badger tail underfur
Hackle:
   D1: Half stripped golden pheasant rump
   D2: Half stripped blue-eared pheasant
   D3: Half turn of teal flank
   D4: Eight strands of red Krystal Flash
Wing: Mallard bronze flank
Collar: Red schlappen
Cheeks: Jungle cock
Comment: Another creation by Steve Sallard that fishes very well in various water conditions.

Thugmeister Spey
Hook size: 6–1
Tag: Peacock herl
Body: Electric blue Flashabou
Rib: Silver Flashabou
Thorax: Kaufmann's black stone angora dubbing
Hackle:
   D1: Half stripped blue-eared pheasant
   D2: Half stripped black marabou
   D3: Rubber hackle
Comment: A versatile pattern that seems to work as well in slow current as it does in the St. Mary's rapids.

Steelhead Stingers
Hook size: Bronze 4–8
Thread: Color to match
Body: Rear half—floss over silver tinsel; front half—seal's fur to match floss
Collar: Hackle to match body color

Wing: Arctic fox tail
Head: 12/0 to match body
Comment: These flies sink quickly and track straight on the swing. Mike Yarnot developed these for steelhead, but they also attract brown trout and coaster brook trout.

Bush Weasel
Hook size: 4–10
Thread: Black
Tag: Medium silver tinsel
Rib: Medium silver tinsel
Hackle: Black schlappen
Collar: Black hen saddle
Wing: Teal
Throat: Teal
Body: Black Mohlon
Comment: This is a Bear Andrews pattern that produces well in the fall. It is named for those of us who spend a lot of time in remote areas.

Boredom
Hook size: 4–8
Thread: Red
Body: Danville fluorescent floss (neon red)
Rib: Pearlescent Mylar
Wings: Chartreuse-dyed badger with underfur
Hackle: Chartreuse schlappen folded over followed with three to four turns of cerise hackle
Comment: This fly, conceived and developed by Fred Vargas, is very effective in the St. Mary's River.

Golddigger Spey
Hook size: Spey hook
Thread: Gold
Tag: Fine oval gold tinsel
Body: Rear half—medium flat gold tinsel; front half—golden yellow seal fur loop-dubbed in fine oval gold tinsel
Rib: Medium oval gold tinsel
Body Hackle: Gray heron substitute over seal fur
Collar 1: Gray/tan ringneck pheasant rump

Collar 2: Golden pheasant back feather
Wing: Pair of golden pheasant back feathers, set low and tentlike
Topping: Three golden pheasant crests
Comment: Intricate, beautiful, and seductive; a Mike Yarnot
  original.

Green Streak Spey
Hook size: Alec Jackson Spey hook
Thread: Black
Tag: Small flat silver tinsel
Body: Rear half—fluorescent green floss
Rib: Small flat silver tinsel
Counter Rib: Small oval silver tinsel
Body Hackle: Black heron substitute over seal fur with two to three
  turns as a collar
Comment: Another Mike Yarnot beauty. This one fishes best
  during late fall and winter in clear water. Fish it in deep runs and
  pools with slow current.

Woolly Spey/Crystal Woolly Spey
Hook size: 4–6
Thread: To match
Tag: Fluorescent wool
Body: Crystal Chenille or wool color is an individual choice—
  experiment
Hackle: Palmered schlappen
Comment: Ray Schmidt is the originator of the Woolly Spey. Jeff
  "Bear" Andrews prefers the brighter crystal version.

Legal Eagle
Hook size: Salmon, 4–3/0
Thread: Black
Tip and Tag: Gold tinsel and yellow floss
Tail: Golden pheasant crest with small red feather topping
Butt: Black ostrich
Body: Black floss
Hackle: Orange-dyed pheasant rump
Throat: Blue-dyed guinea hackle
Underwing: Golden pheasant tippet
Wing: Bronze mallard or mottled turkey

Cheek: Jungle cock
Topping: Golden pheasant crest
Horns: Blue/gold macaw
Comment: Based on the Thunder and Lightning, it works best in
   tinted water.

Purple and Orange Spey
Hook size: Salmon, 4–3/0
Thread: Red, green, or orange—your choice
Body: Dark purple floss/synthetic living fiber/seal
Rib: Flat silver tinsel
Cross Rib: Fine silver wire
Body Hackle: Purple-dyed pheasant rump
Throat: Purple-dyed guinea or teal
Wing: Cock hackle tips, purple-dyed, set back-to-back, or orange
   goose shoulder segments set back-to-back
Comment: Slim floss sinks faster than bulky fur. This fly fishes well
   to spooky fish and in dirty water. Developed by Bob Blumreich
   of Janesville, Wisconsin.

Marabou Spey
Hook size: 2, 4
Thread: To match or contrast
Rear Wing: Orange, yellow, or chartreuse marabou
Rear wing flank: Contrasting or complementary strands of
   Flashabou or Krystal Flash
Front Wing: Contrasting or complementary color of marabou—
   usually darker than rear wing
Collar: Schlappen hackle (optional)
Comment: The most popular of this type of fly is the Popsicle as
   originally developed by George Cook. Ray Schmidt demonstrated
   the great versatility of this tie and showed us how to fish it.

PART II

THE GUIDES

As noted previously, the Great Lakes watershed is an immense, varied chunk of continent, and all steelhead angling in this vast area is not the same. The guided trips recounted in the following chapters represent a sampling of distinct regions within the basin, with action centering on one or two of the best representative tributaries from each region. Our primary goal is to accurately report the experiences we shared with each guide—what the fishing was like, the weather, the terrain, the stream, the strategy—and what we learned that you in turn can put to good use.

The brief biographical paragraphs sprinkled through the guide write-ups, which many times speak to their acomplishments, are not intended as ads or promotions for these professionals, but are designed to lend additional credence to their words and approaches. All have developed specific techniques to accommodate the specific demands of their home waters, and that, along with their widespread reputations for patient teaching, ethics, and sportsmanship, is why we asked them to work with us in the preparation of this book.

For those not inclined to read the entire anecdotal chronology of the day(s) with each guide, there are tactical summaries at the end of every account. This "Cliff Notes" approach is intended as a quick review of salient points, and, while helpful, reading them out of context may not do the justice to the craft of the guide/expert that a full reading would.

Also, if you never plan to fish, say, the far North Shore of Lake Superior (your mistake), we encourage reading the section dealing with that drainage anyway. Many lessons learned in one region can be applied universally.

And finally, we covered Michigan's Pere Marquette on the west side and the Au Sable on the east more than once, with more than one guide, for a couple of reasons: They are fish-filled, extensive flow-ages of such worldwide repute that they deserved it; and we had a nagging curiosity to see what an expert could show us about our favorite home waters, on which we'd previously spent so much time. It was a lot, we were to find.

5

Scott Smith

Spate Streams of the Canadian Shield

There are few highways in North America that present such incredible beauty as Canada's 17 in its long curl around Lake Superior. We first touched 17 one mid-May morning at the foot of the International Bridge in Sault Ste. Marie, Ontario, and followed it due north heading through Agawa Bay, Frater, and Wawa. At White River (the home of the real Winnie the Pooh of WWI fame), 17 turns west and follows the route of the Canadian Pacific Railway along Superior's coastline of ragged scree and nearly impenetrable bush. It then passes through Hemlo, Marathon, Terrace Bay, and on to Nipigon and Thunder Bay.

Our destination was Gurney by the Sea, a rustic cluster of cabins nestled tight to the bay near the village of Rossport. We found Gurney easily enough and were informed that Scott Smith was expecting us, but at the moment was fishing with Bill Boote, a fellow police officer in Thunder Bay. "He'll be back later and meet you two at the second cabin. It's not locked," the manager said.

We unpacked, drained the cooler, and met a friendly couple from Wisconsin who, with their two young dogs, were staying in the cabin next to ours. They had been fishing the smaller streams in the immediate area and catching a fish now and then, but were anxious for the Jackpine and Cypress to drop their levels and start clearing. A hard rain had swollen the lower reaches of both rivers and had made fly-fishing extremely difficult. We patted the pups and decided to take a quick look at the two main rivers rather than sit in the cabin until Scott and Bill returned.

We drove to the bridge over the Cypress and found a two-track that led to a small parking area near the river. The trail continued upstream beyond the small parking spot, but it was too soupy to proceed farther even with four-wheel drive. The Cypress was out of its banks and a 4-foot-wide channel sluiced across the trail before dumping its tea-colored flow back into the dark surge to our right. "A bit moist, don't you think? Let's take a closer look on foot," Steve said as he killed the engine.

We walked the few feet to the river and wasted perhaps a full nanosecond in deciding *not* to don waders. A few kilometers and two large hills to the west, the Jackpine drains several thousand hectares of thinly soiled granite. Just 50 or so kilometers to the north lies the continental divide, and from that point all rivers flow north to Hudson Bay and the Arctic Ocean. There are very few roads. We crested the first hill and Steve reminded me of our debacle on the Steel River just a day earlier.

We had fished the Steel near Lake Superior for an hour without an inkling of success. We had pored over maps and the steelhead study report published by fisheries personnel in Thunder Bay and had decided to explore upstream. No Ontario Hydro facilities showed on the map, and we *assumed* steelhead would be in the upper section of the river where it was bridged by a logging road on our regional chart. Dead Horse Trail had a bit of an ominous ring, but we followed its twisting course upstream for 38 kilometers. The bridge over the river was right where the map said it would be. Peering into the steady flow of chocolate mud at the edge of a ragged clear-cut was disheartening. So was the fact that we had relearned one of the most valuable lessons for fishing in new, foreign, or remote country—always hire a guide or consult closely with knowledgeable local sources; our whole Dead Horse Trail trek had been futile from the outset. A waterfall blocked fish passage far below the upstream environs we had labored mightily to reach.

The Jackpine appeared in a matter of minutes. It rushed in nearly straight-line rapids under the bridge on 17. It was very fast and appeared to be deep, rocky, and difficult to wade at this high water level. A young man in a pickup truck was parked in the small opening close to the river and informed us, after the prerequisite greeting drivel of all anglers, that he had just met Scott Smith, who had said he was on his way back to his cabin to meet some people.

Boxes, waders, coolers, rod cases, and two energetic springers were on the small porch when we pulled into our assigned parking spot. A tall, fair-skinned young man strode purposefully to our vehicle as we stepped into the yard. "I'm Scott Smith." He extended a large hand and smiled. "You must be Bob and Steve, eh?"

Scott is a sergeant in the Thunder Bay Police Department and heads their Tactical Forces Unit. "This is Bill Boote," he added as another well-conditioned young man waded through the gear, coolers, and bouncing dogs. Another strong grip and wide smile.

"The shelf ice is finally gone and this warm rain has brought fish up the river in a rush. They've been holding in the lake because the water was low and very cold until yesterday (it was May 17th), but they're coming in now. The fishing should be good," Scott explained. A quick decision was reached to stow all the gear in the cabin, suit up, and hike to the upper Cypress for the afternoon's fishing. We could sort and unpack later. The steelhead were in the upper runs and pools, excited by the warm rains, and we should get moving as well.

"Put it in four-wheel drive and follow us," Scott directed. We drove across the highway and up a short two-track and parked in the woods perhaps 2 kilometers from the cabin. "This is going to be easy," I said to Steve and stepped eagerly out of the truck.

"Leave your rod broken down. We've got quite a hike through the bush ahead of us," Scott warned. Steve looked at me purposefully, an admonishing stare that said don't ever use the word "easy."

We followed Scott, Bill, and the two dogs, Lightning and Twig, through the bush along the river's edge for 2, perhaps 3 kilometers. The river carried a weak-tea tint and was very fast. There did not appear to be any safe place to wade, and I worried that we might find ourselves in need of a crossing at some point.

We marched on. The dogs flushed several grouse, both spruce and ruffed varieties. Usually the birds would fly up to perch on a limb in plain view just a few feet over Lightning or Twig. Sometimes, after turning to the muffled sound of wingbeats, I would catch a shadow banking around a tree, or gliding farther into the brush.

"We need to cross here and approach that run from the far side. It's one of the better spots on the Cypress." Scott's comment brought me back from thoughts of doubling with my 20-gauge to more imminent exercise. "We're going to cross here?" I asked. The Cypress churned swiftly over rubble and rock. Twisted limbs and trunks lined the near shore. The hydraulic gradient was obviously severe, and I could barely see the bottom. "Yes, it's safe enough. We'll guide you across slowly," Scott replied.

Bill was the first to cross. Thigh-deep in the heavy current, he backed up to our bank and sat on the edge of a twisted spruce. Scott lifted Twig, the larger of the two springers, to Bill's shoulders, and he started

Scott Smith quickly lifts a typical Lake Superior steelhead for the camera.

across, one hand high on the dog's back and the other holding his fly rod out for balance. Redford should have filmed this. It was quite a sight. On the far bank Twig was soon bouncing around, obviously used to crossing rivers on his boss's shoulders. Scott grabbed Lightning, hoisted him, and the scene was repeated. I wondered if they were going to grab *us* and carry *us* across. No photographs, please.

Steve and I made it across with some trepidation but no incident of note beyond needing to be briefly steadied in one narrow chute by the strong arm of Ontario Law. We were on the proper shore to approach the "hot" run. Finally we were going to fish—just as soon as our legs regained some strength.

"This is a pretty deep run and it's deepest at the outside of this sweeping right-to-left curve at the point where it widens and forms the whirlpool on the left." Scott gestured to the heavy black swirl at the base of the run and the tail-out of the pool, where it dumped over a ledge into a narrow chute of white water. "The technique is dead-drift, and a cast usually requires several mends to avoid drag in this tricky current. Rig up a long leader, 12 to 14 feet, with an 8-pound-test tippet. A hot butt section helps in detecting strikes."

He spliced a 12-inch section of red 25-pound-test Amnesia into the butt sections of our leaders and tested the knots. "We'll need split shot to drift the fly at the proper depth. I think we should start with three since the current is heavy with all the recent rain." He rigged a dropper about 18 inches above the point of the tippet for the split shot and suggested we start with an orange Cactus Fly. "It's translucent and catches light filtering through the water. It's very effective here. The run is only starting and the first wave of steelhead just reached this stretch in the past couple of days. We're quite a bit higher than the lake here and the fish have to work up through the rapids, but there are more arriving by the hour."

We both stood, leaving a comfortable seat on an ancient cedar log worn smooth by time. Small black stone flies crawled on our waders and flew clumsily over the water. They appeared to be the same bugs (*Capnia vernalis*) that were so busy on the Pere Marquette 2 months earlier. I waded up to the head of the run while Scott and Steve elected to try a spot farther upstream with Bill, who had returned with a report that it would be worth another moderate hike to a swift run that "should be holding fish."

The stream thermometer read 42 degrees F (6 degrees C) and my watch showed 11:10 AM. Scott grinned, pointed to the run, and said, "I think it's about time to show up for work." With Scott's patient coaching, I began to sense the hidden underwater currents, the personality of our selected stretch of river.

Each cast did indeed require several upstream mends, and a drift at the farthest edge, near the opposite bank, insisted on a hard upstream reach cast as well.

We worked the run in tandem. Scott fished the Cactus, confident in its seductive essence. I switched to a Micro-Egg dropper and size 12 Black Stone Fly nymph as a point fly, one of my favorite duos.

Scott suddenly yelled, "Here!" I thought he was addressing Lightning, but my glance at the beach detected a calm, but intrigued, Lightning staring intently at Scott. I turned and saw Scott's rod in a bow and a fresh, silver steelhead thrashing at the surface in midcurrent. The fish fought gallantly, but soon Scott had donned his cotton landing glove and had a firm grasp just forward of the tail. The barbless hook was out, and the fish was swimming away before I could retrieve my camera (left on the beach) for a photograph.

"Whew, that was fun. I guess about 23 inches, a male." Scott smiled in the general direction of the run, the cedared hillside, the heavens.

"I would have liked to photograph that fish and its release. It was gorgeous," I said and then noticed Lightning's still moist, perfectly centered noseprint on the zoom lens.

"More to come, Bob. Keep the camera handy. Go get one!"

Back to a cool, thigh-deep condition, I was into the umpteenth drift and about midway down the run when the red Amnesia made a noticeable upstream twitch. I lifted the rod and was answered with a swift surge of speed and power. The hen ran upstream for several yards, then darted left and right downstream where she put on a greyhound surface display in the whirlpool before I was able to lead her to the beach and Scott's gloved hand. She was taped (28 inches), photographed, and quickly returned to the Cypress. She required virtually no hand-held revitalization, thrusting strong and fast into the pool as soon as the grip on her tail was relaxed.

"Nice job," I heard Steve's congratulatory remark. He and Bill had returned from their venture, each having hooked fish. We shook hands all around and I sat down to test the connecting knots on my leader and to revel in the afterglow of keen pleasure and satisfaction.

Steve soon hooked and landed a mint-bright 21-inch male on a chartreuse Glo-Bug, and we had just finished our usual postrelease babble when Scott appeared to our right. He was in concert with a large fish that required his close attention.

"What fly?" I asked as he shuffled and skipped along in the heavy flow.

"Orange Cactus," he answered. Then, "Hard take near the bank; I think it's a male, but I'm not sure."

The steelhead, a large male with a hooked jaw and a deepening red band, ran out of steam at the edge of the tail-out. Scott eased him to the shallows and disengaged the hook without touching the fish. "Neatly done," said Steve.

Scott fishes the base of the falls, the upstream barrier for steelhead on the Cypress River.

We gathered near the ledge that dropped into the white, frothy chute and Scott advised that we should start fishing our way back downstream. I thought about the prospect of another white-knuckle, arm-locked, "I love you, God and I'm looking forward to continuing your work," crossing of the turbulent Cypress. Steve obviously was reading my mind, and bored with the unintrepid text, said, "Let's go, wimp."

We crossed three times on our way back, none of which proved eventful, although all three necessitated shoulder rides for the two eager spaniels. Scott hooked and lost a good fish that just would not be slowed, and Bill jumped a bright hen in a deep slot tight to a steep graveled bank studded with the witchy arms of ancient driftwood.

Our last crossing was to the path nearest the vehicles, and I took the temperature before leaving the water. It was 46 degrees F (8 degrees C) at 7:20 PM. The river seemed to have dropped and cleared slightly. It had definitely warmed. I reported the reading and Scott opined that more steelhead would be hurrying upstream and that tomorrow's fishing should improve. Hard to imagine.

Dawn cast a warm, golden tint on the calm waters of the bay as we rustled through the head scratches, coffee spills, spaniel licks, and prerequisite aimless wander of early morning in trout camp. Two gulls circled the small dock and settled on a small, tethered rowboat. A loon called and I thought all of this represented a package of good omens.

Now we were hiking again, uphill through the bush but on a better pathway, a faint, washed-out trail. It was cool (near freezing) but we were perspiring freely when we reached the same run we had first fished the previous day. It was 7:15 AM and there was hard frost, soon to melt, on the gravel beach.

During the course of the day we hooked and played several good fish, but most of our attention was directed to the study of specific techniques for the North Shore's rapid-fall spate rivers. Scott coached Steve on his tuck cast and emphasized to both of us the importance of long leaders for this type of fishing—a long leader helps you to keep your fly line off the water. This is critical in eliminating or reducing drag. When a floating fly line is drifting in complex currents, it moves the fly unnaturally and this fly movement is bad karma to a steelhead. Scott explained that his theory on leaders seems, on the surface, the direct antithesis of conventional wisdom. "I use a 14-foot, or longer, tapered leader in high water and a 9- or 10-foot leader in low clear water. The length is only critical in that the longer the leader, the deeper the water that can be fished with the least line resistance. I *always* use a section of Amnesia in the butt to serve as a strike indicator."

Scott continued the demonstration while fishing through the deep upstream run to the head of the whirlpool. He had moved a few steps into the slower, deeper flow when his rod bowed and a heavy swirl showed at the surface. The steelhead moved, somewhat doggedly but surely, toward the tail-out and the crashing foam of the downstream chute.

Scott literally ran to the shore and down to get below the fish, and during the scramble, managed to throw a hard downstream loop that pulled the fly line into the chute and applied hard pressure from below. A very neat trick, well executed, and the steelhead, feeling the pull, moved back up into the pool where it was soon tailed and released.

Scott explained that in the high-gradient streams of the North Shore, an angler must apply pressure from below the fish when near such rapids or chutes. The only way to do this is to get downstream from the fish by running like hell, or to seem to be downstream by throwing the downstream loop. "The fish will almost always resist that pressure and pull back to a more desirable position," he added.

Steve asked about his tailing technique and Scott explained that a soft cotton or wool glove (wet) allows you to grasp a steelhead just forward of the tail with a firm grip and control the fish for a release without damage. "The glove gives you enough friction to hold the fish without squeezing too hard. It saves carrying a net, which is a real pain in this heavy bush."

We each were entertained by another fish or two. They took Scott's Cactus Fly, wooed I think by the translucence and subtle, natural colors. We gloried in the sounds of the river, its dash of clearing, tea-stained spate against the weathered deadfall and tumbled granite. Too soon, it was time to leave.

"Come back in the fall if you can. We have some pretty good brook trout fishing up here. My good friend Bruce Miller caught one over 6 pounds on a streamer not far from here, and the Nipigon is close by. It's strictly catch-and-release, and the weather and scenery are, well— look around you."

While Steve and I were sorry to leave the beautiful setting and our gracious, knowledgeable host, for once neither of us dreaded the long drive ahead. "Let's be sure to stop several times and take photographs of the overlooks, the bays and islands, the waterfalls, the . . . "

And the anticipation of viewing all this natural splendor was sweet-ened, oh so much, by our smug knowledge that we had a one-day jump on the infamous Far North Black Fly/Mosquito Jamboree; said festival we had once attended years before and had a most lively time as the centers of attention. Some things need no re-experiencing.

TACTICAL SUMMARY

- Specialized casts such as the tuck cast and reach cast are manda-tory in specific situations.
- A series of short (or small), quick mends is often more effective than one or two larger mends.
- You must turn a powerful fish before it gets too far below you into heavy water. Either run to get downstream of the fish or throw a (very hard) loop of line below the fish. The pressure usually turns the fight back into a more desirable arena.
- Long leaders are recommended. They aid in keeping your fly line off the water.
- Scott recommends a cotton glove as an aid in tailing steelhead.

Make sure the glove is wet and grip just forward of the tail.

- A "hot-butt" section of Amnesia serves as an effective strike indicator and does not impair casting.
- He recommends translucent flies that gather light for the tea-colored streams of the North Shore.
- Fish the water closest to you first, and fish it thoroughly. Steelhead often rest near shore and are spooked by careless anglers.

RECOMMENDED TACKLE

- Scott prefers Sage rods. He uses 8-weight and 6-weight, 9- and 9½-foot models, and recommends that visitors to the North Shore consider bringing four-piece pack rods for hiking.
- His favorite reels are the newer Hardy models with rim control. "They're lightweight, they do the job, and they play beautiful music."
- Scientific Anglers fly lines, both floaters and sink tips, are on those Hardys.
- Maxima leaders for abrasion resistance and cold-water knot strength and Amnesia butts are connected to the fly lines.
- He carries a Minolta waterproof camera. "Sometimes it rains. Sometimes I slip."

6

Eric DiCarlo

Ontario's Michipicoten River—A New Drift

In the damp cool of the early May evening, the North Shore Lake Superior bay received the tumbling, slate-hued waters of the Magpie River much as it has for untold hundreds of years. Craggy, weathered rock cliffs dotted with dark spruces stood sentinel over the inlet, and thickly forested hills rolled back as far as one could see, with little of man's impact visible even this close to a town. Our wader-clad presence on the black basalt rocks at the base of the falls seemed a paltry thing; nature certainly took no notice of three men momentarily interfering with her landscape, but the view surely gave *us* pause.

As we drank it in, Eric DiCarlo, our Wawa area local contact, pointed to the far shore of the forested bay. "The first Hudson Bay post sat right over there, and the Northwest Trading Company set up shop just over that way," he informed us. The picture of bearded early voyageurs plying paddles to move their large freight canoes flashed to mind. To be standing where the first commerce as we know it moved whole native cultures out of the hunter/gatherer age added an almost eerie fillip to the awed feeling engendered in us by the raw power of the rumbling falls and the frigid lake.

"Musket parts, ax heads, and similar artifacts from that time are still found in spots like these," Eric added as we eventually began rigging rods, remembering the steelhead that also lurked in these ancient waters. His historical knowledge was much appreciated, as was the fact that we found him as fishing guide in the first place. Guides are scarce in this part of Ontario, as are fly-fishers in general, we were to find. Even Eric, a 43-year-old former Guelph, Ontario, transplant, isn't guiding per se anymore, since he has a full-time job in a Wawa ore-processing plant, but he welcomes contact with fly-fishers under the "local expert willing to help" label. "There are no Trout

Unlimited groups or similar clubs nearby," he lamented. "I'm pretty much all alone here when it comes to taking steelhead on flies."

We were fast getting a sample of his versatility. His knowledge of local lore as well as his fish-taking techniques were enlightening. Eric is a family man with a wife and two children. He is into music, art, photography, and auto racing, so the conversation never lacked for variety either.

But we were here to sample the steelhead fishing, and once rigged we slipped easily into our standard, "O.K., we're a couple of aspiring steelheaders . . . show us how it's done around here" approach. He sort of tossed it back at us.

"Where would you start if I wasn't with you?"

I had already been inching toward the obvious pool at the very base of the falls, so I indicated the same.

"Logical choice," he responded. "Fish often hold there and you can take them, particularly in the seams where the river current works against the static water of the lake. But do you see that boulder sticking out of the water about 50 feet from that peninsula over there?"

Leaving me to fish the falls pool, he took Bob around a little inlet to a spot where he could cast his weighted nymph to the rock. The granite chunk sat in a side eddy with very little current action around it, but Eric told Bob that fish often held on either side and behind it, rather than stage at the base of the falls. A previous client had, in quick succession, taken a 5- and an 8-pounder from the lie. Bob's patient casting from varied angles produced no action this day, however, and I had a similar lack of response to Spruce streamers and Marabou Muddlers near the falls.

As the evening gloom deepened, we voted for creature comforts and headed for our motel. Eric, who considers history almost as intriguing as fishing, had one quick detour for us. We pulled off the road near a bluff above the bay, and he pointed through the brush to some ancient tombstones, barely visible in the shadows. "Several of the earliest settlers rest here," he explained. "Among them is a relative of Alexander Mackenzie. Native Americans would camp on these same bluffs and fish and hunt through the summer and fall."

A discussion of the harsh conditions they endured in those times led us to a more immediate, somewhat selfish concern: How did the current winter, which was so severe that Lake Superior froze over, affect the spring steelhead runs? "They're definitely later," Eric said. "And we're not getting as much spring precipitation, so streams are lower. It seems fewer fish come up now than in past years. Hopefully that will change."

"What is normal regarding runs?"

"They move up from the river mouth right at ice-out. Of course in many of these rivers there are only short stretches, sometimes just a hundred yards or so, before a waterfall that fish can't pass. Then they can be in and out in a day or two."

"So if a guy was to pick the wrong 2 or 3 days for a fishing trip, he could be S.O.L. up here, eh?" Bob said. "Makes calling ahead more of a consideration than in other areas, I suppose?"

"Well, yeah, on some of the streams. But we have pretty dependable waters too. Bigger rivers with longer, unobstructed stretches may hold fish all year." As examples of the latter, Eric named the Nipigon, Batchawanna, Goulais, Agawa, and Michipicoten. We intended to fish the Michipicoten the next day, so it was good to know that holdovers were a possibility, and we wouldn't have to bank entirely on the more capricious spring runs.

That evening we got into local fly patterns—Eric DiCarlo patterns, that is, since there are no nearby fly shops. As is often the case on foreign turf, we saw some interesting variations and adaptations.

The first thing you notice about a DiCarlo-tied nymph is size. He ties them on size 6 to 10, 2X long, up-eye salmon hooks (Redditch design) and bulks up the bodies. "I use the heavier hook and weight the fly itself, in most cases, rather than cast sinkers," he said. "And I prefer a fat, soft-bodied nymph because I believe a steelhead will hold it, perhaps even chew it, with less chance of rejection."

His nymphs somewhat resemble a Whitlock Fox Squirrel nymph, a sort of generic stone fly in brown, black, and combinations thereof— uniformly fat and buggy-looking.

He was particularly high on a Casual Dress look-alike tied with red squirrel tail, a rabbit fur body with gold wire overwrap, and a black wool head.

One exception to the "portly" look is his Sculpin pattern; it is austere compared with most of these minnow imitations. The body is simply lead foil (gleaned from the tops of French wine bottles) overwrapped with brown floss and lacquered. The head is more loosely flared than the normal tightly spun and clipped deer hair head. "I think the secret to its success is the peach-tan hue of the body, which is really close to the color of the sculpins in our local rivers. It is easy to tie, and it *works,*" Eric said, emphasizing the last word.

Another fly he likes to drift in front of steelhead is a foam-bodied, rubber-legged dragonfly nymph. Bob and I were reminded of past success with similar patterns like the Black Girdle Bug and our own June Wiggler, so we figured to try this "local" creation the next day.

Where to fish in the morning, seeing as there were well over 100 streams and rivers in the DiCarlo stomping grounds (the Sault to Wawa and on north . . .), we left up to Eric. He suggested the Old Woman River. "It's smaller, so you can read the water easier, and it's one of our more dependable steelhead producers."

Early morning found us at the Highway 17 bridge near the mouth of the aforementioned stream. The water looked great—low, due to little spring precipitation, but carrying a tinge of color after a light, nighttime rain. It also had a nice, even flow so wading would not be a hazard, as it can be on some of the rushing North Shore streams during spring runoff.

"This really looks good," I enthused as we clunked along the gravelly dry river edge exposed by the low-water conditions. "I'm for working upstream all day if there's a chance for a fish." The lure of the unknown had its hold on me.

Eric was quick to point out that while my attitude was admirable, leapfrogging upstream for any distance here (and on many area rivers) just wasn't feasible. When you hit narrow chutes or other unwadable spots, as we were about to, getting out and moving through the bush is generally impossible. Thick, he made it clear, is a laughably mild adjective for the bankside tangles hereabouts.

"Risque de bushé," Bob chimed in. "Très formidable, eh?" He was rapidly becoming bilingual (sort of) due to guessing his way through countless miles of Ontario road signs.

"Yeah, it's bad," Eric agreed (referring maybe to the bush, *probably* to Bob's pidgin French). "Hey!" he exclaimed in the same breath as we paused at the first slight bend. "Try a smelt pattern first. Look at the gulls wheeling over the water out there. While the drop-backs are ravenous and will often hit anything, they key in on smelt if any are around, and gulls are a pretty good indicator of that."

We went for Clousers and Zonkers, and while we prepped our rigs, Eric told us of a lesson he had learned some time ago on a larger river not far from here. "I had been fishing a run from one bank. I was sure it held fish, but I couldn't get a hit. Then a boat motored up, anchored across from me, and they took fish from the other side."

"Was the sun behind you?" Bob asked.

"No. Dark day. But I finally figured a way to get to the other side, and then I took fish. For whatever reason, be it their angle to the current, or dominant eye, or whatever, I've since found that fish sometimes won't strike to one side of the river, and you have to experiment with location."

Bob and I recalled a popular pool on the Pere Marquette that everyone fishes from the obvious side—except for a couple of knowledgeable locals who get consistent hook-ups from the "tough side." It can be well worth standing up to your scuppers with your back in a bush on occasion.

We worked our minnow patterns for quite awhile, but if any steelhead were in, they didn't show. Nymphs and egg patterns also went untouched. Spruce grouse walked up to us, so close we could have bopped them with sticks, but the steelhead weren't so trusting. After a couple of hours we implemented plan B and walked down to the mouth.

"If you wondered why the river is so named," Eric said, "you can look across the bay here, and with a little imagination, see the likeness of an old woman's face formed by the rocks on the cliff." While Bob took the lake temperature—0 degrees C (32 degrees F) compared with 8 degrees C (46 F) upstream—Eric continued the history lesson, telling us of a Loch Ness–ish local legend about the Michipeshu, a half-lynx, half-lizard denizen of the Superior shore. The Native Americans reportedly appeased this creature by leaving offerings of tobacco at points around the bay.

After striking out around the mouth also (due, no doubt, to unmollified monsters) we headed for bigger water—the Upper Michipicoten just below the Scott Falls power dam, which is the stopping point for anadromous fish. On the drive up, Eric indicated a small stream near the gravel road we were traveling. "That's one of very few closed as a sanctuary for spawners," he said. "Most streams are open all year. I lobbied for a season to get fish numbers up, but nothing has changed yet. I'd also like to see lower limits. Five fish a day is high to my thinking, and a lot of people will take the maximum."

"That's too bad," Bob agreed. "You'd like to see a resource like this better appreciated, especially since these are basically wild fish."

"That's right. The lineage goes back so far they are, for all intents, wild. I haven't caught a tagged or fin-clipped fish in the last 10 years. They only stock at Thunder Bay and the Soo. We also have resident rainbows in all summer. They are very aggressive and can top the 5-pound mark."

Eric DiCarlo (foreground) and Steve at the Magpie River Falls

As we jounced along, Eric closed out his commentary by observing that if the steelhead were given anywhere near the same attention as the thriving Ontario moose population, they could have a spectacular—not just good—fishery.

When we reached our destination, it was heartening to see three or four steelhead holding just below the dam in an off-limits area. "They obviously haven't all dropped back," I noted as we gingerly picked our way over immense jumbles of rocks, boulders, logs, and assorted ankle-twisters to the far side of the river. Lower water enabled us to move downstream this way rather than high-bank it through the bush. I'm not sure which is worse, though. A slip in rubble would result in memorable contusions, but we made it intact.

The Michipicoten is wide in many stretches below the dam, so we were able to wade well out from the banks and position ourselves above an area Eric knew to contain good bedding gravel—and make full backcasts. It was here that a favored DiCarlo technique was revealed. Eric had, over the years, watched "float fishermen" or "drifters" with their center-pin reels, bobbers, and spawn or yarn rigs stand well above runs and make extremely long, free-line drifts. Noting the fish-taking effectiveness of the way they methodically combed all the holding water, he adapted part of the procedure for his fly-fishing arsenal.

"I had used the lift technique, you know, rod high, tight line, follow . . . but I found this other method even more effective." He demonstrated with my rod, rigged with weight-forward 8F, a 10-foot, 6-pound leader, and tipped with one of his Casual Dress look-alike nymphs. "Picture the grid of water you want to cover, beginning from across and below you, cast well upstream of this target with a reach and mend, then when the line gets even with you, throw a big upstream loop and as the line dead-drifts below you, keep it on your chosen line with a continuous series of small mends."

"O.K., I can do that all right," I said.

"But keep feeding line out as it goes below you. See how I have all this slack off the reel hanging in the water? I'm letting it run smoothly over my finger so the float continues with no tension."

He pulled more line, and more, and still he let it go. The backing appeared and *still* the drift continued.

"Holy smokes. Do you have any problems detecting strikes when your fly is a couple of hundred feet below you?" I asked.

"No, you develop a feel for it, and these fish are pretty aggressive. They usually smack it hard."

I took over after a bit and worked the suggested grid, moving each successive float a foot or two farther from me, letting it dead-drift into what appeared to be oblivion before retrieving and repeating.

"Bang your rod at the end of the drift to drop the fly even more before it starts up on the swing," Eric advised.

It didn't take me long to feel at home with this, since it was basically the greased-line technique I've used a lot—with the exception of the extreme length. Barely 5 minutes into my long-drift experimentation and well into my backing, as if to make a prophet of Eric, my rod throbbed with the take of a fish. I lifted, and a silver form vaulted out of the water so far below me that I was momentarily taken aback. Reflex took over and I quickly had him on the reel, almost thankful that it was a smaller steelie, and I wouldn't have to try to move quickly over the treacherous rocky riverbed to control him.

The male was brilliantly colored, and we photographed and released him with all due care. "You're right about them smacking it," I told Eric. "I'm more used to those subtle takes. It's nice to have the guesswork taken out."

"That seems to be the rule," he said. "You may not detect the odd fish, but it's infrequent, I think."

Eric told us that he fishes his sculpin pattern the same way most of the time. He rooted around in the rocks near shore and showed us the local minnow his sparse ties imitated. "And look at these," he enthused, showing us a couple of small, squirming crayfish he had grabbed. "I think steelheaders are missing a bet by not imitating these guys more than they do. This river is full of them."

He talked of how many of the area rivers are sterile, but some, particularly those with dams, which lead to silting, have good insect and "critter" habitat, and imitative flies as well as attractors are successful.

We fished some more of the runs, riffles, and eddies below the dam, but time was limited and we couldn't give a fair test to these imitator patterns. Bob and I had to head farther north to explore rivers between Wawa and Nipigon. Work, work, work . . .

I talked to Eric the following December, and once again, in an even more impassioned fashion, he voiced his concerns for the future of the steelhead fishery in his part of Ontario. He spoke of how many of the smaller rivers get only spring runs; in the fall the fish concentrate on bigger, open rivers and stack up in the lower holes, where they are sitting ducks for meat fishermen. "*Too* many fish are ending up in freezers," he warned. "People from the whole Great Lakes region—anywhere, for that matter—who used to fish these rivers but don't anymore, and people who want to experience them for the first time, should write letters to the Ontario Ministry of National Resources (in Wawa). Suggest lowering limits. The current five fish per day is ridiculous. It would be great, too, to see a closed season, if only during primary spawning times. We *have* to protect this resource, and we need help."

He is right. Once you experience the wild, rugged beauty of the North Shore of Lake Superior, you will know that a continuing, thriving steelhead population is its perfect complement.

TACTICAL SUMMARY

- Where feasible, extend your drift; don't be afraid to lengthen it beyond what is normally your supposed control zone.
- Keep a low profile when wading. Wearing camo doesn't hurt.
- Be ready to go at first ice-out.
- Don't fish a run too long . . . no "poke," move on.
- Fog coming in from the lake (Superior) usually means poor fishing.
- Bring plenty of gear since few places carry any fly-fishing paraphernalia.

- Gulls can mean baitfish are present.
- Try fishing a promising run or pool from even the most unlikely looking side or angle.
- "Bang" your rod or otherwise activate the fly at the end of a drift; don't be overly quick to retrieve.
- If a once- or twice-a-year angler, consider practicing your casting *before* a trip so you can get more quickly into the rhythm.

RECOMMENDED TACKLE

- Eric uses a Loomis 10-foot, 6-weight rod.
- He likes Hardy reels, particularly the Marquis, with a Scientific Anglers double-taper, 6-weight floating line and *lots* of backing.
- He favors Aeon tippet material for its lack of memory and good knot strength in cold water.
- Weighted, bulky nymphs in larger sizes are his first-choice flies; his home-tied sculpin rates high also.

7

John Ramsay

West Coast Influences in the Huron River Wilderness

"Big Mac" is not just a cholesterol bomb sandwich in this part of the world. In Michigan the term refers more properly to the nation's most magnificent bridge. Five miles long, 600 feet high, and purely awesome, the Mackinac (pronounced Mackinaw) Bridge spans the straits that join Lakes Huron and Michigan, and links the lower peninsula to the upper at Mackinaw City and St. Ignace. High winds can cause this elevated stretch of I-75 to sway noticeably and necessitate a police-escorted crawl to reach land safely on either side. That eventuality makes for an interesting day, something on the order of driving from Silver City, through Bear Tooth Pass, to Red Lodge, Montana. In a misty rain with bald tires. It is a passage you will long remember.

There had been no measurable precipitation for weeks, though early May is normally pretty damp in Michigan. The western and central regions of the Upper Peninsula were approaching drought conditions, complete with stern warnings from the US Forest Service about the danger of flash fires throughout the range. We were on our way to meet John Ramsay (aka Black River John), a fly-fishing guide and blues-jazz-boogie musician and vocalist from Black River Harbor. His neighborhood streams, the Black, Presque Isle, Montreal, and Ontonagon, were showing few steelhead this spring. Low water was the prime suspect in this circumstance, so he had been scouting eastward and had arranged to meet us at the campground bridge over the Huron River northeast of L'Anse later in the afternoon.

John was waiting, hands on hips, staring intently into the Huron as we pulled across the bridge on Big Erick Road. Big Erick's Brook enters the Huron at this point and the public campground is simply called Big Erick's. There must be some colorful local history involved here, I thought, as we parked and exchanged greetings.

The Huron River headwaters near Mount Arvon, Michigan's high-

131

est point of land at 1979 feet and flows due north through some of the wildest country remaining in the continental United States to Lake Superior at the Baraga and Marquette county line. It is a swift stream, granite-based, with large boulders and ledge rock, coarse gravel, and sand. It is remarkably clear for an "Iron Country" river, and only shows its tea stain at depths over 2 feet. It was very low this day.

John warned that we would be fishing under the toughest possible conditions. "The snowmelt runoff is long gone and we've had *no* rain. The low water has kept most of the steelhead from ascending. There are a few in, fish that came up early, but many of them have gone back out to the lake."

Steve commented, "They rarely come easy. Should we rig up or wait until later in the afternoon?"

John had located some deep bend pools downstream that he thought would be the best bet to hold fish. He suggested that the wiser course of action would be to defer setting up camp and to begin fishing as soon as possible. "The river's level is still falling," he said. "We'll need to use long leaders, fine tippets, and *lightly* weighted flies. Even the smallest split shot makes too much entry disturbance under these conditions. That soft 'ploink' when the shot hits the water can spook steelhead."

We knotted fresh tippets, tied on small (size 12) Stone Fly nymphs, and followed John down the faint trail on the east bank of the Huron. We traversed several smallish spring seeps on the 30-minute hike, and John pointed out their practical value to steelhead anglers. "Where they gather and form rivulets and enter the main river, particularly if it is near a fairly deep run or pool, they cool the water and act as a magnet for game fish."

We started fishing at the head of a deep bend to the right. The Huron washed over a lip of granite boulders onto a short gravel run that quickly widened, slowed, and rolled into a deep cut at the base of a steep hill littered with spruce slashings and new-growth pine.

The stream thermometer read 48 degrees F (9 degrees C) and John advised that although the water temperature was ideal, the fish would be found, if at all, only in the deepest holes. "They want to avoid the direct sunlight," he added, "but the stream is *so low* there isn't much deep water."

Steve and I fished through the deep hole alternately. We tried the Stone Fly nymphs without a touch and then began to switch and search for the magic pattern. I tried a Micro-Egg, an Egg-Sucking

Leech, a Hare's Ear, and finally, a Marabou Spey. Steve fished a chartreuse Glo-Bug, a Wiggler, a standard Woolly Bugger, and a Frammus. No luck. John worked his favorite fly, an orange-and-white bucktail, methodically through the very head of the pool near where the deep run channeled its power and pushed hard against a nest of twisted driftwood. No luck.

We continued downstream, walking along the bank toward the next spot John had scouted. He was deeply troubled about tribal rights as they impacted the steelhead fishery. Gill nets near the mouths of spawning streams were a serious problem, and he recited several cases in point where he had witnessed illegal operations in process. Despite discussions with the Department of Natural Resources, no action had been taken. "It's discouraging," he added. "The sport fishery along the south shore of Lake Superior should be one of the real jewels of this country. The fish are lean and hard; they have specifically adapted to their natal watershed over generations; each drainage system has produced a unique, exquisite animal that deserves a fair chance. And it's not just the nets. A lot of people consider any large fish as their personal protein source, obtainable by any means at any time."

We approached a high bank with a dark slide of deeper water. This was the best-looking water we had seen so far in our ramble. A long riffle slowly thickened at the far edge and merged to black water against the boulders, ledge rock, and sand of the high bank.

"This hole usually stacks up with fish. If there are any in this area they will have moved into this deep stretch to wait out the high sun and clear sky. With such light pressure [we had seen only one other angler in the roughly 3-mile hike], the fish will likely take or show somehow if we can get a good dead drift next to the bank." John suggested Steve try the lower end of the holding water with a traditional Skunk pattern, and then directed my efforts to the head of the dark water. "Try an Orange-and-White," he said and handed me one from his fly book.

Nearly an hour later, after several passes through the most promising water without a hint of action, I retired to the bank to commit notes to paper and to reflect. I noticed that Steve had disappeared around a bend downstream, and that John was sitting on a large granite slab, poring through his fly boxes. I waved him over and we decided to finish out the afternoon and rethink during the evening hours in camp.

John Ramsay and Steve run classic West Coast patterns through a riffle.

"Maybe we should drop down to the mouth and fish the surf with big streamers. Maybe they're staging there—waiting for rain," I offered.

"When fishing is *really* tough like this, I usually move my clients to larger systems, rivers with more water like the Black, the Presque Isle, or the Montreal. But I've just been on those rivers and the runs are way late there due to the long and very hard winter and no rain. It's probably just not worth the drive. We're as well off right here as we would be anywhere else, so let's tough it out for now."

For a moment I wondered if perhaps Steve was "felts up" in a logjam, but John started to talk about techniques and I quickly refocused to more critical matters. "Under normal water levels—a *lot* more water than this—I recommend high-density, sink-tip lines, usually class III or IV, and more heavily weighted flies." He continued, "Fly-fishing for steelhead in the Upper Peninsula is quite close, I think, to angling for *winter* fish on the West Coast. We'll normally have high, often clear water, with temperatures in the 30s. Most of the patterns I use are of West Coast origin or are adaptations of western flies."

I asked about pattern selection, and John stated that he usually starts with a fairly bright attractor. "They're pretty effective up here.

If I raise a fish, if one shows and doesn't take the fly, I'll switch to a nymph, or dark streamer. That will usually induce a solid take. A fish rarely comes twice to a bright attractor, even if you change patterns. They take it hard the first time, or at least show themselves, so the advantage is clear."

We looked hard at the beautiful, seemingly fishless river. Still no Steve, and I was working myself into a dither of fret. "What do you do when you've fished through a promising piece of water and there's nothing—no take, no swirl, no shadow?" I asked.

"Well," he answered, "I've used a bright fly on that first pass, so I'll rest the water for 10 minutes and then fish through with a dark pattern. That's my normal procedure. It's usually effective. Sometimes, I'll add a split shot to the leader if I feel it is absolutely necessary in order to achieve a deeper drift, but I prefer to fish without the extra lead."

John explained that there was little history of steelhead fly-fishing in the Upper Peninsula, and few fly-fishers even now. "Most people who utilize fly gear are really drift-fishing with spawn or yarn. They're not fly-fishing at all. Even drift-fishing with true fly patterns bored me and I switched to fly-casting with fly lines."

I asked how that resolution affected his success and he guessed that, after he rethought his approach and how he would present the fly, his production had remained relatively constant. "When I began experimenting with patterns I had to rely solely on books based on the Pacific sport fishery, and I found that those patterns work just fine. I began taking fish in the surf off the Presque Isle River. They were small fish, 12 to 16 inches, but they gave me confidence in those early days."

John explained that a drop-back technique at the end of an across-and-downstream swing will often bring a strike from curious, previously uncommitted steelhead. "I'll hold it steady at the end of the drift, straight downstream, then pop the rod and let out 6 inches or so of slack. The fish hit when the fly pulls tight the second time."

The conversation lapsed for a moment and as I stood to stretch and de-kink, I noticed Steve attentively fishing the run below the pool where we had been sitting. He had been obscured by a narrow tongue of cedars. Looking our way, he waved and began slogging upstream.

"It's about 3 miles uphill to the bridge and campground. We should start back," John offered as soon as Steve, huffing, rejoined us.

"Anything to report?" I asked.

"No, not even a shadow. I covered some great-looking water, deep, broken surface runs and holes, but no takes." Steve was still optimistic, though.

On the way back (did I *emphasize* uphill?) Steve asked John how he had settled in the wilds of the Upper Peninsula. "I grew up in Elmhurst, Illinois. The city life tired and depressed me. It was a move that was made for the soul," he paused, "and for brook trout and steelhead. I met my wife Nancy up here. We have two neat kids, Max and Maisie. I have the forests, the rivers, the trout, my music, and a fine family. I'm very content; it was a good move." He stopped and looked at the river. "I don't miss Chicago," he said and led onward and upward.

Back at the bridge we wheezed out of neoprene waders that were as wet inside from condensation as if they had leaked.

That evening around a small fire we were able to learn a bit more about John Ramsay and his sylvan philosophy. "I much prefer the April dance of mating woodcock and the thunder of Lake Superior to the sights and sounds of *any* city," he answered to Steve's rhetorical, "What is the lure of this wild place?"

It is clear that John holds a special reverence for the wild, bush and beast alike. He likes the simple, self-sufficient life and practices a concerned and enlightened stewardship over his perceived responsibilities to the natural world. "Grouse, deer, coyotes, woodcock, brook trout, steelhead—are the essence of what makes this country special to me. The steelhead really need man's help, or at least man's forbearance, so that they can help themselves." He went on to point out that total fish kills were too high and made an interesting case for licensed "kill tags" for sport fishing and stricter, enforceable regulations for netting. "A steelhead stamp would include three, five—pick a realistic number under ten—kill tags for an entire calendar year. Any steelhead dead or on a stringer must be tagged. An angler could use all tags in a single day, dole them out throughout the year, or hopefully, burn them," he concluded.

The next morning was brisk for early May, but the cloudless sky promised a quick warm-up. We cleared camp, artfully and thoroughly, I thought, after years and years of practice, but John made a slow, final turn around the site to be sure we had overlooked nothing before heading to the river.

This day we would drive farther downstream in hopes of finding pooled fish in larger water closer to Lake Superior. We drove north a few short miles and turned east to intercept a path down to the Huron through a heavy roll of hills timbered by hemlock, balsam, and spruce, and seeping with countless tiny springs.

"The water should be cooler down here," he said as we sideslipped (felts are not ideal for *all* angling terrain) toward the river on a steep slope permeated with the pungent odor of forest rot.

We found the river pretty much as we had left it the previous evening. The Huron was wider here, and for the most part slightly deeper. The riffles, runs, and deep pools were of the same characteristics as the upstream water, that is, inviting, spectacularly beautiful, and empty of fish, at least of fish willing to show an interest in our flies.

John was apologetic. "I'm really sorry about this weather. As soon as the rains hit, the fish will storm up this river. They'll be bright silver and aggressive. Can you wait for the rain?" He looked at us and added, "It'll be worth it."

"It might not rain for quite a while, but we can come back," Steve answered. We reeled up, broke down our rods, and crabbed up the wild hills to our vehicles.

John was going back to Black River Harbor. His wife Nancy, a prominent potter, was returning from a show in Wisconsin and he was looking forward to seeing her and the children. He had been away from home, fishing and scouting, for several days. "I'll fish the Black and the Presque Isle, my backyard streams, for a few days," he said.

"We're bound for the North Shore and then the St. Mary's," I offered.

We shook hands and John pulled two samples of his favorite pattern, the Orange-and-White, from his box and handed them to us. "This one really works. Come back and try it."

We will.

TACTICAL SUMMARY

- When conditions are tough, John recommends long leaders, relatively fine tippets, and lightly weighted flies to achieve a seductive drift. He feels split shot causes unnecessary surface disturbance and spooks fish, especially in a low, clear water situation.
- When temperatures rise, look for spring seeps that freshen the river. Steelhead seek out the cooler water and will often hold near the first decent downstream cover.
- When the sun is high and the sky is clear, fish the deepest water as your first priority.

- Fish stream structures such as logjams thoroughly. Fresh from the lake and out of the comfort zone provided by great depths, steelhead seek out shade and cover.
- He suggests his clients use sink-tip lines, usually class III or IV, under normal flows. The quickly sinking line and a weighted fly can get to the proper level without the nuisance of extra lead.
- Fish in the steep-gradient Upper Peninsula streams respond well to classic West Coast patterns. John usually starts with a bright attractor, then follows with a smaller, darker pattern.
- He thinks that many steelhead fly-anglers hurry too much and do not fish the water thoroughly. "Change patterns two or three times and work a piece of water methodically and patiently. Not all fish want the same fly."
- The "drop-back" technique is productive on Lake Superior rivers.
- Fish stage at river mouths and in the deepest pools in the lower reaches, waiting for enough water to feel safe.
- Use a stream thermometer. Be aware that a change of only 2 or 3 degrees can turn fish on, or off. Optimal temperature is about 50 degrees F (10 degrees C).

RECOMMENDED TACKLE

- John's favorite rod is an Orvis 9 foot 3 inch, in 7 weight.
- He prefers Hardy reels, particularly the Golden Prince. "A Hardy plays the sweetest music."
- Scientific Anglers lines are his first choice, and HiD class III and IV sink tips are used most often.
- John makes his own leaders with Mason hard nylon butt sections and Orvis tippet material.

8

Dan Donarski

Angler's Paradise—The St. Mary's Rapids

Something akin to a triumphant Johnny Weismueller/Tarzan bellow boomed out above the turbulence of the rushing St. Mary's River rapids. A bigger-than-usual grin split the mustachioed face of Dan Donarski, who had just landed our first steelhead of the day. Then, in case someone in St. Ignace hadn't heard him, the exultant yell split the air again. "I can't help it," he said while we quickly photographed the 5-pound female prior to release. "I'm the proverbial kid in a candy store when I'm fishing here."

"Here" was rubbing elbows with history: The skyline of Sault Ste. Marie, North America's third oldest city, was visible; the famous Soo Locks with attendant parks and walkways were nearby; awesome Great Lakes freighters plied the waters; best of all, some of the finest steelhead fishing anywhere can be had here.

Hooking, fighting, and landing a good fish in the tumbling, rocky rapids was a worthy accomplishment in itself; getting a rod in Dan's hands to begin with was nearly as difficult. "Guides do not fish," he had insisted. "Maybe late in the day I'll go over some water you've thoroughly worked."

"You have to, dammit. We learn best by example," and additional reminders of the intent of our project eventually had the desired effect. Good thing, too, because it was eye-opening to watch a veteran familiar with this water, an accomplished wader, slowly, almost gingerly, work his way downstream, trying to stay somewhere within handling range of his adversary and not take a header in the process.

"In a worst case scenario, you could die here," Dan told us as we approached the river. "There is a 20-foot drop, plus or minus, in a few hundred yards, so it rips along pretty good." The rocks and rubble are obvious, but their varied hues, shapes, and sizes under the ultra-clear, very fast water distort perception. Cautious wading is an im-

139

mediate requisite; complacent waders often get wet. (We saw three tumbles just this one day.)

"I know it sounds self-promoting," he told us as we entered the water from the Canadian shore (no access permitted from the US side), "but anglers should always get a guide for the first day on a new river. If you didn't know, for instance, that it's best to ford to the berm at the head of this little island, you could waste an hour just trying to cross to the main flow."

This berm or dike, by the way, has been in place for about 10 years. It is a concrete structure roughly one-fourth of the way out into the river from the Canadian side, rising 4 or 5 feet above the riverbed and extending from the compensating gates that hold back Lake Superior to the bottom of the rapids. It was put in by the Ontario Ministry of Natural Resources and the Edison Soo Electric Company to keep the river level constant and create spawning habitat. According to Dan, it works well. The river rarely gets high or muddy, especially inside (Canadian side) the dike. It also creates a convenient catwalk for stalking fish.

Referring to this water as "my little slice of paradise," Dan has guided and fished at the Sault since 1989. From 1984 to 1989 he had been in Alaska, and previous to that he was involved in the charter-boat fishery on the Wisconsin side. He lives on the American side with his wife Kristen and daughter Karen. The 35-year-old Donarski is a busy man. Besides his job as Executive Director of the Sault Convention and Visitors Bureau, he is president of the Sault Area Sportsmen Club, a member of the Michigan Outdoor Writers Association, Trout Unlimited, Ducks Unlimited, and the National Rifle Association. He ties flies and is a fanatical pursuer of feather as well as fin; the latter, however, command most of his attention on the productive waters of the St. Mary's River.

This fishery has good natural reproduction and, in addition, is heavily stocked by both Michigan and Ontario. Dan was effusive in his praise of this cooperative management and also pointed out that the local power company, Edison Soo, turned over one-third of its power plant (area) to create a hatchery. He credited movers and shakers like Bill Gregory, Roger Griel, Joe Cain, and Dr. David Behmer, as well as many local volunteers, for keeping things running—and run they do. The river is host to not only our presently sought steelhead, but Atlantics, pinks, kings, cohos, browns, and brook trout.

There were four or five other fishermen present when we reached

Dan Donarski congratulates Marc Linsenman.

the berm adjacent to the main flow. While we tied on the meat-and-potatoes fly of the St. Mary's rapids—Green Caddis Pupa—I commented to Dan that there sure weren't many rods present, considering we were into the front end of the projected "hot time" on what has come to be known in most serious steelhead circles as one of *the* primo areas in the Great Lakes Basin.

"On weekends you might have to get here early, but generally it's not crowded. In fact, I'd like to see *more* fly-fishermen get on to this bonanza. The more people who fish it and appreciate it, the more care the resource will receive."

We waded out to a section that looked much like all the other water for hundreds of yards in both directions. Some large boulders protruded here and there, breaking the current and creating the seams and slicks and lies that steelhead favor. Rods of 9½ to 10½ feet were our choices today, with floating lines for the greased-line dead-drift and/or shorter tight-line follow, approaches usually effective in shallow, fast rivers.

Dan fished his caddis point fly below an egg attractor relatively close in since we were fishing blind at this point; the sky was gray, and long casts weren't necessary yet. I watched him change hands and lean downstream at the end of each pass to get an extra few feet out of the drift.

Early on I fished close to Dan, asking questions and enjoying his ebullient responses. "We're going to hook fish!" he exclaimed. "We're up in what is called 'The American Pool,' and a fish hooked here will go downstream. Go with him *carefully* to the next ('Canadian') pool, and he'll usually hang there. You can finish the fight at that point."

"Why the 'American' and 'Canadian' pool names?" I asked, envisioning some international fish-related bit of local color.

"Who knows. That's just what they're called."

Since Dan hooked the aforementioned first fish, I got to do the pool-to-pool downstream trek as photographer/observer rather than fish-fighter, for which I was a bit thankful. It gave me a chance to adjust to current speed and rock conditions without a reel-screaming distraction.

Dan discoursed on the way down, exhorting the fish, then turning to me, "She isn't real big, maybe 5 or 6 pounds, but with the sharp gradient we have here, you get a better fight. They can really make the current work to their advantage. This is another instance where a long rod comes in handy. As far as that fish is away from us (well over 100 feet at that point), you need to keep the line as high above the water as possible to clear rocks."

After landing this first fish, we attracted an audience. Two official-looking persons clambered over the rocks in our direction, leading me to think that Dan's exuberant vocalizations were going to win him an excessive-noise citation. But this meeting with local bureaucracy was enlightening.

Arriving just as we released the fish, a Ms. Kathleen McLaren said, "Oh, that's too bad. We needed a female."

My puzzled look led this pleasant employee of the local Ontario hatchery to explain that this was how they obtained eggs and milt for their program, that is, from fish that anglers allowed them to "milk" into coolers. She would station herself at a central vantage point, watch for a person fighting a fish, and head for the angler with her equipment. The collected eggs and milt were then taken to the hatchery and processed within 12 hours—usually within 3 or 4 hours. When I spoke with her this day, their year's goal of 110,000 fertilized steelhead eggs "looked reachable."

"Come on, let's get you into a fish," Dan said. "I get a bigger kick out of seeing someone else land one." We headed back up the berm toward Bob and found him doggedly working his way down to us, rod bent with the weight of another strong Lake Huron steelhead.

He got the fish all the way down into the quieter water we had just left; the hatchery consortium regrouped expectantly, but then the fish rolled, the hook inexplicably came out, and that was that.

"At least I got to see that she'd taken the point fly," Bob told us. "They really go after those Green Caddis. I was running it below a Black Stone Fly."

"I like to use the caddis below a pink-and-chartreuse egg fly," Dan added. "I will, of course, vary the egg fly colors if I'm not getting any action. I also like to try variations on the Green Caddis pattern. I've had good success with Swannundaze ribbing over the body. I generally keep the peacock herl head."

Fly boxes appeared and we compared notes on various patterns and personal variations on them.

"I tie my caddis on heavy wire egg hooks in sizes 4 to 8, and I check points frequently for sharpness—and to ensure I even have a point, what with all the rocks," Dan said.

"Any reason for the upturned-eye hook?"

"Yeah . . . I'm not positive but what a downturned eye might not act as weed guard of sorts, deflecting the hook from a fish's jaw. Might as well give yourself every little advantage."

"Any luck with these stone flies?" I asked, noticing a couple of interesting patterns in Dan's collection.

"On occasion. There are those who say there aren't any in the St. Mary's here, but I've taken fish on them. I like to jazz up the Black Stone Fly by tying in a fluorescent thorax or sometimes a Flashabou wing case. I will use yellow stones sometimes also." He brought out another box. "Look at this. It's just a big, black ugly bug with black rubber legs and upturned antennae. But note the fluorescent green butt. Color is so important for steelhead, where it's more silhouette and action for other trout."

"I noticed you pinch on a split shot or three. Do you think that's the best weighting system for this rapid water?" Bob asked.

"Well, sinking lines are tough in most spots here, so I don't often use them. I like to fish traditional fly gear and dead-drift, but the most effective way to get to fish is the slinky rig. I'll have clients switch to it if they get frustrated. Personally, I prefer to hook one fish on regular fly gear to ten on any other setup."

Dan pulled up Bob's 9½-foot Graphite-USA. "This is what you need in a rod," he said approvingly. "Plenty of backbone. The wind can kick butt through here. Twenty-knot breezes aren't uncommon,

Dan coaches as Marc battles another big fish.

and you have to be able to drive casts sometimes. I've had people come with 5- and 6-weight rods, and I often end up giving them my rod so they can fish effectively."

"Speaking of which, let's get back to it," I said, still skunked at midmorning and wanting to end that. "What's it like on the other side of the dike?"

"I'll show you," Dan said. We waded to a section where some huge boulders broke the gentler current close to the Canadian shore. "This is a neat feature of this area. While lots of people can't break a big river into sections, or workable pieces, over here it's a bit smaller, and holds are easier to recognize in much of it."

"There are a couple of fish," I exclaimed. "Aren't there? In that fast water just up from the big black rock? Boy, they're hard to see."

As if to facilitate matters for my suspect eyes, a darker male slid in and there was no further doubt. However, they wanted no part of our offerings, and shortly they disappeared. We waited a while, but no reappearance, so it was back to the main river.

While stalking around fishing likely spots and just looking for holding fish, I ran into a guiding friend of Dan's, one Ray Ebertt, who showed me another bit of local lore, a feature of the area that tied in with Dan's observation about breaking a big river into workable pieces. The dike separating the river had occasional narrow breaks built into it where water can channel through from the Canadian side into the main St. Mary's. One of these breaks, considerably downstream from the more popular area, let water through into a configuration of rocks that channeled the flow somewhat for a while before it merged with the river proper.

Ray explained that fish apparently felt they were entering a tributary here, and would often come up it and hold at the top of this "channel" as they might in a smaller spawning stream. We found none this day, but he assured me it gave up fish to him on more than one occasion.

A bit later I rejoined Bob and Dan upstream and found that both had landed fish since I had departed. Bob had, in fact, lost another one just minutes before. "It got too far out from him," Dan explained. "He couldn't keep his line high enough to clear rocks and the fish hung him on something."

"Or else my dropper fly snagged up," Bob speculated. "Maybe I should go to one fly. One of life's eternal dilemmas."

I tried the main rapids some more, but with no success, so I hiked back across the dike to where I had earlier worked those visible fish off a little island. They were back. This time I stationed myself *way* above them, marking their holding area by a large rock to one side. My fly would hit the water a good 50 feet above them, and my downstream swing should finish right in the dining room. It did. A half-dozen swings brought that longed-for boil, rod-bend, and surge of a heavy fish. I had to quickstep down the shallows to let my line clear the top of the large boulder the fish had chosen to drop below on the side opposite me. This accomplished, I looked below to see where I might end up. I had been down there earlier with Dan, who had advised me of where not to wade if I got below the island. Things looked unfamiliar now, so I decided to slug it out from where I stood if possible.

This took quite a while, as the fish was below me in heavier water. Occasionally I could pry him out and up a bit, but he would slide back and the stalemate went on. I would glance up to where Dan and Bob were fishing and wave now and again, hoping one of them would see, but not really needing any help.

About the time the fish was giving it up, I saw the boys working my way, along with the egg-taking crew. I turned my attention back to the fish and missed seeing Donarski take a header into the frigid water, testimony to the difficult wading conditions.

When they reached me, both wet, Bob having punctured his 5-mm neoprenes on a stumble into a sharp rock, I had the fish beat, tailed, and waiting in the shallows for a picture. "Jeez, you cause a lot of trouble when you finally catch something," Bob complained. But he measured the fish, a 27-inch male of about 8 pounds, and got a photo or two before the release. The hatchery folks had enough milt already, which was probably a good thing as this fish, exhausted after the overlong fight, needed no further depletion of strength. We spent a long time resuscitating him in the current, and I hope he made it. I suspect that may have been a fish I should have kept, hindsight being what it is . . .

In addition to constant wading care, brought to mind again by "The Donarski Immersion" (Is that a Ludlum book title?), another caution peculiar to the St. Mary's rapids is in order. The dike provides a neat walkway from which to spot fish, but one can become too intent on looking and neglect basic walking skills. Brother Bob *twice* illustrated his version of the space walk to various degrees of pain and tackle damage (hereafter Ludlumized as The Linsenman Splashdowns). But once fish are spotted, the berm can serve as a sight barrier between you and holding fish. A reasonably coordinated person can mark his/her location, climb down from (rather than step off of) the wall, creep along behind it, and cast over the top while staying low and concealed.

Incidentally, I used to think I was really good at spotting steelhead. Due to aging eyeballs (?), I'm not as proficient as I once was. Here I was downright inept. "Is it me or what?" I whined to Dan, who had just indicated two fish holding about 50 feet out from the berm. "I can't see anything there I'd bet heavily on as being fish."

"It's not you entirely. This water is really clear, but the current motions, bottom colors, and the many fresh (meaning light-hued) fish make spotting tougher than in most places."

When I finally did see a fish on my own in the main flow, a kicking female my grandmother could have spotted, I felt better. But when the hen quit flashing, she was invisible again. Maddening. Be advised and persevere.

Fortunately, Bob and I, like most steelheaders, don't have to have visible fish in front of us. We subscribe to the bromide about an ignorant person being constantly surprised. A good-looking hold with reasonable potential—with which the St. Mary's abounds—is enough for us to while away many happy finger-numbing, nose-dripping hours. Which we did, jumping more fish and generally having one of our best-ever steelhead experiences.

Bob was, in fact, so taken with the abundance of wild, or as Dan refers to them, "naturalized," fish, that on a later trip he brought his son Marc, who had yet to land a steelhead, to these rapids—this in the face of literally dozens of other rivers we have explored recently and in past successful years. Marc was finally christened, hooking several and landing two, one near 15 pounds.

Like so many of the guides and local aficionados we have worked with in preparing this book, Dan is worried that this beautiful picture could fade. He is active in calling for fly-fishermen to work together to preserve what we have, not just in the St. Mary's River, but in all Great Lakes tributaries.

A recent Donarski article in *Fly Fisher* (Autumn '94) gives a concise, balanced appraisal of the threats to steelhead, citing overly liberal creel limits, lengthy seasons, too few closed streams, tribal netting, offshore charter boats, huge increases in river angling, new licensing guidelines for dams, and zeroing in on steelhead as salmon numbers decline as major problems needing remedy.

Dan is not a gloom-and-doomer, either. Quite the contrary. He simply wants, as so many of us do, the good times to continue rolling, and he sees rule and regulation changes as the major steps in preserving the fishery.

TACTICAL SUMMARY (especially for St. Mary's River)

- Put plenty of backing on your reel.
- Watch your shadows *very* carefully. Fish spook easily in clear water.
- On chilly days try the shallower, sun-warmed pocket water (particularly on the Canadian side of the berm when on the St. Mary's).
- Break a big river into manageable pieces and work these thoroughly.
- Use cover (e.g., the berm) whenever possible.
- Keep as much line off the water as possible when playing a fish.
- Allow fish to move down into slower, deeper water where they can find a "haven" and will pause.
- Wear felts, studs, or cleats—a must.
- A net can prevent injury in landing a fish among the many rocks in northern rivers.

RECOMMENDED TACKLE

- Dan favors the Loomis GLX and Orvis PM-10 in 7 weight. He emphasizes the need for longer (8½ to 10 feet), fast-action rods with sensitive tips and lots of backbone.
- The Scientific Anglers System II is a good reel choice, as is the Scientific Anglers weight-forward 8F line.
- Abrasion-resistant leaders are needed. Dan likes Maxima green in 6- to 8-pound.
- Heavy wire hooks with upturned eyes are his preference.
- Try egg-fly attractors in pink and chartreuse with a Green Caddis at point. Sculpins, Muddlers, and Stone Flies can also be effective.

9

Karl Vogel

Spotting and Stalking with a Canadian Master

The city of Sault Ste. Marie, Ontario, operates a cold-water hatchery that over the years has planted tens of thousands of sport fish—fry and fingerlings—into the St. Mary's River. These fish grow fat in Lake Huron and ascend the river at various times of the year to spawn in the rapids, providing some of the most challenging and rewarding trophy fly-angling in the world.

The Pacific salmons are represented by pinks, coho (silver), and chinooks (kings). Atlantics in the 30-pound range also use the river. Steelhead ascend in large numbers from late April through early June and again in late fall. Browns, brooks, resident rainbows, and white-fish are also present in substantial numbers. For all but the fiercest days of deep winter, the St. Mary's River, especially the intimidating rapids, provides a sport fishing venue of wide variety and high excitement.

Picture this. You are standing in knee-deep, crystalline, rushing water, legs apart to brace your feet (perhaps wisely studded). You are connected by a 3X tippet to a fresh, 12-pound buck steelhead. He has taken all your line and perhaps 60 yards of backing straight out toward the center of the rapids. You must keep your arm and 9½-foot rod as high in the air as possible so that the line and backing will clear several large boulders. The fish makes several short dashes in a pocket of flat water and turns downstream toward Lake Huron. It is too deep to follow by river, so you scramble over several large rocks and through a waist-deep, bankside slot to chase (I mean *run*) after the fish on the bank. Hold your rod high! Do you get the idea? This is the good stuff—200-proof adrenaline.

Karl Vogel began guiding as a service to his community in general and specifically in support of the efforts of the Sport Fishing Development Organization and the hatchery. The city of Sault Ste. Marie has invested, and continues to invest, heavily in the steelhead program, hoping to lure fly-fishing tourist dollars to the city. To continue operation, the demonstration of viability is a necessity. Return on investment shows as nonresident license sales, motel bookings, guides employed, donations, and so on.

"Many fly-anglers are frightened by the reputation of these rapids. Older anglers in particular feel they cannot safely fish here, and I wanted to show that it can be enjoyed by people throughout the range of physical athletic ability and power." Karl took a few more steps into the current, braced his wading staff, and pointed to three melting, shivering shadows on the near side of a large boulder. "There are at least three fish out there—no, four, by that reddish rock. Cast about 15 feet upstream for the proper drift and see what happens."

I looked around and noticed that Steve had moved downstream, so Karl was obviously addressing me. The second cast seemed decent and a shadow moved a foot toward us and then turned back; my leader stopped. We were connected—for the moment. The steelhead cleared the area immediately, thrashed once, circled the large rock, and rushed upstream. My line had caught on the boulder, and the tippet parted. "You'll need to raise your rod as high as you can, as quickly as you can," Karl said.

We made the short 15-foot wade to the bank, and I sat down to reload as Karl continued his earlier commentary. "I've just had both of my hips replaced, just a few months ago, and I can hook, play, and land fish here—safely. I take it slow and easy and concentrate on spotting fish close to the bank. Many of my clients are past 50 and do not wish to wade too deeply—to dare the power of this river. And they catch steelhead and have a great time without ever having to be scared out of their wits."

I clicked in my advanced mathematics brain cell and was able to calculate that I was past 50 and then remembered that an immersion in 6 degrees C (42 degrees F) water could be unpleasant. Karl's slow, cautious approach had some significant merit and real appeal on this windy, cool morning.

The wind from Lake Superior, about 3 miles due north, came in sharp gusts. High clouds sailed quickly toward Lake Huron, casting city-block-sized shadows on the water, and I found it nearly impossible to spot fish until Karl pointed them out precisely. "Two feet below the third black rock out 30 feet from the shore at 2 o'clock." Straining, squinting, I picked up a faint shimmer, then two, then three.

"Bob, you'll need a longish reach cast for this drift. Remember that you'll lose distance, so throw 12 feet more than you would normally. Drop the fly at least 10 feet above the fish. By the way, what fly do you have on?" I was fishing one of Karl's modified Tellico nymphs, a gray-bodied version on a size 10 unweighted hook with two small split shot, and so responded. "Try it. If they won't eat it we'll switch to another pattern." Two poor casts and four decent drifts did not produce a take or any noticeable movement by the shadows, and I began to wonder if they weren't just shadows. Karl handed me a peacock herl Stone Fly attractor with a moose-mane tail. "They like this one and will usually take it if they don't want a Caddis."

I made the switch, checked my tippet knot, and dropped a pretty decent cast at seemingly the right spot. "Good cast, get ready!" Karl said. "He's got it." He was indeed a he, and *he* proceeded to demonstrate some of the finer points of steelhead rage. The buck ran toward the middle of the rapids (I kept my rod as high as I possibly could), then turned and crashed across the surface on a porpoising run directly at us. I made a downstream lunge, a quick scramble to the bank, and a 30-yard dash. Back out—rod held high. Back at us—reeling like mad—speed-pulling line through the guides to hold tension. Upstream and hold—catch my breath. Whoops! Downstream—around a rock—gone. "Holy pluperfect Jesus," I groaned.

"Nice fish," said Karl. I turned toward the bank and shrugged. Karl smiled, returned the shrug, and repeated, "Nice fish, nice job."

Karl first saw Canada in 1966 while vacationing from his home in Hamburg, Germany. "I'm still on vacation, I guess," he said. He has been guiding professionally for only 2 years and is careful to underline the fact that his interest is in supporting tourism and the growth of the sport fishery in the St. Mary's. "I try to offer a service for people who might not otherwise come here. This is a low-cost operation, no lunches—no frills, but I get people into fish safely and without fear."

His ability to spot game fish in the tricky, shadowy currents and varying depths is uncanny, and he quickly acknowledges this as one of his key strengths. "I can't wade out in the rough water because of my artificial hips, and this has forced me to be more thorough, more analytical when I work the runs closer to shore. Most of my clients like that."

He is partial to only a few fly patterns and strongly supports the theory that presentation is the most influential factor in seducing a steelhead. He uses simple Caddis Larvae, Stone Fly, and Hare's Ear

Karl Vogel fights a large buck that has taken his fly close to shore.

patterns in various shades of tan, gray, and olive, mostly unweighted, in sizes 10 and 12. "A weighted fly just does not seem to work as well here in the St. Mary's as an unweighted fly. I use small split shot on the leader to get the fly to the proper depth. Add a shot, take one off, pretty soon you have the right package and a good drift will usually bring a take."

The stocked versus wild fish controversy hits close to Karl's heart. "A stocked fish *thinks* it's wild, and I sure can't tell much difference in fighting ability. As an angler, I want to hook and play fish. That's why I'm here." He continued, "Some of the biologists want to shut the hatcheries down, and I think that would be terrible. Without the hatchery here in Sault Ste. Marie we wouldn't have the caliber of sport we now enjoy. We have Atlantic salmon, wonderful steelhead, big browns, Pacific salmon, due, in large part, to the continuing work at the hatchery here in Canada."

I had noticed a young woman and young man, dressed in an official-looking manner, taking eggs and milt from landed fish before they were released. "All the eggs and milt are taken here in the river from sport-caught fish. It's a good program," Karl stated and continued, "This berm behind us was put in for the sole purpose of enhancing and protecting habitat for natural reproduction. Another large investment that has proven successful. I guide to support more sport angling, which shows benefit to Sault Ste. Marie, Ontario, so that these programs will continue. Period."

Downstream, to our left, Steve appeared to be working a small flat run rather intently. He looked up and I waved. He saluted and turned back to the run.

Karl suggested we do a "sneak" up the berm to try and spot more fish, and we climbed, carefully, to the top of the concrete wall. We moved slowly up the narrow ledge in a semicrouch. He stopped our progress several times to point out fish at considerable distances. More often than not I had to stare and really concentrate for several moments before I recognized a steelhead.

We had moved upstream perhaps 70 yards when my guide gestured sharply and dropped lower. Five, maybe six, fish were sliding on and off a shallow flat to the bank side of a large granite slab. The fish were about 20 yards out and seemed approachable.

After several casts, it was clear that whatever "touch" I had possessed had fled, and I asked Karl to fish. I wanted to watch him in action. He worked slowly out to my right and let his wading staff swing free. On his second longish reach cast a large female inhaled the small caddis nymph and headed south with real purpose. Rod held high, Karl carefully worked back to shore and slowly followed the panicked hen, methodically stretching and lifting so line and backing would clear obstructions. He never ran (could not), but stayed in control and beached the fish about 200 yards below her lie. The hatchery crew gently took eggs and measured her at 29 inches. She swam away a few ounces lighter and bewildered, but strong. It was quite a show.

"I like to see them swim away," Karl said. "I discourage people from keeping fish. I tell them they are not safe for human consumption." He smiled and we sat down for coffee. It was May 26th, and at 10 AM the air temperature was about 10 degrees C (50 degrees F); the water temperature had not changed from the 7:30 AM reading.

"Very few people are capable of consistently effecting a true dead drift," he began. "The reach cast and the ability to mend properly are critical on this water. If the proper drift is made, the steelhead often take the fly right away. They're not terribly shy here. Then the problem becomes one of strike detection." He went on to say that he strongly recommends use of a strike indicator to aid his clients, and he suggests a very particular way to rig indicator and leader. "My leaders are usually 13 feet long. I start with a 4-foot butt of 25-pound Maxima and a sliding strike indicator. To that I tie a 7½-foot tapered leader plus an extra 18-inch tippet. By sliding the strike indicator up or down, I can instantly change the effective length of my leader to accommodate stream conditions. I rarely use a dropper fly. They hang up on the rocks or the bottom, and good-bye steelhead."

The day had turned bright but not warm. The wind remained a constant, if fluctuating coolant. We moved back down the berm, now accompanied by Steve, and Karl continued to spot and point out *slightly* darker shapes that soon enough shimmered into life and identified themselves as steelhead. We were both amazed at this uncanny ability repeatedly demonstrated under both flat- and bright-light conditions, over various bottom shades, and in rough and calm water alike. I have fished with some high-ranking, professional "ospreys" in the Bahamas and Keys, but never have I observed such a demonstration of concentration and keen eyesight.

We hooked a few more fish, and I roughhoused one up to the shallows, expecting Steve to tail and hold it for one quick photograph. But Steve, ever casual, decided to talk to the (guessing) 28-inch male instead of tailing it. "Hi, how ya doin' big guy. We're not gonna hurt you. Want your picture taken . . . ?" The fish tired of this drivel and dashed back to the current around a rock and snapped the tippet. "Neat release," said Karl. Steve bowed and murmured "adieu" to the general direction the fish had taken. "That's panache," said Karl. I remained silent.

Throughout the day Karl spotted and coached. He demonstrated mid-drift mini-mends, double reach casts, strike detection, and how to keep fish off balance in such a heavy flow with the application of

*Karl's spotting and Steve's careful stalking
produced this handsome steelhead.*

shifts in the direction of rod leverage. He showed us his favorite patterns and described the various food forms in the St. Mary's rapids.

"Spotting fish is difficult in this river, but it is critical to success. Even though there are a lot of fish in the rapids right now, fishing blind is a waste of time, in my opinion. The river is so big you need to concentrate your efforts on specific targets." Karl gestured to the swift current and continued. "The St. Mary's is rich in food for game fish. There are stone fly nymphs, mayfly nymphs, sculpins, and caddis. I prefer nymph patterns, and day after day the caddis is one of the top producers. If you can spot a fish here, drop a caddis nymph 10 feet above it, and achieve a drag-free drift, you will catch a lot of steelhead."

We drank hot coffee and watched the river. Gulls worked the shoreline and several mated pairs of Canada geese swung low over the water. Mighty behemoths, ore and grain freighters over 600 feet long, nudged through the locks on the United States side of this international waterway. Too soon it was time to leave. We said our goodbyes and gave sincere thanks for the lesson, and Karl sat down on a rock. "I think I'll just sit here and watch the river for a while," he said, and waved, "Drive safely."

TACTICAL SUMMARY

• Go slowly. Study the water. Look for fish, or parts of fish, close to shore.
• Keep your fly selection simple. A few pattern types—stone fly, mayfly, and caddis nymphs—in various natural hues and in sizes 10 and 12 will suffice.
• Concentrate on presentation. Make your first cast a good one. Drop the fly 10 to 12 feet above the fish and use quick, small line mends to position your dead drift.
• A long leader, strike indicator, unweighted fly, and variable, small split shot are great aids to success on the St. Mary's.
• The reach cast is a necessary skill for big water.
• To clear obstacles such as boulders, you need a very high rod arc when fighting fish. Shift the rod arc often to keep the fish off balance.
• A dropper fly, regardless of how it is attached, very often snags on a boulder or scrapes the bottom; the result is usually the same—a popped tippet and lost fish.
• Don't eat a steelhead from the St. Mary's; catch-and-release is far preferable.

RECOMMENDED TACKLE

• Karl is very utilitarian and not impressed with one brand name over another when it comes to rods and reels.
• He favors 9- and 9½-foot graphite rods for 6- to 8-weight lines.
• His reels hold "lots of backing."
• He prefers Maxima tippet material over all others.

10

Jerry Pytlik

Near Perfect Timing on the Au Sable

Winter holds hard to the land at the 45th parallel, but by mid-April hints of mercy begin to show through nature's veil. Chickadees still try to kick your windows in if you should fail to keep the feeder neatly topped with sunflower seeds, and some deer (and most of the local citizens) look a bit wan and shaggy. But the snowbanks recede daily, the geese return, and the steelhead start to show in the lower Au Sable.

This awakening is a much anticipated time for Jerry Pytlik, proprietor of the Hexagon Rod and Fly Shop in Bay City, Michigan. Although he does not guide steelhead anglers for a fee, trips can be booked through his shop with the area's top guides. Jerry is recognized, however, as one of the lower Au Sable's "experts" when the word is measured by success in fooling the river's finicky, brutishly powerful steelhead with feathered hooks.

A bachelor, Jerry devotes 20 hours a day to fly-fishing. He is an artist, and bamboo is his medium. Split-cane rods of unique character and delicate, practical beauty are handcrafted against the ideal of perfection, and his customers are more than pleased. Additionally, he builds power graphite sticks for steelhead, salmon, and salt water, teaches a few fly-tying classes, and fishes hard.

The first day available to fish with Jerry was in late April. Happily, this coincided with a rush of fresh fish from Lake Huron that seemed spurred by a combination of early spring rains, high air temperatures soaring into the low 50s F (low double digits C), and the corresponding increase in water flow and warmth. The Au Sable is a "late" river, but when the right conditions merge, the river pops and receives a stampede of aggressive fish.

Jerry had recommended we bring 9½- or 10-foot, 7- or 8-weight rods with both floating and sink-tip lines. "The fish will be moving

157

up to the gravel and holding in the nearby runs. I think these fish are a little stronger per pound than those on the west side of the state, so be sure to test all your connecting knots and bring the very best reels you have. Make sure you have *lots* of flies. The lower Au Sable is filled with drowned timber from the logging days, and it's possible to lose a great many in a day. Bring egg patterns, both medium-sized Glo-Bugs and Micro-Eggs, Gold-Ribbed Hare's Ears in 6 and 8, Hex nymphs, Leeches, and Stone Flies."

The early morning of April 27 was brisk, with winds gusting to 30 mph and air temperatures in the low 40s F (single digits C). The sun was just beginning to provide some warmth as Jerry turned his truck into the boat launch site near Foote Dam.

"You guys bring lots of flies?" were his first words as he wheeled the rig around to back the boat down the ramp.

"Yes, we did—and good morning," Steve answered.

"Let's get going. The sun is likely to be a problem. We were supposed to have some overcast, but there are *no* clouds up there and none on the way. And good morning to you gentlemen."

The drift boat was quickly off the trailer and secured, and Jerry strode purposefully over to the tree that supported our rigged fly rods. Steve's choice on this day was a 10-foot Winston 8-weight with a 9-weight, weight-forward taper on a Heron reel. Jerry picked up my 9-foot 8-weight Graphite-USA. "This is the same blank I use on most of the custom steelhead rods I build. It's extremely rugged. Let's put this gear in the boat and start down the river."

Well, we had both passed our first inspection, it seemed, and we scurried rods, camera bag, lunches, vests, and all the paraphernalia necessary to the day's purpose into the boat. We were perhaps a dozen flies short of equaling the gross weight of the *Edmond Fitzgerald*.

Jerry lifted the drag chain, pulled twice on the oars, and we eased into the current. "The water is about a foot higher than normal for this time of year. It will make wading physically exciting and intellectually stimulating in a few places, and we'll have to experiment with split shot to get the right depth, but the fishing should be quite good."

He continued, "Downstream a short way we'll come to an area called High Banks where the river runs up to the face of a long, slow, curving, steep sandbank next to the road. This long curve creates a very deep run with extensive gravel. It is ideal water, since it affords enough depth for protection and perfect spawning areas. Unfortunately, because it is so close to the highway, it gets fished very hard.

Sometimes it seems like there's an angler for every 5 feet of bank. If it's crowded today, and I think it will be, we'll just float on through. There are plenty of good spots, both above and below, to keep us occupied."

We were drifting through deep runs and over dark, swirling holes of indeterminate depth. The twisted limbs of ancient timbers, perhaps tumbled and trapped in a logjam a hundred years ago, were often visible just below the surface, then faded from sight into the dark.

"Many of these runs and holes have fish in them right now, but they are too deep to fish effectively the way we're set up, and we would have little or no chance of landing a fish because of all the snags. As a retailer of fly-angling goodies, I guess I should encourage a cast or two—I could sell a lot of flies that way." Jerry pulled the boat into a bankside eddy and dropped the chain. "There is a good reach of spawning gravel down here just out from the bend that we can cover by wading. If we see fish, fine, but if we don't it's a very good bet they'll be in the run downstream, or in the pool just above. Let's take a look."

Steve had tied on a chartreuse Bubble Egg as a dropper and a Hex nymph as the point fly, and Jerry, after a quick look, pronounced him ready. I fumbled a bicolor Micro-Egg and Stone Fly nymph combination onto the leader, and we edged away from the boat along a low bank to scan the water.

"I don't see any fish on the redds, so they must be in the pool or in the run. Steve, why don't you try the run and Bob can fish the tail-out of the big pool. Steve, use an upstream reach cast for a drag-free drift, and, Bob, I think you should start with the same technique. If you don't nick the bottom, we'll have to add another split shot."

We moved into position and Jerry eased shoreward, out of range of backcasts, to observe and suggest. He asked Steve to fish the run straight through from top to bottom, then to back out and change flies and fish through again. He suggested I make a few more casts, then change to an Egg-Sucking Leech and walk upstream on the bank and try to spot fish holding next to the sunken timbers.

There were no suspicious pauses, no likely twitches of my leader, and after a dozen more drifts than I thought necessary to cover the water, I moved back to the bank to change patterns. Steve and Jerry were sitting next to each other on a length of log that sported a massive tangle of grotesque roots and a knot that appeared as a subsurface gargoyle in the refracted light.

We changed flies and queried our host about his very large landing net. Jerry explained that the long handle and large opening, while difficult to handle in heavy current, provide a measure of reach often necessary in areas of a river that are particularly heavy on log tangles. "You can't follow the fish as closely as you might like, you can't beach it, and *sometimes* the extra length allows you to release a fish by choice rather than by long distance hang-up."

Steve moved back out to his run freshly armed, and Jerry beckoned me to follow him up a stream along the path by the river. We moved up through the mixture of large, second-growth hardwoods and younger white and red pines. To our left the river made a mild push of 6-inch-deep, 41-degree water against the bank, but 2 feet out the bottom was not visible; only the jackstrawed trunks of ancient white pines showed at mid-depth (guessing) of a long, sweeping, and very dark hole.

"There are small patches of gravel, some as small as a kitchen table, hidden along this bank. They are very attractive to the fish because they're out of the way, rarely fished, and they're next to the protection of deep water. Because of the height of the bank we're on, we'll see fish easily if we're cautious, but hooking and landing one will take a studied approach and a lot of luck," Jerry said as we eased up the bank.

"There are three fish on the edge of the gravel upstream about 50 yards and about 6 feet to the right of that V-shaped stump. Bob, let's think this through before we get too much closer." We paused, and with some difficulty, I managed to locate the fish, one very large, sliding back and forth along the edge of the gravel and the deeper water to the left.

"I wish you were left-handed; you'd have an easier cast," Jerry said as we inched closer. He pointed to a small cut where the bank had collapsed. "If you can deliver from there, the fish won't be able to see you, but you'll need to drop the fly about 10 feet above the fish with an upstream reach to get the proper drift. Want to try it?" I nodded, duck-walked into the conveniently located hiding spot, and thought about exactly how I was going to effect an across-the-body, backhanded, upstream reach cast without inducing terminal hysteria in my watchful guide.

The first attempt was a disaster. Like so many anglers, I focused on the fish, not where my fly needed to land, so the fly dropped on the fish, well short of the target. The largest steelhead, a bright chrome

Jerry Pytlik netted this fine Au Sable hen for Steve.

female, held steady, but the two smaller fish, both males with clearly visible wide red bands, scooted nervously across the patch of fine gravel. "Take a deep breath and let them relax. The larger male will chase the smaller one off and then settle down. Let's wait a bit."

Five minutes passed, enough time to mentally offer sacrifices and donations to the trout gods, before Jerry suggested another attempt. This cast arrived nearer the intended mark, and the black leech pattern with the bright chartreuse nose swung along the seam where the fish held. The larger upstream male moved sharply to the right and then back, but the fly continued past him. "He'll take it next time. When he does he'll probably run up and out or dive for the logs. In either case, you need a high-leverage arc to avoid the snags. Stand up quick and get your rod as high in the air as you can." Then he gestured as if to add "let's get on with it!"

This cast was again fairly decent, although a foot farther to the right (toward the bank) than seemed desirable, but the aggressive male had seen enough egg-sucking intruders and shot forward to intercept. "He's got it, hit him," Jerry yelled as I lifted the rod high and stood to gain height and leverage. The fish zipped back and forth across the gravel several times, seemingly checking avenues of escape, before heading straight out for approximately 30 yards, then taking a 90-degree turn upstream. The fly line and backing looped around the lone deadfall in that part of the river and it was over.

I reeled in and sat on the bank. "Nicely done," Jerry consoled, "We couldn't anticipate that move. He just plain beat us—flat out—no reason to feel bad."

We walked back downstream to check on Steve and I thought that although technically competent (for that grading period), I remained emotionally incomplete and resolved a better result—a quick hand on the fish and a photograph—on the next encounter.

Steve had not touched any fish, nor had he seen any move to the redds, so we elected to float on and perhaps reconnoiter with another boat that carried Jerry's father, Jerry Sr., and two friends, Peter Jones and Don Check. It was likely that we would run into them in the general area of the High Banks, and we would have the opportunity to compare notes.

Jerry asked about my tippet, particularly what pound test I had been using, adding that "it seemed pretty light." My tippet was R10 5-pound test, and Jerry explained that 5-pound was a bit fine. "The fish in the Au Sable are not terribly leader-shy: Even in low, clear water 8-pound test is not too heavy. In the fall, when the water is like air, we can use 8-pound test—it's perfectly viable. It doesn't frighten the fish, and it allows an extra margin of safety."

Peter Jones's boat was snugged up to a large cedar on the north shore of the High Banks, and we slid into a small cove just downstream to compare notes and share coffee.

"We were hoping to be able to fish the runs next to the gravel here at the High Banks, but there are too many people on both sides. We'll just finish here and float on down," Peter stated.

"The pressure here can be tremendous, especially when the fish are in plain view. Many fish hooked here are fouled, sometimes intentionally by people with little, if any, angling skill or sense of responsibility. If people would just make an effort to learn the fundamentals, they'd have a great time, but some are simply poachers and thieves," replied Jerry. "Let's leave this zoo and move down a few bends."

Jerry and Peter decided to keep their respective boats in sight on the float to a predetermined spot where we would have lunch and fish a long, productive run. Jerry suggested that Steve try a Sparrow nymph, a very effective fly on the Au Sable, and that I should tie on a double Micro-Egg dropper with a Jeff's Hex as the point fly.

"Are there any singular keys to successful fly-rod steelhead fishing on the Au Sable?" Steve asked.

"Effectively delivering the fly in a drag-free drift line is fundamental. In order to accomplish drag-free drift, an assortment of delivery casts are required; the most important two of these are the reach cast and the roll cast," Jerry answered.

"The roll cast, with a high-density sink tip, or heavy floater with split shot on the leader, is a little tricky. Everything needs to be under tight control to work properly. The rod is raised slowly until everything—line, leader, fly—is *on* the surface before the forward cast, or roll, is made. If *anything* is subsurface, just the point fly for example, the cast won't deliver. And, remember to slow everything down, the lift and the forward power stroke, or you could be wearing a painful hood ornament."

I asked for an opinion on a top-quality, wide-purpose steelhead outfit, and Jerry replied without hesitation. "I like 9½-foot, 7- or 8-weight rods. Graphite-USA is a good choice for lots of people because the rods are so tough. The Scientific Anglers System II reels are affordable and of very high quality. Their drag system is smooth and they have plenty of room for backing. I use Scientific Anglers fly lines and Maxima tippet material."

We centered on a midriver run and passed through a chute where twisted stumps and long, smooth trunks, only partially submerged, bordered the narrow passage. Peter's boat was bankside on the left about 200 yards distant, and it looked as though someone was playing a fish. As we pulled in next to Peter's boat, Jerry Sr. puffed on his pipe and retied a leader, seeming not to notice the angler excitement just upstream. "That fish has been wearing Peter out. It might be time soon enough for a net job though." We looked up in time to see Don make a calculated lunge and lift the net with a shimmering 28-inch buck.

"He took a Green Caddis right off the seam in the deep water. I think this whole ledge is stacked with fish," Peter opined.

We spread out along the river's edge fired with enthusiasm, and Jerry spent time with both Steve and me coaching the "5-ton" roll cast that was demanded by the high sandbank to our immediate backside. "Slow everything down, Bob. And remember, make sure *everything*, fly included, is on top of the water before you apply forward power." His teaching technique was effective, and soon we were both dropping our flies on target with minimal problems.

Steve hooked up quickly and a chrome hen sailed into the air with the Sparrow nymph point fly showing in the corner of her jaw. Pound for pound, or inch for inch, whichever you may prefer, this was one of the strongest fish in recent memory. It took several minutes of strict attention before she was netted and released. Steve rubbed his forearm and elbow and grimaced.

A few minutes later my roll-cast Green Caddis enticed a 21-inch male that gave every indication (until he jumped) of a much larger fish. "Wow, these fish are strong," I muttered as Jerry suggested that the big fish, say 30 inches or so, *really* wear you out.

We hooked up a few more times during the day, managing to invent new ways to lose our connection. I recall a largish flash of silver greyhounding downstream with my Hex nymph, and Steve lured a big, red-sided male into a logjam for a quick release. It was dusk when we reached the take-out point, and as we unloaded gear, Jerry continued his steady stream of information. "Streamers, make that *big* streamers, work well when fished through gravel areas before the fish are actively spawning. The males are very aggressive and territorial. And they're particularly testy because the females are not yet ready. They'll smack an invading fish without hesitation. When the females start to release eggs, a Micro-Egg pattern fished in the runs below her is a good bet, but the best all-around flies on the Au Sable are nymphs. The Sparrow, Caddis, and realistic Hex patterns like Jeff's Hex are the top producers day after day."

We winched the boats up on the trailers and double-checked the surrounding area by flashlight for any tackle, pop bottles, or sandwich bags that might have been dropped. "You should fish here in the fall," he said as full darkness closed in. "The fish are more aggressive, and there are very few anglers because people have switched to ducks and grouse or bowhunting for deer. And, the fish fight harder in the fall."

The Au Sable reflected black and ominous in silent passage to Lake Huron as we pulled up the boat ramp and back to the never-ending horror, for a Red Wing fan, of the Stanley Cup play-offs.

TACTICAL SUMMARY

- Use tippet with enough strength to subdue big, strong fish.
- Jerry believes two of the most important casts for the Au Sable are the reach cast and the roll cast. Practice them.
- Look for fish *near* gravel. Then fish the dark water—runs, riffles,

holes, undercuts—both up- and downstream with different fly patterns.

- Keep your rod as high as you can when fighting fish near snags. Apply side pressure only after you've cleared the obstruction.
- Jerry prefers fall steelhead angling to the more popular "spring madness." "The weather is nicer, the fish are more aggressive, and it's less crowded."
- The key to steelhead recovery is a short, hard fight and a quick release.
- Carry and use a quality hook hone. The points *must* be needle sharp.

RECOMMENDED TACKLE

- 9½-foot graphite rods for 7- and 8-weight lines are suggested for the Au Sable. Jerry favors Graphite-USA, Thomas and Thomas, and Powell.
- Scientific Anglers System II reels are a top value in Jerry's opinion. He is also very fond of Harris reels and uses them extensively.
- Scientific Anglers Mastery floating weight-forwards, and class III and IV sink tips, are his lines of choice.
- Maxima is the tippet material he uses most often.

11
John Skrobot

Innovation for Big Water

"Bring lots of flies. Fifty for a day should be safe."

Bob and I looked at each other. We never travel light. We are of that old school that advocates, "Carry 500 flies (and use both of them)," but the implication that we could go through anywhere near 50 was an eye-opener. This numbers recommendation came in a confirmation letter from John Skrobot, a well-known guide who runs Calypso Charters on Lake Huron out of Oscoda. More to our purpose, he also guides for steelhead on the lower Au Sable River.

"I really would like to build up greater interest in fly-fishing for steelhead over here on the east side of Michigan," he told us when first we talked. "I've guided some clients who have done well, and I have some ideas and angles you might be interested in."

One of these ideas involves applying to fly-fishing the successful techniques he has employed in drop-back fishing with plugs. This is something we have toyed with a little, but here was a chance to get input from an expert—and perhaps use 50 flies. The drop-back technique involves going deep and well under logjams, sweepers, and other fly-grabbing, fishy cover.

John is one of those guides who sees himself as a river steward, we learned early in the course of our day with him. (Most of the guiding guild share this sense of responsibility, fortunately for all of us.) Our morning conversation centered not so much on strategy for taking steelhead, but on concerns for bettering the resource. He felt that generating increased interest in fly-angling, its challenges and rewards being what they are, would bring in more types who would take an active interest in the steelhead stream fishery. "There are fewer streams over here (east coast), and an increase in the big-lake fishery, especially if the scum line continues to be targeted, could impact negatively on the streams," he said.

167

John has taken a big role in positive improvements for steelhead fishing in his bailiwick. He worked to have plantings made later in the day and in different spots so the new arrivals would have a better chance against predation from humans and animals. He had a hand in the experimental stocking of 100,000 micro-tagged smolts in the river and a like number off the Lake Huron beach to see if survival rates differed. And he was instrumental in leading and continuing the fight that brought an end to salmon snagging in his area. (It's now illegal in the entire state.) "I got some serious threats to my health and property when that snagging issue was going hot," he told us. "And when I was guarding newly planted smolt by firing a shotgun to scare gulls away, somebody sent the police to get me for harassing birds."

We reached the launch below Foote Dam before we had time to delve deeply into other issues usually discussed by fly-rodding steelheaders, but a couple of them got fair treatment in the course of our drift.

Our first stop put us 20 feet above a deep pool, logs and debris forming a rough horseshoe shape with the opening toward us. This was a favorite spot for drop-back plug fishermen, and we were anxious to see if it would produce for us also. We didn't have John maneuver the boat to work the flies as he can do with "set" rods and plugs; he simply held us above the hole by rowing, and we plied our rods to each side. We tried the fairly traditional drop-back approach of letting several feet of line play out down a chosen lane, working the fly for several seconds, then letting out a couple more feet of line, working the fly, and repeating this process until we were into the farthest reaches of the pool. Then we would retrieve it in similar staggered intervals, try another lane a couple of feet over, and do it all over again.

"I know it will work," John said. "It's a matter of the right color and action. Plug anglers have been hitting fish recently using combinations of green and gold on lures. I'm tying flies right now to try and incorporate those shades."

"I have read," said Bob, "that it's the diving-digging-wiggling action of the plugs like Tadpolies and Flatfish that really bring on the hits. If you could add that action to your fly, maybe with a Dahlberg Diver kind of lip . . . Hey, you've got the 'Finn-gineer' right here. Nevala could be your consultant and . . . "

"I recommend duct tape instead of epoxy. It is quite durable, comes in different colors, and I have a large supply."

John Skrobot in his favorite element

"Well, I'm not sure where a fly stops being a fly and becomes a plug, and I don't want to get into that issue with fly-fishermen," John ventured. "I'm getting close to a good pattern with a modification of the Carey fly, the Jolly Green Giant. I'm going for a thicker-bodied version with just the right hue of imitation seal fur and pheasant-rump color."

John talked of West Coast patterns and the fun he had in Spokane in the '70s learning to tie under the expert tutelage of Joe King, while Bob and I tried some of our green- and olive-hued patterns in Speys and Woolly Buggers and Sparrow flies, putting them—and leaving several—in the tightest, deepest confines of the snaggy pool. Still no hits. "Let's move on," said John. "There's a brushy, bank-tight bed just below us that usually has fish around it."

There were a couple of fish holding in the spot John mentioned, and there was no way bank fishermen could have approached them. They were tight against a high, brush-choked cliff, and deep water and blowdowns above and below them prevented any wading attack. Overhanging trees made even casting from the boat a matter of extreme finesse.

"What did you do, pull in here once to hide and take a nap and then notice fish?" I asked.

"I was floating by once and saw a slight surge of water when one of them moved up onto the redd. I don't think too many people know that fish hold here regularly."

Since tree limbs prevented lengthy casts from the river, John held us in position again by backrowing just above and a *short* distance from the fish. Little sidearm curve casts through openings in the overhanging branches could put a fly in front of the visible quarry.

"Sometimes they are so intent on spawning, I can almost touch them with an oar, and still they will pick up a fly."

The spawners this day did hold and didn't appear spooky, but they had no inclination to strike. We couldn't help but think that our close proximity and rowing activity, gentle and feathered as it was, made them nervous and close-mouthed.

"Any rule of thumb on how long you should work a particular holding fish?" Bob asked as we headed down in search of more cooperative players.

"It depends. If there are good numbers of them about, usually 10 casts—good ones that give the fish a look—and then I'm gone. If fish are scarce, I'll work longer, you know, change flies, sizes, colors, angles," he answered.

We floated on, searching for other hidden pockets or midriver runs and redds that had not been depth-charged by lead-slinging bank fishermen. The drift boat is an obvious two-edged sword here: You can find midriver fish that wading/shore fishermen can't readily see, but by the time *you* notice them (glare and shadow blend), you are often right on top of them.

This was the case when from my standing lookout position I spotted several fish over a midriver gravel span. "Fish dead off the port bow! Hard a-helm! Avast! Back water!" and other seminautical gibberish didn't slow our progress.

"I see them," was John's laconic response. "Check out the bottom configuration and snag situation as we go by. If they spook, they'll come back. We'll beach below, walk up, and wait for them."

We checked, they spooked, we waited. I have mixed feelings on this tactic, preferring to give fish a wide berth, but there is certainly logic in John's tactic.

"They have to dodge a number of boats anyway," he said while we waited for steelhead to reassemble. "But if they're heavy into spawning, and these appear to be, we won't have to rest them long. The advantage is that now you know there is a log just at the back of the main bed, and you'll hang it, lose rigs, and make commotion if you don't swim your fly over it carefully. Also, did you see the raised lip on the front of the bed? That's going to be a consideration."

The fish did come back and we let them settle in before casting. We went with floating lines with nymph and egg-fly attractor combos, staying far away in the clear, bright conditions. The deeper water near our bank necessitated long casts anyway, since wading closer courted serious dampness. John was high up on the bank calling shots, which creates shared excitement *and* is very helpful; it was tough for us to see the fish from our water-level angle.

"That's perfect," he'd call. "You're swinging in . . . now you're right in front of them . . . Oh, man! The smaller male threw a feint at that fly, but didn't hit." This combination of casting with inspirational dialogue went on for half an hour. We changed patterns, colors, tippets (lighter), angles, but no takes.

Then I noticed that what had been deep, forbidding water between us and our targets now looked more fordable. "Let's try to get to that bar about 40 feet to the side of those fish," I suggested to Bob. "I think we can stay low and not spook them and get a more controlled drift from close in."

Inside the next 20 minutes we hooked, fought, and quick-released (forceps to fly and 'bye) three of the dozen or so fish ranged out over this extensive gravel area. Then everything shut down. The remaining fish disappeared. This was somewhat puzzling, since our battles had gone immediately downstream, not riling the other fish much, we thought. Nor had we touched a female.

"That's fairly typical on this river," John said when we clumped up the bank with this conundrum. "They release water for power at Foote Dam, and then as the surge lessens some, the fish often turn on. When you were able to wade to that bar, you were in that diminishing stage. But when it gets even lower, as has now happened, the fish become uncomfortable and head for deeper water."

"Shucks. We thought it was our low-profile, close-in, controlled-mend presentations that turned the odds," Bob ventured, taking a seat on the edge of the bluff.

"In part, probably," John said. "And that's a neat thing about fly-fishing on this river this time of year. You can get fairly close in many instances. You don't have to be an expert who can throw tight loops and lay out 90 feet of line to hit two or three fish a day with fly gear. It's not like fishing a dry fly to summer fish out West. I think some

Steve uses John's long-handled net to capture a wild hen for Bob.

people shy away from fly-fishing for steelhead because they think it's complicated and difficult, but it really isn't."

"By the way, it was good to see you guys put the hammer to those fish when you hooked up. You know, rods low to the side, keep 'em fighting. I've seen some people who hook up and then stand with vertical rod and let the fish dictate the fight."

Conversation drifted on to strike detection problems. "I try to position people above a redd or a fishy run whenever possible. The take is hard to miss when you can swing the fly down to and in front of the fish on a tight line," he stated.

"And I can see where with a boat you can maintain optimum position to work some of these deeper, midriver holds. A wader would be neck-deep or swimming from the same position," Bob observed.

"One would never know there were fish out there. And midcurrent beds can be tough to cast to from closer to shore," John added. "There's the problem of backcast room, plus the other difficulties involved in making long casts, then mending for a good, clean drift. With the boat I can give the angler different angles of presentation from above and eliminate a lot of problems."

As we had been floating and searching for fish, I had occasionally picked up one of the rods rigged with a floating line and made some casts. With judicious mending relative to the boat speed, long drifts could be maintained. I was doing it more to occupy time, but John acknowledged that it can produce. "You have to stay in tune with it though," he had commented, "because a boat generally moves more quickly on a surface current than a weighted fly does near the bottom. Current speeds differ from top to bottom."

We located a fish or two a bit later, but they were nervous. Other anglers were nearby and had obviously put lines, lures, and who knows what past them this day. "Let's not waste our time on those guys," John said. "There's an area just up from that big tree lying in the water that always holds fish. It's deep and they feel secure, but they're near gravel so they like to move up and check things out occasionally, and they will hit."

Bob went to a multicolored Woolly Bugger recommended by Steve Pensinger, one of the best trout fishermen we have had the good fortune to know. He had recently jumped a bunch of western rainbows with it when other favorites were being rejected. Bob figured these anadromous Michigan "cousins" might also find it attractive.

Before he committed it to the deeps, John came over and explained what to do if the hoped-for hook-up occurred, because this was a tricky place.

"A hooked fish may hang in and fight right out from you here, but more than likely it will run toward midriver where the current gives it a greater advantage."

"And go downstream, I fear," said the apprehensive Robert.

"Oh, yeah. And most anglers lose them when their line catches on up-sticking branches of fallen trees and the fish keeps going down. But, if you get right down tight to the roots of the tree, and *if* the fish is far enough out, it's possible to raise your rod, hold the line high, and just clear the top of the highest branches. You're tall and you've got a 9½-foot rod. Once you're by that snag, it's open water below and the advantage is all yours."

"If the fish stays in close . . . ?"

"You do your best to keep him out of the jam in front of the tree. But it's tough to do, so let 'em run if they head up and out, and take your chances with plan A."

I climbed the bank after 15 minutes and started down toward Bob and John . . . but saw the latter hurrying toward me and figured something was up. Since the boat was closer to me, I detoured down to it and grabbed John's net. He saw this move, waved me to come down with it, and headed back toward Bob.

I reached them just in time to hear John say, "It's going to work. Take it over the top!" Bob was 5 minutes into the battle, the fish had indeed run out toward midriver, and the fallen tree was about to come into play. The fish turned in the heavier current and began moving down, wallowing on the surface occasionally to show us her silvery bulk.

With raised rod Bob held his line as high and as tight to the fish as he could and took his shot. His line caught the top inch of the highest portion of the last branch (I think he did it on purpose to heighten the drama), held for a couple of seconds, then scraped over.

"Bring her back up and see if you can do it right," I yelled.

"Just get in here with that net. This is a good fish."

A few minutes more and Bob steered her into the large, waiting mouth of John's boat net. I brought her into off-current water and we did the usual photo, fly removal, release business. She was indeed a fine, fresh fish of about 8 pounds, brilliantly colored and nicely proportioned.

"A little pregame strategy pays off," Bob said by way of credit to John's earlier advice.

"Once you see a fish or two lost in the same spot, you do learn." John answered. "I think a lot more people could avoid trouble if they surveyed the battlefield more carefully first, then fished. Sometimes just snapping off a dead branch hanging yards below or above you will pay dividends."

I had to add, "Speaking of pregame coaching, you might have said something about what it's like to stick a boat net with a bag as big as a pup tent into that current out there. I like to beat you guys to Oscoda."

John grinned. "Takes some talent and muscle when up near your wader tops, hey." That's an understatement. Watch yourself if you've never tried it before, and be sure you're planted solidly.

John looked more closely at the Woolly Bugger that Bob had christened, commenting, "I like browns and blacks in fly colors too. This is a good idea, working them into an attractor type of streamer like this."

"Hey, I noticed you got a little jumpy when we held the fish above the tail for the photo. Not your recommended tactic?" I asked.

"If possible, catch-and-releasers shouldn't touch them at all," he stated. "I know it's difficult to position them (for photo) sometimes, but handling can displace scales, and I think it sets the stage for fungus to start in. This is especially true when the water warms even more. It's not so crucial now when it's colder."

Our last destination was near a bend known as "Three Pipes," a wide, slow section with gradual shallows, well graveled, what current there is on the shallow side passing a long, sandy expanse of low bank.

Light was low now, making it tough to spot fish, but from the vantage point of the raised sandbank, we could make out a couple of different groups of holding fish only a few feet out from the water's edge. There was so little current along this slack-water side of the river that it was tough to get a consistent drift; one could work the fly with a retrieve just as well. It was almost like fishing a lakeshore.

Bob and I both had takes, but were slow to set or something because our flies came sailing back at us. "I could see a noodle-rodder with ultralight tippet and strike indicator doing well here," I posed to John as much a question as an opinion.

"Boy, I don't like that," he was quick to reply. "I know you can hook a lot of fish that way, but it wears them out too much if you plan to release them, and the longer battles disrupt the fishing of others nearby. Also, if you use a long, light leader (as many do) and break a fish off, it trails along with the steelhead and can hang him up somewhere on debris. I don't see it as a sound way to fish."

An increasingly cold wind and waning light decided the day for us. "Crank up that engine, Captain," voted Bob. "Let's blaze down to the bright lights and fleshpots of Oscoda."

TACTICAL SUMMARY

- Apply what you have learned from related sports (e.g., fly hues similar to successful lure colors).
- Survey the entire "battleground" before commencing; planning can circumvent later problems with snags, holes, and so on, and prevent loss of fish.
- If possible, don't touch a fish you plan to release.
- Use barbless hooks for catch-and-release—and check the points often for breakage or dulling.
- Don't spend too much time on reluctant fish when others are bound to be around.
- Take time to climb to high ground (or up trees) to aid in spotting fish.
- Know river tendencies, e.g., the Au Sable steelhead turn on when a water surge (from a dam) is diminishing.
- Be prepared for all forms of nasty weather—even when it isn't in the forecast.
- Have your valid fishing license and trout stamp *on* your person.

RECOMMENDED TACKLE

- A Fenwick HMG 8½- to 9½-foot rod for at least a 7-weight line gets John's endorsement.
- Scientific Anglers reels in larger capacity for adequate backing and SA lines are his choices.
- He uses Maxima tippet material.
- John likes thicker-bodied marabou streamers in greens, olives, and golds. The Egg-Attractor patterns with or without dropper nymphs are in his arsenal, as are Egg-Sucking Leeches in blacks, browns, and greens with heads of hot pink, chartreuse, and orange.

12

Bud Hoffman

Lake Huron's Canadian Shore

Nottawasaga Bay is the southernmost reach of the huge arm of Lake Huron known as Georgian Bay. Approximately 150 kilometers north of Toronto, and 350 kilometers northeast of Detroit and Windsor, Nottawasaga's clear, fertile waters teem with splake, whitefish, brown trout, several species of salmon, and, of course, steelhead.

The coastline and bordering countryside are more likely to remind a visitor of New England than the fertile agricultural expanse of the central continent. There are rolling hills dotted with ski runs and apple orchards, deep welcoming valleys with picturesque villages, and handsome, lively streams that offer quality fly-fishing for stream trout as well as the anadromous denizens of big water.

Nestled in a striking valley surrounded by massive hills, Bud Hoffman's home and fly-fishing school near Kimberley are within a short stroll of the Beaver River. The Beaver and the equally accessible Bighead River host impressive spring and fall runs of steelhead. Bud's willingness to share his tactical approach to these productive waters presented the opportunity to fish with an internationally regarded expert in beautiful country at the peak of the fall colors.

Bud Hoffman's fishing and casting programs, videos, and international exploration have earned him a deserved reputation, but it was his knowledge of his backyard, the fishery of the eastern shore of Lake Huron and Georgian Bay, that brought us together.

"We've had very little rain through the late summer and so far this fall. The Beaver and Bighead are so low that the fish are stacking up in the bay at the mouths of the rivers. The very lowest reaches will hold some fish and we'll try there, but we're better advised to work the big river in this area, the Saugeen. Its flow is stabilized enough by Denny's Dam at Southampton to welcome the fish." Bud went on to explain that the steelhead fishing at the mouth of the Beaver at the

Bud Hoffman on the shore of his beloved Saugeen River

village of Thornbury, and at the mouth of the Bighead at Meaford can be very good during the low-light conditions of dawn and dusk. "Both nymph and streamer patterns will work. They need to be fished *slowly* on a fairly long leader, not less than 8 feet, and a floating line. A 9½-foot, 8-weight rod will be a good choice."

On our drive to the water for the evening's activities, Bud directed us on a circuitous route along the upper Beaver and Bighead Rivers. We stopped often and our host pointed out various holding and staging lies that under normal flows would provide excellent fly-fishing conditions and opportunities.

We drove on toward Meaford and Bud talked about the seemingly endless variables that affect the outcome of each attempt to seduce a steelhead with fur and feather. "I won't try to prioritize these, but they are all very important factors in achieving success. A novice angler tends to underestimate one, some, or all of the critical elements that influence a steelhead's decision, or reactive impulse, to take a fly."

Steve asked Bud to start with the fish. "What about the creature itself? Independent of weather, what makes it tick, in your opinion?" Bud answered with his belief that the senses of sight, smell, and sound are altered when the fish moves from the big lake into moving water and its predilection adjusts from feeding to spawning. He definitely feels that the sense of sight (and perhaps also the senses of smell and hearing) deteriorate as fat reserves are utilized.

"The number-one critical factor in choosing a fly for steelhead is visual impact. First—will the fish notice it? Does it have flash or flutter or some vibrant lifelike essence? Does it approximate the color and form of a natural food source?" He also feels that sound is important, especially so in still or slowly moving water, and that the fly should move water or "create subtle currents" to stimulate interest and a possible take. He did not elaborate on the sense of smell beyond the obvious—odors from insect repellents, tobacco, and so on are not likely to enhance one's success.

Bud's passion for exploration often leads him to remote and exotic destinations. Bonefish on isolated Cuban flats, immense northern pike in desolate flowages near Hudson Bay, near-record grayling in Manitoba are typical of his yearly excursions. Still, he pointed out as we neared the mouth of the Bighead, the continual investigation of his own neighborhood waters, especially the Saugeen River, provides his highest level of satisfaction and pleasure. In addition to regularly float-tubing the Saugeen from country road to country road (he utilizes a stashed bicycle as his shuttle vehicle), he often fly-fishes the big water, both Lake Huron and Georgian Bay, from his Fenwick U-Boat. His understated caution was, "It's a productive way to fish for staging salmonids, but one needs to exercise some common sense. The winds and currents can push you into harm's way."

Steve and I shuffled into layers of fleece and neoprene in a biting wind as Bud lined a 9-foot, 8-weight Fenwick with a weight-forward floater and a 10-foot leader. "Normally I like to fish a 9-foot, 9-inch, 5-weight out here, but the wind is a bit too strong so I'll go with a heavier rod," Bud explained. This surprised me and I said so, stating that such a preference seemed on the light side. Bud said that his 9-foot, 9-inch, 5-weight is a very different tool with a wider range of capabilities than a typical 9-foot, 5-weight. "It serves very well out here with increased line control, and it has the muscle to move up two line weights and punch a class VII, even VIII under some conditions. I also like the rod's extra length for the advantage it provides in mending line for a drag-free drift in rivers. But this wind . . . well, this is an 8-weight evening all the way."

We traversed the boulder-studded, fine-gravel beach on the south side of the Beaver River and made our way, thankful for felt soles, over and between slick rocks to the reassuring traction of a long sandbar that ran parallel to the spread of the river's channel to the bay.

I tied on an Oswego Smelt, reasoning that it was a pretty fair prey imitation for the area and might interest a cruising trout. Steve and Bud both thought a nymph, drifting ever so slowly in the mix of current and wave action, would be the right choice for starters.

Three large wakes and a heavy boil midway across the mouth focused my attention and I managed several less-than-graceful long-line deliveries into the wind and to their vicinity without a hint of interest. As I changed flies, a flowing loop of fly line caught my attention. Watching Bud cast with total control, waist-deep in swells, into quartering gusts was an opportunity not to be wasted. His line lift and backcast came after a slow hand-twist retrieve and were crisp, high, and powerful. The line sprayed mist as it accelerated and straightened behind him, and again as it surged forward in a tight, speeding loop. Bud was casting 80-plus feet into the wind, seemingly without effort. No strain, no line slap marred the performance of coordination and timing. It is no wonder that Bud's casting and fishing schools are so popular.

I selected a flashy, pearlescent Clouser Minnow for the next assault and waded out a bit closer to Bud and Steve, who had both stopped casting and appeared to be changing patterns as well.

Steve asked Bud about fly selection criteria as I bobbed through the swell. "What factors affect your initial selection on a given day? Why did you decide to start with a nymph as opposed to a streamer this evening?"

"What we have right here, right now, is a classic example of mixed conditions that complicate fly selection. We have low, clear, summer-like flows in the river blending with colder, heavier water in the lake. We have a front moving in from the west. We have low-light conditions and frustrated fish. Now, I'm guessing about the frustration part of that, but it's my feeling that they want to be somewhere else— upstream in the river—and they are nervous or disturbed or whatever because there is insufficient flow in the river for them to feel safe. My instinct and my experience tell me small and dark is better than large and gaudy when steelhead are nervous, so I started with a dark Hare's Ear."

Steve looked down into his fly box, and I broke off the glittering Clouser as Bud went on.

"In flowing water—small streams or big rivers—I like small dark flies, imitative or highly suggestive of specific food forms. Hare's Ears, Stone Fly Nymphs, and Oscar's Hex are all good when fished on a long, fine leader absolutely drag-free. When the weather changes and we move to winter/spring conditions with heavier, off-color water, I use larger, brighter flies and shorter leaders. It's really pretty simple.

"Fly line selection is an important part of the equation, and although I much prefer to fish a full-floating line, I'll very quickly change to a sink tip. In really heavy water in the spring, I'll go to a full-sinking line if necessary to get the fly down to the fish.

"And there's another way to accomplish flexibility in this regard— without carrying several spools, or reels, but it's pretty dark now, and I'd prefer to show you this technique in the morning."

We waded back to shore through the building swells and slippery boulders in a chill wind. The dome light in the truck was a welcome aid to peeling waders and stowing gear, and as we double-checked the ground around our vehicle (some of us have been known to drop-leave-forget wallets, fly boxes, cameras, and other assorted valuables), Bud offered his opinion that some of the very best fly-fishing in the world is within the Great Lakes Basin. "We have steelhead, trophy brown trout, lake trout, world record whitefish, not to mention muskellunge, northerns, bass, panfish. It's fabulous." He added a somber note, though, as we drove back toward dinner and rest: "Poaching is a problem here, though I guess that is true everywhere you might find trophy-class sport fish that are even marginally edible.

"And, we have to find a realistic balance, a fair understanding of *equity* between native peoples' rights and the rights of the rest of the country's citizens. Over-harvesting can destroy a year class, even a total strain in a short time. Netting, particularly near stream mouths, can be devastating to our steelhead."

Dawn found us on the back roads south of Owen Sound. Bud led the way west through the countryside to Southampton on Lake Huron and the mighty Saugeen River.

The Saugeen hosts some of the heaviest spring and fall runs of steelhead on the Canadian side of Lake Huron. With the aid of fish ladders at Denny's Dam in Southampton, steelhead have open access to 50-plus miles of river, much of it prime spawning gravel, and two new fish ladders have been recently installed upstream from Walkerton, providing access to the river as far as Maple Hill.

The Saugeen is fed by a number of small creeks that enliven the system upstream from Hanover. Carrick Creek, the South Saugeen, the Beatty, Kemp Creek, Rocky Saugeen, and the Habermehl swell the river to a width of 50-plus feet near Hanover and make it wider yet in the upper limits for steelhead between Maple Hill and Walkerton. We would be fishing more than 50 miles downstream, below the sanctuary at Denny's Dam, where the Saugeen is over 100 feet wide. Here it pounds through quick-scare rapids into dark ledgerock pools more than 12 feet deep even in low-water flows.

At this point, perhaps 200 yards downstream from the dam, the Saugeen is nearly 200 feet across. We were presented with a wide riffle that flattened and deepened into a long, gently curving pool and a gradual tail-out that was split by a small island into a choppy run nearest our bank and a new, smaller pool on the far side of the island. Maples, aspen, and sumac in the deep blush of fall colored the steep hillsides in mirrored complement to the silky flow of the river. A fish rolled. It was time.

Bud suggested we start with floating lines and nymphs in the slower current seams of the pool, and he planned to show us his portable sink-tip system as we worked downstream through the deeper sections.

We dispersed across a 50-yard stretch and assumed the heronlike stance of intent nymph anglers. Steve was fishing a Hex pattern upstream and to my left. I centered the formation and worked a size 12 Black Stone Fly over the cobble bottom. Bud stood downstream and artfully cast long-line Hare's Ear deliveries to the heart of the pool. No takers. We continued with this method for about 20 minutes, adjusting only the fly pattern, the length of cast, and our relative position in the pool.

A long cast on a beautiful riffle

We had each worked downstream about 40 yards when Bud reeled in, turned, and headed back to shore. "We need to get deeper and put our flies right on their noses. It doesn't seem like they are going to come to us. Let's try the portable sink tips." He reached into his vest and removed several small plastic bags that contained lengths of plastic-coated, lead-core trolling line. "These range in length from 3 inches to 2 feet. They have loop-to-loop connectors at each end and provide a lot of flexibility in adapting to various water depths and current speeds," he explained.

Bud looped a section of about 1 foot to another of equal length and handed it to Steve. He passed me a 15-inch piece and described how to assemble and use the "sink tips" to best advantage. "First and foremost, I don't have to carry extra spools loaded with several types of fly lines to meet different conditions head-on. Several lengths of sink tips, a floating fly line, and a heavily greased 7½-foot leader are all you need for most situations. Here's how it works." He threaded a foam strike indicator onto the 7-foot leader that was already on his floating line, positioning it very near the nail knot. He then tied a loop on the end of the leader and looped a 12-inch section of sink tip to the leader. Finally he looped an 18-inch section of 6-pound tippet to the sink tip and tied on an Oscar's Hex to the business end. "We have hinging effects with this and most fly-anglers think of hinges in

184 GREAT LAKES STEELHEAD

the fly line and leader as a problem, but these are actually helpful to the cause. They allow the sink tip, tippet, and fly to ride at the desired depth *without* pulling the strike indicator and fly line under the water so far as to be ineffectual. Therefore, the fly sinks properly and rides more evenly, more uniformly with the current."

Steve and Bud loaded up with the "in-line" system and waded back out for round two. I decided to slog back up the path to get another cup of coffee. It was getting colder. At the crest of the small hill I heard a whoop and turned to see Bud's rod pulse and bow. A heavy fish swirled and bulged the surface and his rod pulsed, but just as quickly the line went slack. Timing is everything, I thought, and turned into the wind in search of the thermos.

My companions were working the second pool on the far side of the small island when I returned. Every few minutes a king salmon would roll, its darkening olive sides a definitive ID. "Lots of salmon, very few rainbows in from the lake," Bud said as he waded back to shore. "I'm really sorry the water's so low and the fish are holding back, but that's the hard reality. The fish I hooked was a steelhead— about 6 pounds, about average—I saw it clearly, but there aren't many others around."

"Could it be a simple case of lockjaw induced by some fishy voodoo as yet unfathomed by man?" I asked.

"Well, of course, but I don't think that's the case. They're just not here in any numbers. As a last resort I'm going to try this fly down through that riffle at the end of the island." He showed me a black leechlike pattern with an epoxy body and head. It had painted eyes, the glimmer of red, and black Krystal Flash showed through the hard coating. The tail was a strip of black rabbit fur. It was very sexy. "This is a scaled-down (no pun) version of a fly I use for giant northerns and muskies. I think a steelhead will like it if I can find one."

He waded to the head of the riffle and cast his magic, flawless casts. Seagulls worried and quarreled over coveted patches of shore and streams of geese paraded low against the building, lead-colored clouds. Steve panted over, shooed a gull off a comfy-looking rock, and sat beside me. We watched in silent admiration until Bud eventually stopped, looked heavenward, shrugged, and reeled in.

We were shucking waders and summarizing our notes at the rear of my truck when a full-sized classic yellow school bus wheeled into the parking lot and disgorged about 40 rod-waving, wader-clad (one boy wore plastic bags over his pants and sneakers), gleeful teenagers.

Bud wandered over to the bus and talked with several youngsters and an adult before returning. "This is quite a deal," he said. "These kids are from the Clarke Road School in London. The students have a fishing club and they come to the Saugeen twice a year, spring and fall, for an outing. I think that's really wonderful. Two teachers, 45 kids, a day on the water."

"Why didn't I think of that," exclaimed Steve, recently retired from 26 years in education. "I could have had my English classes diagram sentences in the mud banks while I fished."

It was a good time to say good-bye and thank you. The thought of young people learning to enjoy, and hopefully, to protect the sport was heartening punctuation to our time with Bud Hoffman. We shook hands and buckled up.

TACTICAL SUMMARY

- On small streams, particularly under clear water conditions, long, soft-action rods with light (5-weight) lines and fine tippets are highly recommended.
- Clear water also demands delicate presentation. Be careful to avoid disturbing the water's surface on delivery and pickup.
- Drag-free drifts with small dark nymphs are the key to continued success. Bud feels strongly that fly-anglers try to manipulate the fly far too much.
- The judicious use of a float tube greatly enhances an angler's mobility when fishing for staging steelhead at or near river mouths.
- Various lengths of plastic-coated, lead-core line with loop connectors at each end will allow maximum flexibility and allow you to adequately cover a wide range of water depths.
- Don't overlook very slow-moving stretches of river. They often feature silt bottoms and banks that support Hex nymphs, and steelhead often rest and feed in these areas.

RECOMMENDED TACKLE

- Fenwick 9- or 9½-foot, 8-weight, and 9-foot, 9-inch Fenwick Iron Feather, 5-weight rods are Bud's favorites.
- He favors Fenwick World Class reels.
- Fenwick fly lines, leaders, and tippet material are his first choices.

13

John Kluesing

Nymphing with a Spey Rod

I wish John Kluesing could have been at my side at a recent social gathering when a gentleman overheard me telling someone of an experience involving drift-boating on the Pere Marquette. The man wandered over and said something like, "You know, I used to fish that river for brown trout years ago, but they [?] turned it into a steelhead river and ruined it."

Had John been there, the party would have livened up considerably. Nothing puts a knot in this western Michigan river guide's neoprene knickers quicker than this particular "attack" on steelhead. It was one of the initial topics of conversation he brought up when, in the early 1990s, we first ran into him in a restaurant in Baldwin, Michigan.

He fairly bristles when someone slanders the steelhead with remarks to the effect that they have disrupted the spawning habits and habitats of the "native brown trout" and are responsible for (supposed) declines in other trout numbers.

"A common misconception," John would have expostulated to the soon-to-be enlightened gentleman, "is that the steelhead came in a mere 30 years or so back, along with the salmon. Many people don't realize that the steelhead were here in 1876 and are more native than the browns, which first were planted a few years later."

Since they spawn at different times of the year, they don't compete for gravel, he would point out. And Bob and I have noted, as have most people who have fished Michigan rivers over the years, that some of the best steelhead rivers like the Pere Marquette, Big Manistee, Little Manistee, Betsie, White, and others, maintain healthy brown trout populations. We have caught many browns (on the Pere Marquette in particular) in recent years, and steelhead runs in these same rivers have been significant. Some of these browns have been in the 20-inch range, indicating they can withstand even the fall incursions of salmon, share spawning areas, and grow to decent size.

John *is* a fan of the brown trout—don't be misled. But one can detect in him a deeper fascination with the majestic steelhead. Here is a man who has fought them on flies in California, Washington, British Columbia, Alaska, and many Great Lakes tributaries. That he has settled in Michigan and chose to take us to the Pere Marquette for this March sharing of tactics, techniques, and philosophies shows his high regard for this area's steelhead potential.

On that early April morning, we hadn't drifted very far below the MI 37 bridge when we got the first demonstration of his abiding respect for our quarry. Two anglers were in the final stages of landing a steelhead, one of them ready with a net, the other leading his catch to the meshes. The dark male they came up with wasn't a prime specimen, and the three of us were surprised when they got out a stringer—for reason of its condition as well as for the fact that it is much more common practice to release fish in this flies-only section.

John tried his best, calling out, "You ought to put that fish back. You'll probably catch a bigger one." He was hoping (we inferred) that they would not and end up killing no fish. They looked at him skeptically and tethered their catch.

John muttered a bit, but took some consolation in that it hadn't been a ripe hen, and the episode did give him reason to make a point. "Did you notice the knotted nylon net they used? Those knots can beat up a thrashing fish, and those large openings can catch gills." He reached down and picked up his own net, holding it for our view with a definitive gesture. "*This* is something all catch-and-releasers should have." The soft cotton bag was fine meshed, with maybe ½-inch-square openings, and there were no knots.

"Would that you get to use it several times today," said Bob. And the fish gods heard, and they smiled, and it was good . . .

When we reached the first large pool John had in mind (he had fished it the previous day with considerable success), a couple of guys were already working it. We moored a respectful distance above them and walked the shoreline down to a spot well below the two—who, by the way, graciously invited us to step in with them.

"Thanks, we'll come back up in awhile," John said.

We moved down to some promising water where clean, white-graveled redds, now untenanted, indicated active fish were nearby.

I was in a lather to christen a 10-foot Winston prototype steelhead rod (I have since come to love it), which I had balanced nicely with a silent-drag Heron reel spooled with a 2-weight floating line. I had intended to rig a hefty pencil lead/surgical tubing weight on my 10 feet of straight 6-pound leader and tight-line my fly down through their dining room.

But in the 20-minute float to this spot, John had discoursed on the merits of various techniques and had made one almost paradoxical observation: "You know, you don't always have to fish in the most effective manner. You *are* likely to get more hook-ups when you put the (weighted) offering right in the fish's face, and that's O.K., but it can be really challenging to drift a fly with floating line and minimal, if any, weight. You give the fish more choice. He has to want that fly and come to the presentation."

Good point. And it was fairly open where we were, so I went with the suggestion. It is more fun to actually fly-cast than to lob weights, and I was using my new rod more as the makers intended, getting the true feel of the flex, the load, the overall smoothness of its action.

Yet after a time even the joy of a precision rod in hand and the somewhat sanctimonious feeling of being a real sport began to fade in the face of the reality that while *I* was giving the fish a choice, *they* were making the wrong one. Forty minutes of thorough coverage of some first-rate holding water had produced not a touch.

Meanwhile, Bob and John had moved up into the recently vacated big pool, and I could see much gesturing and head-bobbing, evidence that some sort of fish-gittin' plot was brewing. I moved up and watched with growing interest and some veiled amusement as my usually proficient fly-casting coauthor bungled and flubbed in a most ungraceful fashion—with a 14-foot Spey rod.

John had hinted earlier that he had "a new toy" for us to play with, and Bobby got the initial turn at bat. It had been some 15 years back when he had for the first time (and last until now) handled one for a few casts in someone's backyard. He had written it off then as a quaint European affectation, little thinking that the time-tested, two-handed rod would make the North American invasion it appears to be making.

With John at his elbow coaching (and ducking), Bob was soon laying out decent-looking roll casts with fair regularity. The Sage was rigged with a 10-weight floating line tipped with a two-nymph dropper setup at the end of a 12-foot leader. Two tiny split shot were pinched on about 3 feet above the flies, and a corky-style strike indicator was positioned about 8 feet above the terminal rig. When this indicator paused or dipped, Bob would set in his usual fashion—and place the whole arrangement high in the oaks behind him.

"Just flip the tip," John would remind him. "With all that rod *and* a two-handed grip *and* that heavy fly line, you can set a hook with barely a twitch. And if nothing is there, you can continue the drift."

"I know," Bob would say. "I just can't get used to doing it."

I left him moments later as he gazed ruefully toward the treetops for about the sixth time, and I headed for the upper section of the pool.

"Hey, before you work that deep-running rig, let's try another experiment," John called to me. With some trepidation, branch-yanking Bob still doing his thing just below us, I set my familiar gear streamside and waited to see what mystery was in store.

John's plan for me was simply a 9½-foot rod with one of his Harris reels loaded with a 30-inch sink-tip line, an 8-foot leader, and a streamer fly: nothing I hadn't handled before. The presentation involved going to the head of the pool, casting across and slightly down, and letting the streamer sink and sweep across to end up below me in the current. I had, of course, done this sort of thing over the years in a desultory manner, but John wanted me to be very thorough. "It's basically drop-back fishing like the boat pluggers do," he said. "When you reach the end of the drift, just let it ride there a bit, raise it, give it slack, twitch it, then move it over a bit and repeat. Cover the same water for a few casts, then move down a step and repeat until you've covered the whole pool."

I found I could do this and still watch Bob manfully persevering with the Spey rod just a few yards below me, his sets now modified and sojourns with the squirrels subsequently fewer. In fact, one of his twitch sets soon produced a rod bend, a throb, and the dreaded early release. Bob harumphed and "frammelled" for a moment or two, but the first action of the day inspired us all. He reloaded and I continued my streamer efforts with heightened interest.

"This (drop-back) is an easy and effective way to cover water," John commented. "I'll quite often have clients who haven't fished a lot do this." (My antennae perked at this suggestion of a dig, but he never missed a beat.) "Like this Japanese gentleman last March. I had him do this in the MI 37 pool just below the launch site, and he took a 10-pound chrome buck. And you probably know when a fish hits in this situation, there's no mistaking a strike, so the soft takes so many people miss aren't a factor."

Bob becomes a believer in John Kluesing's Spey rod nymphing technique.

I opined as I knew but would like to be retaught by a big chromer myself. As I picked a bit of weed from the fly at one point, John asked what I thought of the pattern. "I like the looks of it," I said candidly. "The yellowish olive grizzly wing has the parr-markings look, and . . ."

"That's what it's supposed to imitate—a young salmon. Have you noticed the fly in the shallows? Walt Grau [another top-notch area guide and fly-tier] came up with this pattern. He calls it the Tiger Fly. They just smack the stripes off it on some occasions."

This not being one of those occasions, I got out when I had stepped down to Bob at the tail of the long pool and rested my aching shoulders. Then Bob joined me, so John took his Spey and continued the assault on the pool. His adroit manipulations soon produced a hook-up and a scramble for cameras, but it turned out to be a brown trout— a nice 15-incher—but not what we were after.

My turn with the Spey was less than spectacular, but I stayed out of serious tree trouble and managed to hang another brown, nearly a twin to the earlier 15-incher. It came out of the same off-current slack from which John had taken his. "The steelhead we caught the other day were in that froggy water too," John said. "Other times they like to stay more out in the current right along that bubble line."

After an hour in this spot, we moved downstream, keeping an eye out for visible fish and exchanging theories and opinions on why some people can spot steelhead and some have difficulty. John said that he has been accused of having Polaroid eyeballs, and he soon put the mark on some fish we would have missed. He attributes spotting success to "seeing the bottom," an intimate knowledge of this water, and an understanding of the fish's habitat.

We moored and got out to put our best moves on these newly discovered holding fish, Bob and John preparing to introduce them to Mr. Spey rod. I moved downstream a couple of hundred feet and found what I usually consider to be the ideal scenario: a half-dozen steelhead maintaining steady position in the darker, deeper water adjacent to a shallow redd, attendants to a female barely visible above them in a deep bed she was apparently still forming. They didn't appear to be the least bit goosey, though a few other boats had been through earlier. Maybe, just maybe, they hadn't even been fished to . . .

Salivating ever so genteelly, I decided to stay well above them, cast across, and let the fly swing down and in front of the phalanx of males. No danger of lining or foul-hooking with this approach, and the female was off my line of drift. As I made the first cast, I was already mentally rehearsing whether I should call out, "Fish on!" or "Camera boy, please," or one of the other smug, bent-rod bons mots we bandy about.

A half hour, a hundred passes, and several size and color fly changes later, I was cursing rather than rehearsing. Not a touch. I couldn't figure it. They did not act like pestered fish; they just didn't like me or my bugs.

Bob and John had hooked, fought, and lost one of their two "holders," and they now moved down toward me with the boat. I gestured meaningfully at the run (with its stubborn fish) down and across from me; my companions nodded and tied the boat higher up, then waded cautiously down.

"This is a lock," were John's first words after appraising the scene. I nearly dislocated my already sore casting arm reaching for my wallet, hoping my $100 stash bill was still there and that John was a betting man. Some glimmer of good sense stayed me, however; perhaps it was a vague consideration that this guy made his living doing this stuff. So I relaxed on a half-submerged log to watch . . . and prepared to commiserate politely when they too struck out. As if to further defy the fish gods, John positioned Bob *directly* across from the fish. Maybe he figures he'll drop that big rod and conk one, I thought dispiritedly.

I barely had half my re-rig prepped (for when my turn at futility came again), when the Spey rod bent and Bob exclaimed, "There's one!" *I* played camera boy, Bob handled the gear like he'd been there before, and John gave us a fine demonstration of hustle and savvy with that tight-meshed net he was so happy with. The fish was long and sleek and soon released. He swam away with hardly a scale out of place after a quick taping and photo moment.

Bob and I took a breather, so John moved back to "position Spey"— and promptly hooked another fish. It threw the hook after a moment but I was rapidly becoming a believer.

If I may digress for a moment (the chronology of incidents insists), Bob and I have fished a lot out West—Madison, Green, Bighorn—and witnessed some guide rivalry, with ensuing boat races, name-calling, and near fisticuffs. It would lead one to believe that many of these guys look out for old number one to the exclusion of good sense. If what happened with us at this point is typical, hats off to Great Lakes guides; if a fluke, it was still a heartwarming incident and one we'll remember. "You know," John said, "there are still fish holding here and we could get them. Why don't we move on down so the guide and his client above us there (we could see them a bend away) can have a crack at them? They hadn't had any hits when I last talked to them."

Bob and I are pretty flexible, so John waded up to give them the skinny while we walked the boat down a bit to wait. Waves and thanks from the other party were appreciated, and we left feeling as good as we felt all day.

A quarter of an hour later found us by Simmy Nolf's (a local leg-end) cabin, fishing the run in the snaggy, narrow chute there.

We elected to stay in this log- and debris-choked section for a pretty good length of time. I like to try to figure out clean drifts through snaggy areas, even if I can only get a 6- to 10-foot run. Moments later I was in the midst of one of these tackle-losing undertakings when I had a head-shaking take on a Green Egg Fly. I brought the fish up top, and he immediately started down, as I hoped he would. I clambered into shallow water to move with him and keep him on a short line, but just as I figured the field advantage was mine, he turned and powered back up into the narrow, log-infested chute, mowing me off on a submerged timber.

Even at this writing, with the benefits of hindsight, I probably would do the same thing, but John did make an observation worth consid-ering. "Sometimes when they start down and away from trouble,

John demonstrates precision line mending with the long rod.

you're farther ahead to just stay in place and let them get way below you. Then they're not as apt to run back to their original cover." Maybe it varies from fish to fish . . . I'll file this with my ever-growing list of options. Meanwhile, Bob hooked a fish and played it for maybe 10 seconds before it spit out the fly.

"What were you using?" asked John.

"That fly you gave me a while ago, the flashy, blue-bodied, wood-duck-winged streamer . . . Greenberg? Iceberg? What did you call it?"

"The *Blue*berg. It's designed to imitate Pacific salmon fry. I've had good luck with it, particularly on a floating line."

"Any other favorites you're willing to divulge?"

John regaled us with a recent episode where two clients took four fish in the 38- to 40-inch range . . . "That's the 20-pound variety, kids" . . . in a 5-day span in early November. Instrumental in this success story was the Sarps Seducer.

It is now one of his fall favorites.

"How about nymphs?" I asked.

"You noticed that when I rigged them today they were olive-hued—the Hare's Ears and Hexs, that is. And in early spring I'll also work the Green Rock Worm (caddis larvae) imitations, as well as Black Stones in 8s and 10s, slender bodied."

"Steve and I have about 10 Hex nymph variations," Bob interjected. "Do you play around with that tie?"

"Oh yeah, I go for wiggle. Marabou is good, and the filoplume Hex, while delicate, is easy to tie and has plenty of motion even on a dead-drift. Amber has been a good shade in that pattern."

We floated on, now only a half hour or so from our take-out spot at the Green Cabin, and John waxed incredulous at the low number of fishermen for a Sunday.

"We're well into the walk-in water, and hardly anyone's around. It's not *that* cold, and there are plenty of fish in the river."

"Got to be yesterday's weather report." Bob speculated. "It called for wind, sleet, snow, slime, and basic havoc. A lot of people must have said 'Bag it' and stayed home."

"Whatever the reason, this is great. Look at that. There are fish holding right there, and we're almost in sight of the Green Cabin! This never happens."

But it did, and we moored for one last Spey session. I had used that rod once briefly early in the day, but now promptly forgot the proper casting technique. I struggled and flopped line in the general vicinity of my target, John at my side coaching and spotting. After about the tenth decent drift, the indicator paused, I twitched, and all hell broke loose—as much at my end of the rod as at the fish's end. I hadn't had occasion to use the reel, hadn't really even thought about it as John had stripped line and readied the rod for me. I've always held the rod and fought fish with my right hand and handled line and reeled with a left crank. This was a right-hand crank. Couple that revelation with a rod several feet longer and several ounces heavier than what you are used to, attached to a rampaging steelhead on which you are trying to keep a tight line. I must have looked like someone handed me a hot poker as I flipped my hands, the rod, the reel in various postures. "Oh Jeez, oh no! Do this. No, not that. Left hand *above* the reel. Oh God!" John didn't know quite what to make of this Chevy-Chase-goes-fishing routine.

After what seemed several minutes but was more likely about 30 seconds, I got my act together and brought the fish up where we could see that it had been fouled. John simply slid his hand down the line, got the hook, and popped it loose. This was a fortuitous episode, though, because moments later I tied into a big male from the same hold, and with the earlier practice session, managed a creditable performance for a neophyte Spey-rodder.

John did one of his high-speed net jobs. We took the 8- or 9-pound buck off the main current for pictures (fly nicely in the corner of his jaw) and sent him on his way.

Bob took the big rod from me and made two drifts by the remaining fish; the indicator paused. The fish swam toward Bob, who had momentarily shorted out or something. He was oblivious. We yelled and then he set. Once firmly attached, he fought and landed it in record time, and we stood shaking our heads.

"Now is this just a gimmick that had its flukey moment in the sun, or . . . "

"I'm not about to give away my one-hander," John said. "But the Spey rod certainly gives you better line control, which aids in getting that much-sought dead drift, and you've seen how the added leverage and heavy line facilitate a solid hook set."

"Yeah, even Bob . . . " I bit my tongue; I needed a ride home.

"It's so versatile, too," he went on. "You can run floating lines, sink tips—any type of line or method of presentation—from the same rod with better results than from a one-hander. It's really effective with streamers in the fall. I can work them parallel to the current in a much wider area—and it's easier."

"Get me one or two for Christmas, Steve," the poor, deluded Bob suggested.

"It's a good tool to have in your arsenal," John concluded as we saw the Green Cabin take-out spot ahead. "When I approach certain holes on this river, I reach for the two-hander and feel really confident."

After leaving the river, John dropped us off at our vehicle. He had a couple of errands to run, then we planned to meet for a final few minutes at the Johnson's Lodge Orvis Shop on MI 37. When Bob and I came out of the shop after browsing and schmoozing for a bit, there was John off to the side of the parking lot—practicing casting with some other combo he hadn't been able to fish during our float.

"My God," I said. "You're worse than we are. Don't you ever *not* fish?"

"I can't remember not fishing," he answered. "I've done it all my life. It has been my life."

This 35-year-old fanatic was exaggerating a bit: He has managed to work in a wife, two young sons, skiing (he instructs that and fly-casting for the L.L. Bean Fly-Fishing School), bicycling, fly-tying, and he is a member of numerous fishing-related associations.

We even talked with him a little about the adventures he had during five summers he spent guiding in Alaska. One of the best features of guiding, he said, is that it allows him to *share* his lifelong passion and instill respect for rivers and fish and fellow anglers.

"John," Bob called as we pulled away, "Next time you see a duo of Spey-rodders on the Pere Marquette, check close. It'll likely be us. And we'll need more flies."

"You'll be easy to spot."

TACTICAL SUMMARY

- Fish often hold on the inside (shallow side) of a bend pool, especially in cold or discolored water, so fish that first before attacking the deeper part.
- Fish a holding area very thoroughly when the water is cold; when the water temperature is warmer, make fewer passes and move on—you better your odds by covering *more* water.
- Use a large-bag cotton net. The net person should let the angler know when he's going for the fish (e.g., say "Now") so the angler can drop the rod tip and the line won't hold the fish from the net. Net a fish headfirst.
- So long as a steelhead is at least 24 inches in length, you can estimate its weight (without removing it from the water) by measuring it, calculating one pound for the first 20 inches, and adding one more pound for each inch over 20. A 24-inch fish, for example, would have an estimated weight of 5 pounds.
- Be extra careful in the first and last 5 seconds of a steelhead fight; that seems to be when most are lost.
- Know your limitations when wading in cold steelhead streams. Go slowly at all times.
- If you hook a fish in heavy cover and it comes right out, don't *always* be in a huge hurry to get it on a short line; sometimes too much pressure too quickly drives it right back to the cover.
- Don't go too light with tippet material and leave hooks in fish unnecessarily.
- Try a Spey rod. It allows you to employ many methods with the same rod.

RECOMMENDED TACKLE

- In one-handed rods John's recommendation is an L.L. Bean 9- to 10-foot for a 7- to 9-weight in fast-action graphite. He likes the

Sage and the Orvis two-handed (Spey) rods in the 12- to 14-foot range with a 10-weight, double-taper line.

- He uses a Harris reel. It has a very smooth drag with fine-tune adjustment capabilities, holds the ample backing needed, and performs well under all weather conditions.
- The L.L. Bean Super Head sinking shooting lines in 250, 350, and 450 grains are his choices for subsurface work.
- Maxima ultragreen is his favored leader material.
- John likes streamers, notably his Blueberg, the Tiger Fly, Bunny Strips, and Sarp's Seducer. For nymph fishing, some favorites are Olive Hare's Ears and Hexs, and the filoplume Hex in amber.

14

Jac Ford

Pocket Water on the Pere Marquette

Bright sun and blue skies with low, clear water, and heavy angler traffic equate to problematic fly-fishing for steelhead. This day promised to be tough indeed. A high-pressure system dominated the entire Great Lakes region, and the local forecast was for a partly cloudy and clearing day with a high temperature of 46 degrees F (8 degrees C). The Pere Marquette was low and crystalline. We expected early morning water temperatures near 38 degrees F (3 degrees C) and afternoon readings approaching 44 degrees F (7 degrees C).

Jac Ford wheeled into the parking lot of the All Seasons Restaurant in Baldwin, Michigan, exactly on time. We had been fretting over the difficult fishing conditions by telephone for several days, and the previous evening had finally decided that the weather was not going to change just to appease us. "Let's go tomorrow. The 5-day forecast is for more of the same—no rain, no clouds. We can't wait forever." I had quickly agreed and made the drive westward through 100 miles of deer crossings in predawn terror, but on time, without any extra bucktail in the grill.

Jac is an active conservationist and serves as the president of the William B. Mershon Chapter of Trout Unlimited. The chapter's spring banquet was nearing, his guide service was tightly booked, his commercial fly-tying was backlogged, and his grandchildren missed him. It seemed prudent to accept the date and get on the river.

"We'll fish pocket water today," Jac advised as the boat was readied and we slipped into waders, vests, and neoprene gloves. He is an advocate of precision when it comes to fly-fishing for steelhead, and this advocacy turns to total commitment and strict adherence as the conditions become more difficult. "The sun, low water, and angling pressure will keep the fish off the gravel. Their first instinct is to stay hidden, so they'll move to the obvious deep holes and runs where

199

they feel safe. And, of course, all the other anglers will fish these same areas. When enough pressure is applied, the fish will move out of all but the deepest, most snag-infested holes and into the small, secretive pockets. Very few people know where to look for fish when this happens. Jump in. I'll show you some precision pocket fishing."

We pushed into the current and slid under the MI 37 bridge at 8:30 AM, which seemed late. "We want the other boats to be ahead of us. Along with the walk-in anglers, they'll push the fish into those unlikely spots I mentioned, and we *should* do well."

"We will need to be quite precise about fly patterns under these conditions; of course this is a process of educated opinion being *strongly* influenced by success or failure. Size *will* be a factor. We'll need to fish small nymphs, or very small egg patterns on light tippets with a natural dead drift."

The other guide boats were well ahead of us, and the air warmed as the sun angled higher. We floated by several deep, inviting holes and through a promising dark run before Jac pulled hard on the oars and dropped the anchor; we sidled into a sand cove on the sunlit side of a long, straight stretch roughly midway between two sweeping bends with deep water. There had been two people casting heavy sinking lines into the upper pool. They had given us a helpless, telling shrug as we passed. It looked like at least one angler was working the bend 90 yards below us.

"Look closely at that small pocket in the shade directly across from the boat," Jac directed. It was no more than 10 yards in length, perhaps 15 feet in width, and it was dark and lay with the broken surface of quick current over irregular bottom. A miniature bankside log tangle completed the picture. Below the pocket was a stretch of gravel that extended for roughly 30 yards.

"This is an unlikely looking spot, one that many anglers will pass by in favor of the deeper holes." Jac smiled and pointed to the head of the pocket, specifically to the tree stump where the water deepened and formed a backside current just upstream from the miniature log-jam. "Put a Micro-Egg on the dropper and a small Black Stone Fly nymph on the point. Try to drop your flies at the seam and as close to the stump as you can; this will put the flies at the right depth when they swing through the pocket."

The line-to-leader connection paused, and then twitched distinctly downward; I lifted the rod with malice in my heart. Nothing. The flies slowly resettled and began to swing. "Allow me to show you a more subtle and more *effective* way to strike a steelhead," he suggested and reached for my rod. Flipping out just a few feet of line, he allowed the flies to sink and then made the rod tip rise sharply 3 to 4 inches. "Do this with the wrist. Hold the line against the grip with very little slack. *Pop* the rod tip up—try to make it move only 1 inch—which is impossible. If the rod tip moves 4 inches against a tight line, the line and leader moves 2 to 3 inches. With needle-sharp hooks this will set the hook. If a fish is there, you'll feel it and can set again—if you feel it is necessary. If a fish did not take, you only moved your fly a small distance—mere inches, and you did not ruin the rest of your drift. Your cast will still be working."

I practiced with a short line so as not to spook the fish in the pocket. Jac was right; I could see the advantage clearly. After the short, sharp, upward *pop*, the flies settled back quickly and continued their drift. After my *hard* strike, the flies lifted too far, and the entire drift was made ineffective.

Four casts later my offering stopped, just plain stopped, in mid drift. "Pop him," commanded Jac, but too late. I popped an empty hole in the water and the drift continued. Then it stopped again. This time the strike took hold and a much larger fish rolled on the surface before diving into the logs. Zing went my heartstring. "I bet it was the Leech again." I reeled in, was proven correct, and sat down on the bank to steady my jangled nerves and shaking hands before tying on another new tippet and fly.

When Steve had been pressed into family affairs and couldn't make this trip, Jac asked me if I would mind if his son, Jeff, came along. Jeff was, of course, welcome and it was clearly his turn now in the "pocket of despair."

It was the fifth, maybe the sixth cast, before Jeff whooped loudly. I was busy with a devilish knot and Jac was arranging his gear in the boat when we looked up to a frantic Jeff backing up the bank very quickly while trying to control several loops of slack fly line with his left hand. At his feet, a *very* large buck steelhead swirled and ran with passion for Lake Michigan. The fish was gone. "Did you see that? He charged right at me. I couldn't get rid of the slack fast enough. Did you see that stripe? WOW!"

"One more time, gents. Let's give it a few more casts and then we'll leave these darlings alone and move down to the next pocket. Who's on first?"

"Bob is," said Jeff. "He's all rigged and ready. I'm a wreck!"

My fourth cast was perfect. The flies plopped and settled like they had eyes. The drift was clean, and the twitch came about halfway down into the little pocket. I had been following the line-to-leader connection closely, and the short, upward set was true. "We have ignition, we have a lift-off! Man the camera, captain!" Our engagement, however thrilling, was brief, too brief. As Jac reached for the camera, the big hen soared through the thickest brush and dove into the upper end of the logjam. The line went slack.

"We're out of here. Let's move on down. We've put enough heat on this little place." Jac held the boat as Jeff and I clambered over the side. "What do you call this place, Dad? Does it have a name?" Jeff asked.

"It sure is an unlikely looking spot." I added. "We shed a tear or two here."

"That's it," Jac offered. "We'll call it Tear Drop Run."

As we drifted toward our next stop, we passed a pair of napping anglers. A third member of the group was pawing through his vest when he noticed our boat. "I bought all new tippet spools last night," he offered. "I should have invested in sunscreen. Seen any fish on the gravel?"

"Not a one. It's too bright," Jac answered. "Good luck." He then continued. "Steelhead behave differently under these conditions. Not only do they seek out more secretive havens, but they definitely react in a more erratic, violent manner when hooked. Under normal spring conditions this river is about 10 to 16 inches deeper, with a bit of color from snowmelt or rain. A hooked fish can ramble around and take some time deciding just where and how it wants to break your heart. What we're dealing with today is a totally different situation. As soon as a fish is hooked and feels any rod pressure, it panics. It is terrified of leaving the security of its little pocket. If they decide to leave, they do so very quickly."

I asked Jac if heavier tippet would help, even though it might mean fewer takes. "No, I really do not think so," he answered. "These fish are so strong and so frenetic under these conditions that they can snap 8-pound test very easily. We're using 5-pound test, 3X, about as heavy as we can use and expect the fish to take the fly. The two fish that broke off in the logs did so very quickly. They were *not* going to leave their protection. They were strong, felt pressure, and blasted into the thickest cover they could find. If you had been using 12-pound test the result would have been the same."

Winter fish hold no mystery for Jac Ford.

We drifted on and I noticed that our captain lifted his oars whenever we approached cleaned gravel. The explanation was that, even through it was highly *improbable* that any fish would actually be spawning during the daylight hours in such thin flow, it was *possible,* and Jac feels (strongly) that oar movement (not the passage of the boat) and the resultant water turbulence badly frighten fish and alter their normal behavior. He uses only dark green oars, feeling that lighter colors, particularly yellow, have an adverse impact.

We were greeted by a rare sight as we floated past the Green Cottage. Three eagles, two of them mature adults, wheeled lazily then glided to the nest and out of view. "My clients and I saw a pair of otters down here yesterday. They were playing on the bank just around the next bend. They sat up, and I *swear* they waved at us when we went by."

We stopped at a spot Jac referred to as the Alligator Alley. Downstream we could see several anglers casting to the runs and edges of a wide gravel spread. The Alley was a slow, 150-foot south bank curve with the obligatory menacing logjam every 20 feet. Three pockets within the run seemed to fit Jac's criteria for potential. They had darker water and a more wrinkled surface than the rest of the sweep. They were tucked between log tangles, and they were small.

The shallow water at our feet showed a bottom mix of sand and medium gravel, and we were advised to pick up our feet when we walked, not to shuffle, which is standard wading practice, and to try to walk on sand rather than gravel. When Jeff asked, "Why?" his father answered that sound vibrations travel much faster and more distinctly through water than through air. "These fish are nervous enough. They've been pushed up here by all that traffic we see downstream on the gravel. Besides, dragging your feet through gravel kills bugs and crushes eggs. If the current is slow and there is no danger, I lift my feet."

Jac prefers to have his clients fish runs and holes rather than sight-fish the gravel. "My customers represent the complete spectrum of fly-fishing experience and skill, and it seems that, regardless of ability, a very high percentage of them will melt down when they *see* these big fish in shallow water over clean gravel. I've had very knowledgeable, widely traveled people put *perfect* casts to very specific locations in pockets and runs, and then trash 10 casts in a row when they see a 10-pound female and several bucks holding on a redd. They cast into a tree, they line the fish, they snag their waders, they cannot, under any circumstance, tie a new knot because they have buck fever. Because of this I want clients to use my gear when we work visible fish. Antireverse reels (I prefer Fin-Nor) preclude problems caused by an excited angler trying to reel when a fish is running."

I checked my knots ever so carefully (fearful of having to retie) and studied the pocket in front of me (even more fearful that I would throw "trash"). I thanked the trout gods that there were no visible fish and began to cast. To my left and upstream Jeff was drifting a Micro-Egg-and-Leech combination. Jac fussed with the grill, a pile of steaks, and a loaf of Bavarian rye.

Suddenly, Jeff grunted, "Fish on," and I turned just in time to see the bright, very large hen vault over a log. She ran up to the edge of the run and the shallow tail-out of the pool above us, then quickly zigged back and forth to both banks before tearing straight downstream.

Ten minutes and five jumps later Jac carefully netted the big silver female for his son. She was 33 inches long with deep heavy shoulders and a girth of 18½ inches. The small Leech was backed out of her jaw and I snapped a quick picture before Jac released her. She needed no long resuscitation and bolted as soon as he loosened his grip on her tail.

We waded back upstream to the boat and lunched on prime steak sandwiches and fresh fruit. The sun was warm and we lingered awhile. "What are the key elements, as you see them, to be successful in fly-fishing for steelhead?" I asked.

"Number one is a careful consideration of the conditions. Water temperature and clarity are critical to your plan. The fish become more active as the water reaches and exceeds the 40-degree F [4-degree C] mark. They begin to feed on the active bug or bugs. Know the cycle of the insect life in the stream you are fishing. Black stones are becoming active now, and when the water moves up a few more degrees, the Hex nymphs will become popular. Little green caddis larvae are effective, too."

"What about fly sizes?" I asked.

"Steelhead are picky, but not so much as stream trout that really zero in on a bug. The smart thing is to start with what they *should* be looking for and *reduce* size first, then change patterns. Independent of insect activity, I like to use Egg-Sucking Leeches with a chartreuse head, in size 8 and 10 whenever I'm baffled. They are working today. Lastly, stealth is important. Careful wading and casting are a real factor in success. Try to keep low, minimize arm and rod movement, and wade *slowly*."

We piled back into the 15-foot Lavro and began the last leg of our float to Gleason's Landing, the downstream limit of the flies-only section of the beautiful Pere Marquette. I looked over my water-spotted gear bouncing on the seat, and opened a soft drink.

"We introduced ourselves to quite a few steelhead today. I wonder how many?" was Jeff's comment from the stern.

"Enough, certainly," answered his father, "to qualify as a banner day."

Agreed. And we didn't even see the otters.

TACTICAL SUMMARY

- Wade *very* cautiously. Minimize sound traveling through the water by lifting your feet if it is safe to do so. Do not crunch gravel.

- If approaching by boat, lift your oars from the water when near holding lies.
- Look for small, shaded pockets with a broken surface and cover. These will hold a surprising number of fish when bright sun, low water, and angling pressure combine.
- Visualize the delivery and drift two or three times before actually casting. This will aid in precision placement on the first try.
- Quick changes in direction of rod pressure harry the fish, and keep it off balance.
- Double-check *all* knots and pull off *all* of the fly line and at least 20 yards of backing to be sure your spool is not overwrapped.
- Always carry foul-weather clothing.
- Be sure to bring twice as many flies as you think you will need and several extra tippet spools.

RECOMMENDED TACKLE

- Jac prefers Graphite-USA rods, usually a 9½-foot, 8-weight.
- He uses Scientific Anglers fly lines. He prefers a floating weight-forward, but admits to the value of sink tips.
- Maxima is his favorite tippet material.
- For inexperienced anglers Jac suggests antireverse reels and supplies Fin-Nors. Advanced clients usually bring all their own gear, but he carries Scientific Anglers System II reels just in case they are needed.

15

Ray Schmidt

Sinking Lines, Marabou Speys, and the Big Manistee

I watched Ray Schmidt hook, adroitly fight, and quickly release a small steelhead on arguably the most beautiful mid-September Saturday on which a fly-angler could ever hope to fish. One of the most highly regarded river guides in the Midwest, Ray had graciously taken a "boatman's holiday" from his extremely busy, full-time guiding and outfitting schedule to chauffeur Bob and me down a gorgeous stretch of his beloved home water, the Big Manistee.

After a couple of hours of spirited yet fishless casting, he had finally proven that while Bob and I may have turned off the Big Manistee steelies, they could be successfully coaxed to at least one fly . . . his.

But it wasn't this hook-up that caught my attention so much as the *un*-hooking. "Man, short of those chronic long releases brother Bob is notorious for [mumble, grumble from downstream] that's about as quick a divestiture as I've seen. You don't spend much time admiring them, do you?"

Talk about pushing the right button. I had intended to later ask Ray for his thoughts on best release techniques, one of our stock questions, but he warmed to the topic *right* now. "It's best never to touch the fish," he said. "Get it in quick, get your forceps on the fly, and pop it loose. You shouldn't even raise the fish from the water. If a photo is desired, be sure everyone is set, focused, et cetera, then lift the fish by the wrist, snap the picture, and it's back in—fast." Ray is and always has been conservation-minded (in fact is past conservation chairman of the Great Lakes Council of the Federation of Fly Fishers) regarding cold-water fisheries in general, but this present discussion showed the special attention *he* feels the steelhead merits.

He referred to a study done at Queens University in Kingston, Ontario, where test groups of rainbows were exercised, then exposed to air for varying times, one group for a maximum of 60 seconds. Hours later the mortality rate for this high-exposure group was reportedly much higher than for the more briefly exposed fish.

"Obviously you stress a fish when you fight him," Ray went on, "and this causes a lactic acid buildup in its system. When the exhausted fish is exposed to the oxygen we breathe, it damages the gas exchange mechanism in the gills. You can revive the fish and he will generally swim off seemingly O.K., but what you don't usually see is that same fish 12 hours later; he can be dead."

Handling steelhead became a moot concern this day. None of us hooked any other fish, though we could occasionally see them roll in pools and skate over the gravel bars. But this paucity of hook-ups was partly by choice. "If fish count numbers are what you want, we can roll nymphs below egg attractors and split shot off running or floating lines," Ray had said when we were first putting in below Tippy Dam. "If a truer fly-fishing experience is to your liking, let's use sinking lines with unweighted flies."

Ray was hearkening back to his earlier days of fly-fishing the Pacific coast. Sales repping had kept him out there long enough to fish extensively from southern Oregon up into British Columbia, and he had later worked with Bruce Richards of Scientific Anglers, developing shooting heads and sinking lines. Pacific Northwest techniques can't be used effectively everywhere in the Great Lakes region, but . . . "Here on the Big Manistee and on sections of the Muskegon where there is a lot of room for casting and plenty of long holding areas, we can use the sinking lines to good advantage—and it's a fun way to fish."

Of all the variations on fly-fishing for steelhead, throwing a sinking line was the one technique I have used the least, so the additional experience was welcome, especially under the tutelage of an accomplished master like Ray Schmidt. He has fly-fished since he was 12, and now at age 45 is a Federation of Fly Fishers certified instructor and stays involved in fly-casting instruction programs.

"Name your tackle, pilgrim," drawled Bob, watcher of too many old movies.

"Let's rig with Teeny nymph lines. Got any T-300s?"

We did. Some shuffling around in the omnipresent Abel bags, a quick change of spools, and we were ready to attach terminal rigs.

"I don't know how you guys like to rig for this type of fishing, but what I have found to work well is just a couple of feet of heavy butt section, say 15- to 20-pound test, with an additional 2 feet of 6- or 8-

pound leader material—Maxima is a good choice—blood-knotted to the butt," Ray suggested.

He saw my hesitation and added, "You can get away with a short leader if you keep the fly ahead of the belly of the line on your drift."

"Do you ever use lighter tippets?" Bob asked, probably with an eye to the extreme clarity of the water we were about to plumb.

"I'll occasionally go to 4-pound Maxima, but I much prefer the heavier. If you show the fly first, as you can with an across-and-down-stream presentation, they will take it." Again Ray warmed to a point. "We've got one of the greatest game fish in the world available to us. Why not take advantage of it? I like to jump them, fight them *hard,* test their mettle, but get them in quick!" He was obviously not a fan of the noodle-rod, slow-dance school, but we had to ask his opinion on that anyway, just to see if he'd get his shorts in a knot. He did. River guides, as a rule, do not lack for color; Ray can range out to the ultraviolet edge of the spectrum on many issues.

This flair for color is also reflected in many of his flies. A fan of the George Cook Popsicle Marabous, Ray produced an assortment for us to choose from. He has tied commercially from back in his school years and beyond, and his meticulous, shimmering creations seem to breathe life. "Sparse is the key for these (Marabous and schlappen) Speys," he said as he handed me an orange-and-red Tequila Sunrise. "You get more undulation that way. It seems to produce a bit better than the thicker ties."

"I assume since you're foisting this one on me, that it's the expert's first choice for bright-day, clear-water conditions like we see here," I posed. "I shall without a doubt kick finny butt?"

"It's a good all-arounder, but if you don't jump any fish with it after a fair try, run this Checkerboard (red/black Spey), which has a good record under these conditions."

Ray gingerly poked around in my fly boxes and found a few selections he deemed worthy of the water. "You ought to like a couple of those," I said defensively. "I tied them after I saw you demonstrate the Spey tie at Fred Lee's fly shop in Kalamazoo last spring."

"Yeah, well, quick studies are hard to find any more. But these red butt and green butt Speys are decent. Did Bob tie them?"

"He can barely tie his shoes. We can't all be George Cook or Bear Andrews, you know." We bantered some more, but kidding aside (I'm pretty sure he was kidding), one of the connections that found us working with Ray was our admiration for his tying skills. For the

Ray Schmidt on his favorite river—the Big Manistee

past couple of years Bob and I have been trying, with fair results, to tie the definitive crayfish imitation, one that would be quick and easy to tie. Steelhead would love it, and it would also bring up the big browns that sulk deep in the Au Sable and don't often show themselves. We were close with barbell eyes, rubber legs, and a pretty combination of marabou and chenille. Then at the aforementioned Ray Schmidt clinic, we saw him produce basically "our" pattern with a simple improvement to the process that made it look nearly perfect. "Steve, he's even more brilliant than we are," Bob had allowed. "We need to work with this guy."

And here we were. But crayfish patterns weren't in evidence this Spey-day. The cerise-and-purple Showgirl took its place on my fly patch next to Whitey, another of Ray's favorites featuring purple schlappen weaving back over white marabou. Four sprigs of Flashabou top and bottom gave it added dash. If conditions were to change dramatically, the Dark Days pattern, a blend of purple, blue, and black, was waiting in the wings, with several other variations close to hand.

As we boarded the drift boat to head downstream to our first stop, Bob exclaimed, "Just when you think you've seen it all. Is this what I think it is? He was referring to a bunch of 1½-inch "bristles" protruding from the bow decking of Ray's boat.

"Well, if you were figuring it's to keep stripped line from sliding all over, you're right. They're pieces of weed-whacker cord. Works great when fishing from the boat, which we won't have to do since wading conditions are perfect."

Being a fair hand with duct tape, baling wire, and Popsicle sticks myself, I'm always looking for ideas. Bob and I have, of course, gimmicked up our own drift boat some, and another of Ray's little wrinkles we plan to implement was a row of 1-inch-diameter, staggered-length sections of circular PVC tubing backed with some indoor/outdoor carpeting. Attached to the inner forward section of the port side, looking much like a misplaced Pan flute, the device allows anglers to insert delicate rod tips inside the tubing, then lay the rods out of harm's way along the side. Keeps the "mating tangles" to a minimum also. Simple and most effective.

Just barely out of sight of Tippy Dam, we pulled into the shallows of "The Rock Pile," so named for its abundance of gravel, cobble, and larger current-diverting rocks. As was to be the case at every stop, we were given a quick yet thorough rundown on how best to attack this piece of water—where the seams were, how far to wade down into the tail-out, and so on before wading into assigned positions. Ray generally goes through a potentially fishy run or pool twice, beginning at the head, stepping it down, then back to the head, maybe a change of flies, and down through it again. If fish are seen or touched, he will, of course, hit it a few more times.

Some rolling fish kept us there for a half hour, though we suspected they were salmon. "Any Skamania in still?" Bob asked hopefully, eyeing a boiling swirl between him and Ray.

"Oh, maybe. But there wasn't a big run of summer fish this year. We're looking for the fall steelhead of 6 or 7 pounds that are traditional here on the Big M. This is one of the earliest Michigan rivers to get a sizable fall run."

The heralded early birds weren't particularly common at this spot, so we regrouped to float farther down. "Let's head for Suicide Bend and see if we can jump some fish there," Ray said.

This bend lies below a high roll-a-way down which logs cascaded in bygone lumbering days. More than the usual number of accidents occurred here, hence the ominous name, but we found it serene and beautiful this present day.

We fished a long slot below the tail-out, but again no steelhead came to play. We did see trout and salmon being taken by bait anglers, which spoke well for other aspects of the cold-water fishery here, particularly the burgeoning brown trout population—a point of personal satisfaction for Ray in that he has devoted countless hours to the cause.

I had been standing parallel to the current casting to 12 o'clock, working as Ray had advised, to keep the fly leading the shooting head. Results were mixed. The occasional sloppy cast, due in part to tangles in my shooting line, prompted Ray to wade over and coach a bit. His technique with the Teeny nymph line is to strip the desired amount of shooting line, lay the head and some line out in front of you with a roll cast, then pick up line so that the darker shooting head is just coming into the rod tip. Make one backcast loading the rod well and shoot.

I particularly profited from his tips on holding a loop of line in my mouth to avoid tangles and facilitate shooting loops smoothly through the guides. "Ooh 'on 'ewah 'ooze 'ooting 'askets?" I asked him as I worked on this new (to me) technique.

"What?! Oh. Shooting baskets. I prefer holding bigger loops as you see me doing. The loops from baskets are smaller and more apt to jam up in the guides. Another thing I suggest is once you've reached the end of a drift, point your rod down the path of the line as you retrieve. You can get more hours out of this type of line if you minimize hinging and the resultant abrasion. And don't talk with line in your mouth."

Farther downstream we tried another particularly attractive area referred to as "The Gravel Island." As the name indicates, the gravelly shallows are in midstream in this straight stretch, barely over ankle depth, while the deep runs are to the banks. We fished down through this mix of very fine gravel, cobble, and boulders, and saw fish scooting around constantly. Even when you aren't hooking them, their visual presence works wonders at keeping your head in the game.

Ray gives the authors a casting demonstration with a heavy sink tip.

At one point a blue-backed, silver-bellied form cleared the water just a couple of yards in front of me. No salmon, that beauty. Casting intensity was further renewed.

"You might be too close to the deep slot," Ray warned later as I crowded in to better reach where I thought my jumper might be skulking. "If you back away some, your swing can come more up into the shallows. Fish often lie out on the edges of these deep runs, particularly if they haven't been disturbed."

Perhaps the fact that this was a Saturday with considerable boat and angler traffic made for enough disturbance to put them off their feed.

We hit some more of the quick-water areas Ray favors this time of year, but the jinx continued. "You warned us that the fish would really have to *want* the fly," Bob said during a lull in the lull. "Even the salmon, and we've seen quite a few, aren't in the mood."

"Yeah, salmon *hook-ups* are fewer using this approach," Ray enthused, leaving us to infer that this was good, leaving one greater time to search out the more favored steelhead.

"What do you do when you have 'real' clients," and you can see the fish holding as we've seen—but they just won't take?"

"I try them for a reasonable time and then move on. People have to accept that amongst the steelhead there are players and nonplayers.

Perhaps the fish have been harassed earlier, maybe even caught; maybe it's a pressure change or temperature fluctuation; for whatever in a myriad of possible reasons, the bite situation isn't right and they flat out won't hit."

"The 'If I spot 'em, I got 'em' theory doesn't get your heartfelt endorsement?" came the needle.

He smiled. "That doesn't work for everyone. You will more likely line the fish or foul-hook it if you persist for too long. There's an awful lot of good water in our rivers. Look for a player."

We looked. We experimented. We dead-drifted. We twitched. Ray suggested Bob try a riffling hitch that he had used with Speys on other occasions.

"Do you have a knot of choice, by the way?" I asked.

"With these heavier steelhead tippets, the basic clinch knots work well. I'll occasionally go to the Duncan loop or the uni-knot to give the fly more wobble."

We riffled and wobbled a little longer, then gave it all up as one of those gorgeous days when scenery and good company would stand in lieu of fish.

As often happens when steelhead fanatics get together, the state of the fishery—politics, management, et cetera—came up for discussion, and we had a dandy on our short trip back to Ray's home in Wellston.

From creel limits, to charter fishing to . . . you name it, much of this spontaneous confab dealt with the pressing need for changes to improve the Lake Michigan steelhead fishery in particular, changes that should be numerous and will engender controversy in many circles. Ray is no stranger to that, being very well known for developing, promoting, and protecting fly-fishing for steelhead in the Great Lakes region over the past 15 years. His philosophy, recounted briefly in the following couple of paragraphs, reflects some of our discussion relative to his (and our) concerns for the future.

Obviously Ray believes in getting involved to better the resource he both loves and, in part, depends on for his livelihood. As he poetically declaimed, "I smoke it, chew it, it oozes out of my pores." He is an active member of numerous fly clubs and organizations like Trout Unlimited and the Federation of Fly Fishers, was cofounder and past vice president of the Michigan River Guides Association, and is on several committees and councils. His list of awards and distinctions from this involvement is lengthy and impressive.

He would, of course, like to see others get involved in making changes in the Lake Michigan steelhead fishery he sees in some jeopardy. "It may involve something as drastic as limiting an angler to, say, five steelhead per year, perhaps on a punch card or tagging system of some sort. Maybe it's time to get away from fishing to spawners on the redds. And we can't cop out by saying, 'Why change when other states bordering the lake probably won't.' Michigan has to show the way, and hopefully other states will follow."

Ray has the ear of Department of Natural Resources personnel and keeps them apprised of public sentiment gained from clients, fellow guides, and fishermen in general—most of whom have similar sentiments. His statistics, diaries, bar graphs, and unaffected zeal lend added credence to his views. And we give our sincere, unqualified support to his efforts.

TACTICAL SUMMARY

- Work to keep the fly leading the belly of the line.
- Generally dead-drift with Speys, but pump them on occasion.
- Vary your knots to give the fly different action.
- Don't stay too long on one fish; look for "players."
- Fight them hard, get them in quick.
- Avoid exposure of fish to air.
- To better spot fish, look for parts, like the tail or the white of an opening mouth.
- Look for quicker, more oxygenated water, particularly in the fall.
- Fish hard for 20 to ? minutes with frequent intermittent breaks to stay fresh and beat the aching shoulder syndrome.
- Keep laughing. It's just a game.

RECOMMENDED TACKLE

- Sage 9½-foot, 8-weight rod.
- T-300, Scientific Anglers steelhead Sink Tip IV, SA floating fly lines.
- System II 8/9 reel.
- Maxima tippet material.
- Spey flies on classic salmon hooks.

16

John Hunter

In Search of Skamania

"Who owns the blue Suburban out front?"

"Oh oh. What now?" was our first reaction to this late-evening query ringing through the rustic confines of the Stockade Bar on US 10.

We slowed up on the wet burritos we consume for fuel on early spring Michigan steelhead rambles and waved an acknowledgment.

"I had to find out where you got that bumper sticker," the inquirer exclaimed enthusiastically. "It's perfect."

The sticker referred to was a profile of a handsome steelhead done in orange and black upon which was lettered, "Love 'em and Leave 'em." It's seen more often now, but at that time it was a novelty. The sentiment is, of course, much beloved of river guides. This man, we soon learned, was one of that hardworking cadre, John Hunter. A few minutes of conversation, an exchange of cards with Bob's promise to send him one of the decals, and we had garnered another knowledgeable fishing companion.

Late that same summer, as this project began to shape up, we set our sights on the elusive (for us) Skamania, hoping a few of these unpredictable acrobats would be in our rivers. We recalled John's enthusiasm and the fact that he was a West Michigan professional in seeking out steelhead (and other finny creatures). He liked the sound of our proposal, so we set up a late August float on the Pere Marquette, rumor having it that some Skamania had recently been in evidence.

I arrived for our 6 AM meet at the popular All Seasons Restaurant south of Baldwin at 5:30 AM—and beat John by a scant 5 minutes. Over the 10 years he has guided, his eagerness has yet to pall.

"I know you guys have probably heard of the aggressiveness of these summer fish," John related over breakfast, "but we'll likely have a better chance of hanging one by chuckin' and duckin' in the deeper, colder pools down in bigger water."

"We can rig for that," we assured him, adding that we had been amongst a porpoising pod of Skamanias recently on the Big Manistee, and they had spurned makeshift wakers, Bombers, and various lightly weighted streamers we had in our stream-trout vests. They laughed at hoppers. We weren't prepared then to go down and dirty, but if that's what it took . . . That July day at the mouth of Pine Creek had been doubly frustrating; we had to watch a spawn fisherman below us hook, fight, and land at least five of the brutes.

John nodded in sympathy. "We may even find egg flies to be the key," he said. "We can have a lot of fun experimenting, anyway."

As we breakfasted we caught up more on John's life in general. To facilitate his guiding, he headquarters for much of the year in his cottage near Brethren, putting him close to the Pere Marquette, Big Manistee, Little Manistee, and not all that far from Muskegon. He has a wife and family and maintains a year-round home in Leslie, Michigan.

"Other hobbies?"

"Fishing for fun. I get a bigger kick out of catching and releasing a good fish than from any other hobby-related activity."

John ties flies and is active in various organizations of which he is a member, namely the Pere Marquette Watershed Council, Trout Unlimited, the Federation of Fly Fishers, the Red Cedar Fly Fishers, and the Michigan River Guides Association. He has done seminars and written for the Michigan Steelheaders Association publication.

Shortly after daybreak we were jouncing along back roads dodging wild turkeys on our way to the public access just above Rainbow Rapids. No need for two vehicles, even though we were hauling John's 16-foot drift boat; a car shuttle had been arranged. John had also told us to leave our cooler back at the restaurant lot, as he provides snacks, lunch, and soft drinks. We could have even left our rods behind. He carries setups for clients who might be ill-equipped—top-drawer stuff, too.

The Rivermaster aluminum drifter we launched was ideal for what we had in mind. Leg braces at bow and stern made it easy to fish from the boat when so inclined. Even though the Pere Marquette is generally placid, this feeling of security in the event of a rock or log bump greatly enhances concentration. The boat also had low sides so getting in and out never resembled a circus acrobat's performance. We intended mainly to wade-fish—and did, often fishing long runs for an hour or so before in-boating and moving down.

Once on the river, John took us through the fairly tractable Rainbow Rapids like the proverbial man on a mission, bypassing some intriguing water. His goal, it turned out, was to be among early rods on the Sparrow Hole, a huge, right-angle bend just minutes from the launch site.

"This *is* a fish-holding spot," he said, "unlike some of those other good-looking but mostly barren holes on this river. It has a good variety of current seams, and it isn't an all-sand-bottom hole that looks good but doesn't oxygenate enough to hold Skamania or other salmonids. And no one is here. Better yet."

We nodded and grimaced, thinking of the hours we had spent plumbing promising depths with nary a nibble on this same long river system. "Is there an easy way to tell the bad from the good short of just never catching fish in a certain hole?" Bob asked.

"Fishing experience is probably the surest test. But look for clay, sand, or silt suspended in the water. Too much, and fish will avoid the place; the grit gets in their gills."

I had to ask another obvious question: "Why the 'Sparrow Hole' name for this spot?"

"Well, years ago some resident angler/bird fancier noticed all the cliff swallows darting around the opposite bluff—see their nesting holes? So he called it the 'Sparrow Hole' and so it's come to be known." John imparted this bit of river lore with just a touch of an eyebrow lift, implying that there's no flying in the face of local logic.

Convoluted ornithology aside, the place, by look and reputation, was worth a thorough combing. Bob took the middle segment of the big bend while I moved up to the faster water at its head. I began with a lightly weighted Mickey Finn variation, but I also had a healthy length of pencil lead about 20 inches above the streamer.

The lack of grace that goes with delivering the offering has earned it that 'chuck 'n' duck' sobriquet, but after you work at it for a while, especially with a long rod (I use a 10-footer), you can establish a rhythm and let the rod load and work quite smoothly, lobbing your fly with surprising accuracy. I *know* it's not pretty; perhaps it's even the antithesis of tight loops or shadow casts; but hey, Robert Redford won't waste your fishing time pestering you to be in his next movie, and you can cover the deeps and the narrows a heck of a lot better than the Brad Pitts of the world.

After lobbing upstream and ticking my way down in the depths of the hole several times, I eventually found the fly-eating log that always lies lurking. I broke off the streamer, but retained the weight. As I waded into the shallows by the moored boat to reload, John, who had been rummaging in fly boxes, noticed my terminal rig. "What have you got there?" he asked with considerable interest.

He had seen "pencil" lead in surgical tubing before, usually on a piece of dropper mono off a three-way swivel and on the tag end of a blood knot, but I was running it on my main line. It's an old arrangement, but I don't see many anglers use it anymore. Before tying on a fly, I simply run my leader through a ¾-inch length of thick-walled ⅛-inch (inside diameter) surgical tubing purchased from a hospital supply outlet. Years ago I molded lead into ⅛-inch diameter round lengths. I select the length of lead appropriate to the depth I want, and insert it through the tubing, thus pressing my line *tight* between the lead and the latex wall. By using the thick-walled stuff rather than the lighter tubing most tackle shops sell, the weight stays in place on the line during casting, but can be slid up or down manually to vary its distance from the fly.

The simplicity of the arrangement appealed mightily to John. For anyone who fishes a lot in cold weather—and for a Great Lakes steelheader, that is most of the time—the avoidance of even one or two knots is a boon. The only knot required with this setup is to your fly.

"Does it slide over snags like the slinky-weight system?" he asked.

"It's equally as good, better, I think. If the tubed weight hangs up, it often slides down to the fly and springs everything free."

Bob interrupted this "weighty" conversation by touching a fish on one of his egg-and-nymph tandems, then promptly losing it. "I have no idea what that was," he lamented.

It perked our interest nevertheless, and John grabbed one of his ready-rigged 7-weight rods on which he had chartreuse Amnesia running line, a 6-pound leader, and what looked like a large Gold-Ribbed Hare's Ear. He had snap-swiveled a slinky weight above a barrel swivel, and a round bead between the two kept the snap swivel on the slinky from jamming up on the barrel swivel, below which ran his tippet and fly. It is a popular and effective Pere Marquette setup—but requires those pesky knots.

I opted to move to the tail of the bend, so John took my place at the head. Not half a dozen casts later he exclaimed, "There's one." He leaned back on his rod and picked up slack quickly to get the fish on the reel. Bob and I scurried around for best camera angles, hoping to get that elusive leaping steelhead photo, the one you usually snap a

John Hunter and Steve plumb the Sparrow Hole.

second too soon or too late. All we got in this instance were a couple of indistinct shots of the surging, heavy rolls made by a very large fish. After maybe 2 minutes, John's fly pulled loose, and we were not able to confirm our triple diagnosis that this fish had acted more like an early-run chinook than a Skamania. It slugged rather than danced.

"Man, this seems early for salmon to be here," Bob said. "What is this, August 10?"

"They appear to come in earlier every year," John observed. "And spring steelhead are in later. I'm not sure exactly why."

We scratched our collective heads over the unknowns and turned back to the business at hand—catching a Skamania. John was retying his knot at the fly—just in case—after his not-so-gentle tussle with the mystery fish. This prompted me to inquire about knot and leader material preferences.

Maxima is his current choice. He likes its performance in the usually cold steelhead water, feeling that it keeps its knot strength well, particularly so if an Albright knot is tied with due care. "I use the ultragreen most of the time," he added. "It seems less obvious to fish against a sand bottom, and that's a predominant feature in large sections of these area rivers." He keeps his leader material on large-capacity spools, which he has refilled from the bulk spools kept at most fishing shops. Appropriate-sized rubber O-rings (found in hardware stores) keep the line neatly spooled.

"That sounds cost-effective as well as neat. But don't you miss that cool spidery look Bob and I have . . . you know, loose tippet material spiraling out of every pocket in your vest?"

"About like I miss someone parking a Clouser Minnow in my ear."

We continued to probe every seam and angle of the Sparrow Hole for another 30 minutes, then decided to move on. We would stop periodically to wade the most likely runs and pools; others we would work from the boat. Still no summer fish.

"Keep changing patterns and methods of presentation," John advised. "You never know what they'll hit. We're still in the experimental stage with these guys. Sometimes it's bright streamers that will produce, but I've also seen small Stone Flies do the trick." Frequent change of fly is something we are prone to do anyway when the action is slow. It's a good time to test-drive new variations, to see if, for instance, that Flash-Back nymph with marabou tail looks as good in the water as it did in the vise.

A medium-sized fly shop could have operated for a year out of the supply of patterns John had in his boat. He ties his own in just about every style, size, color—whatever might be needed for client preference or river conditions, and we dampened a bunch of them. Even though it wasn't the best time of year for egg flies, we worked them too. Like a lot of steelheaders, we like them for an attractor/strike indicator above another fly.

John said, "As we move into fall, I like to go from the oranges to cheeses to nearly white Glo-Bugs, to imitate the real egg changes. I also try to match the size of the egg under normal water conditions, but will go bigger for dirtier water."

We compared egg-fly patterns, concurring that while the tight-clipped and enveloped body (bubble-style) imitations sure look good in the water and take their share of fish, there is something to be said for the "fluffing" action of a looser yarn tie. And there are those who feel these loose fibers are more likely to tangle in the teeth of a steelhead, making a quick reject less likely. A moot point in my experience. As John accurately concluded, "They all take fish when *presented* properly under the right circumstances."

He added a caveat: "I avoid fishing egg patterns near a bedding hen with males in attendance. The female, in my experience, will take the egg more quickly, and then the show's over. Stone Fly nymphs will often enable you to pick off the males first."

Regardless of fly choice, our combined yeoman efforts produced no further strikes. The day lengthened and we approached the take-out spot at Sulac. Since there weren't any "reasonable" (stupid?) fish around, we hypothesized: "Let's say there were some Skamania in, maybe we could see them here and there, but they were tight-lipped for whatever reason. Any particular fly you'd go to?"

"Sure is," John replied. "We've already used it today, but I'll still stick by the yellow Marabou Muddler. I've seen it be a real arouser during the afternoon doldrums, and it can be a lifesaver on spooky fish that have seen about everything and are sliding on and off the redds. I carry it mainly in size 8."

Talk drifted on to other subjects, one being how the Pere Marquette has become so much more popular in the past few years that angler traffic is a greater concern. More and more drift boats are in evidence, and Bob and I have seen them launching *early* and simply blowing by us (walk-ins), heading down with cased rods to beat the competition to favored stretches.

"Yeah, the boat races do happen," John laughed, "but mostly during what people *see* as the best couple of weeks—late March and early April. More people should fish in December; there's little competition and often some really fine fishing occurs then."

After trailering the boat at Sulac with a pretty full day on the water behind us, John couldn't resist a drive up to the Lower Bridge area so we could still try a couple of other pools. "There's a good spot to walk in and fish a decent stretch," he would indicate as we drove along. "And take that two-track about 200 yards in. There's a great riffle area to fish the gray drake in the spring." And so it went. I don't know if all guides are as free with their tips, but John's theory is that the average fly-angler isn't going to be hitting all the good areas at the same moment he is, so why not be generous.

Hopefully this share-the-wealth attitude may someday extend to better sharing of the favored runs on our more popular rivers. Wouldn't it be great to have the step-down-go-back-and-through-again approach that exists on some waters so a dozen guys could have a chance at a good run or pool rather than just three or four?

TACTICAL SUMMARY

- *Chest* waders and polarized sunglasses are essential items.
- If a hole or pool has considerable suspended sand or silt, don't spend inordinate time there.

- When using egg flies, try to imitate the size and hue of eggs in normal water. Try larger flies in dirty water.
- Avoid fishing egg patterns around females on redds.
- Go with a hooked fish; keep distance short and angles sharp.
- Keep a beaten fish in some current; there is less sand than in shallows where, unfortunately, a lot of photo-taking is done.
- Call a fly shop or local contact during a winter warm snap. If water temperature has risen (to above 35 degrees F, or 1 degree C), it's well worth a try and there will be little competition.
- Try Caddis and Stone Fly nymphs in the winter; Hex nymphs can be effective if there's a lot of snowmelt.

RECOMMENDED TACKLE

- John advocates 9- or 10-foot rods of 6- or 7-weight. He uses a 9½-foot Sage 7-weight.
- A sturdy single-action reel with 100 yards of backing is called for. The Billy Pate reel is his choice.
- He favors Maxima leader material, ultragreen over sand bottoms.
- Popular fly patterns are egg flies in various colors, and varied sizes of Spring Wigglers, Woolly Buggers, Stone Fly nymphs, Caddis nymphs (green), and Hare's Ear nymphs. His "troubleshooter" fly is a yellow Marabou Muddler, size 8.

17

Bob Blumreich and Mike Yarnot

Classic Flies on a Wisconsin Sunshine River

Back in Michigan in the mid-1960s and into the 70s when a particularly vibrant steelhead with a tinge of green in its coloring was caught, say on the Little Manistee, I can recall hearing it referred to uncertainly as "one of those Wisconsin strain fish." Be that appraisal accurate or not, I have always held fond memories of those fish, and the chance to cast flies on Wisconsin streams was particularly appealing.

So was the opportunity to work with a pair of Wisconsin guides, veteran Bob Blumreich and upcoming Spey traditionalist Mike Yarnot. As Bob Linsenman and I have discovered over oh-these-so-many-years, there are a lot of benefits in working/fishing with a partner (technique tips, safety, handy joke-butt), and we were both curious to see if their team effort was anything akin to ours. Not to worry. (Note: For the remainder of this write-up, Bob Blumreich will be referred to simply as "Blumreich"—only to clearly distinguish him from Bob Linsenman, who will be simply "Bob." For this distinction Blumreich shall undoubtedly be eternally grateful.)

We had arranged to meet in Manitowoc, Wisconsin, on Sunday evening and fish the Manitowoc River the following day. Blumreich and Mike were huddled around their fly-tying table. A foam block impaled with a rainbow of Spey flies, which they (Mike especially) prefer to fish over most other patterns, gave evidence that the past couple of hours had been spent tying.

I held up a striking Spey creation incorporating red over gold with hackle woven carefully between an intricate cross-wrap of tinsel. "This looks like a killer," I said to Blumreich. "What is your favorite shade for these rivers?"

"Any color, as long as it's purple," he stated emphatically.

Never one to miss a begged question, I supplied the "And why is that?"

"We have lots of brown, stained water in our rivers. They come out of cedar marshes and run through farmland. We don't have spring creek structure here that you lucky guys have in Michigan."

He went on to discuss advantages of the silhouette created by a purple-over-purple Spey in these water conditions and under the usually darker skies encountered when steelhead are running. The 47-year-old Blumreich is on the Wisconsin rivers 200 to 220 days a year. He is single and devotes considerable time to guiding—and to the art of putting his own fly in front of steelhead on his off time. We listened attentively to his discourse on colors for area conditions.

"When a sunny day occurs," Mike chimed in, "be on the water. It's our experience that all Wisconsin rivers fish better on sunny days."

"Order one up for tomorrow," said Bob, but a serious fog had settled in with nightfall, and his request was but wishful thinking.

Blumreich had opened two or three of his fly boxes for us to peruse. I was admiring some bead-eyed Comets in orange and white and in orange and purple. "I'll use those when the water is high," he explained, "though I prefer an unweighted fly with a floating line. It's easier to control."

"This has a Bitch Creek nymph look to it," I commented, holding up a rubber-legged (black), buggy creation with a green thorax and black abdomen.

"It's a Bright-Butt Stone Fly simulator," Blumreich said as I returned it to the box and closed the lid. He quickly grabbed the box, reopened it, and handed me another fly. "How come you didn't say anything about this?"

"I missed it," I said, "but I don't see how. Is that a staple through the body?" I was turning a streamer in the light, one whose body was made of silver Mylar prism tape folded and indeed stapled over the hook.

"Yup," he affirmed proudly. "Sure is easy to tie. Those are glo-in-the-dark eyes and that Zonker-style strip along the back is white rabbit."

"Used for . . . ?"

"Fresh-run steelhead. They remember smelt from out in the lake. They do remember . . . " He trailed off and gazed ceilingward in a smiling, contemplative manner that intimated vast numbers of steelhead with superior power of recall had fallen for this "staple" streamer.

Conversely, 24-year-old Mike, who had remained busy at the vise during most of the evening exchanges, is already a Spey fly traditionalist. About the only way you could get this Milwaukee native to fish anything else would be to pull a switcheroo when he wasn't looking. His ties are gorgeous and are already gaining acclaim; he was a recent invitee to tie at the Great Lakes Council of Federation of Fly Fishers conclave. He is a utility forester and is just getting into guiding.

Mike eventually left the tying bench to lie back in an armchair and suggested we talk fish rather than flies. This is quite a departure for Mike who had told us in earlier contacts, "I would rather be known as a good fly-tier . . . " (above all other facets of the sport), but he had just taken a 38-inch steelhead a day or two ago, and he was inclined to talk of the beast itself.

"The first warm rains of spring bring a big push of the Chambers (strain) up, and they'll be around into April. Then we get them again in the winter—now," he proclaimed.

We learned that Chambers Creek strain will occasionally take baetis and caddis dries with classic head and tail rises.

"Any Skamania action?" I asked, always curious about this relatively new summer fish.

"Yeah, from early July through September, but they're up and down, in and out. They won't stay up in the rivers when they get warm, so it's kind of a crap shoot with them," Mike answered. "But from late April and into May we also get a run of the Ganaraska strain of steelhead. They were stocked from eggs purchased from the Province of Ontario. They are smaller, averaging 5 to 6 pounds, but they will reach 12 pounds."

"The cohos of the steelhead world," said Blumreich in testimony to their aggressiveness.

We had picked up the 1994 *Wisconsin Trout Fishing Regulations and Guide*, 30-some pages of regulations, advice, and color-coded maps (yes, maps!), and I mentioned to Blumreich and Mike that the brochure claimed that the majority of some 2500 trout streams have some degree of natural reproduction. "Does that go for steelhead?" I wondered.

Both of them were of the inclination that very little natural reproduction takes place with area steelhead, but they had praise for the state's stocking program. They figured that roughly a half million steelhead a year are stocked in this (Wisconsin side of Lake Michigan) drainage.

The following morning found us on the Manitowoc River, one of the favored haunts of these two devotees. If we had been on the Michigan side of the big lake, we'd have deemed it a perfect steelhead day—air temperature around 38 degrees F (3 degrees C), gloomy, overcast sky, a fine, cold drizzle in the air—but we were in the land of "sunshine rivers" so we were unsure. Our hosts were optimistic anyway. "It rained during the night," Blumreich reminded us, "and look at the leaf rubble over there (pointing). That wasn't there when I was here yesterday. The water has come up *and* gone back down a bit. That should activate fish even more, and we hit a couple here the other day under static conditions."

"Sure is carrying a lot of color," I made the mistake of observing. I took a pretty big ration of grief re relative water clarity in Wisconsin versus Michigan rivers, the upshot of which was something about "if you could see one's toes when ankle deep here, it was clear, and if we spoiled Michigan guys cared otherwise, the fish didn't." In fact, Mike pointed out, it had an added benefit in that we could fish 8- to 10-pound tippets and not spook fish.

Mike then took Bob upstream with him, since both had rigged Spey rods, 13- and 11-footers respectively, to what he knew from experience to be good water for this approach. Blumreich and I stayed nearer the parking area to fish a promising configuration of riffle-pool, riffle-pool water in a narrower stretch. I was rigged with a 9½-foot rod for an 8-weight and had chosen the floating line tipped with 6-pound Maxima. As I was tying on a Green-Butted Black Bear with Spey-style hackles (I *try* to start with a little chartreuse in darker waters), I noticed Blumreich looking on attentively. He approved my fly choice, though he was going with his favored purple and was waiting for me to finish so I could watch him rig up. "I wanted you to watch this," he said, "because I haven't seen many people ever use this knot as I do, and I think it has a lot going for it."

I expected to see a riffling hitch of some sort tied on his Spey fly, but instead he knotted a Duncan loop on his tippet, pinched the front of the 2-inch loop together, pushed this through the eye far enough to bring the fly through the loop, then held the two sides of the tippet *behind* the eye of the hook while tightening the loop to where the knot snugged up below the eye. "This allows for a straight pull, yet distributes pressure equally on both sides," he pronounced as he finished.

I had to admit it was pretty slick. "I see you have a little twist-on lead a couple of feet above your fly."

"Yeah, it doesn't hang up much. I'll also pinch lead on the tag end of the blood knot under some conditions, but if I have to use weight at all, I prefer this."

We entered the river adjacent to a run that quickly tailed out into faster riffles. "Can you see the old chinook beds below us?" Blumreich asked. "Much of the riffle water in our rivers has been created by the lips and depressions of salmon redds. The steelhead hang beside and below this kind of structure."

We fished at the head of our chosen stretch for quite a while before slowly stepping down its length. I had to get out and rerig after losing fly and tippet to a snag, and I noticed Blumreich below me in the process of changing also. Moments after he had resumed fishing, I saw him raise his rod in the set mode, then again, more emphatically, to drive the hook home. The fish moved down a few feet, rolled, and was gone.

"He just came off," he explained when I moved down to commiserate.

"What did he hit?"

"Well, I had a bump, I thought, on the purple Spey, so I switched to this." The Spey he held up was hunter-orange hackle wrapped over a pink body. "I figured to stir him into really hitting or send him packing for Ludington. He hit, but as you know, they don't always stay attached."

We took a break and walked the bank upstream to see how the all-Spey crew was doing. Mike was experimenting with Bob's Graphite-USA 11½-footer and had nothing but good things to say as he rolled long deliveries within inches of the far bank.

However, they had had no bumps of any sort. We all practiced our Spey casting for awhile, Bob and I still being greenhorns in the discipline, then walked back down to the water Blumreich and I had left. We figured the hour's rest would be sufficient.

A pretty extensive blanket of white foam had collected against the far bank just off the seam of a good-looking run. As I prepared to fish it, I asked the local opinion of such "structure," just on the off chance Wisconsin fish shunned it for whatever obscure reason.

"Just like 'boom cover,' [floating logs and woody debris]" Blumreich said. "Steelhead are trout—they will seek whatever cover is available, and when they feel safe, they eat."

As I fished it, being forced to throw downstream mends at times to get a decent dead drift in the conflicting currents, Blumreich said that he often advises regular customers to follow the foam lines

Bob Blumreich readies a leader.

with their drifts if they are uncertain of best avenues.

"Any other wrinkles you employ with people who don't steelhead fish much?" I asked.

"Strike indicators, good-sized ones in some instances. I've rigged novice clients with ice-fishing bobbers, and some still don't detect the hit. You'd be surprised how many people can't believe that so large a fish will be so subtle in its take. It doesn't seem reasonable to them."

The four of us hit the 200-yard stretch hard for another hour, but no hits, subtle or otherwise, came our way. Blumreich and Mike conferred, reasoned that with water temperature up to 39 degrees F (4 degrees C) from the previous day's 33 degrees F (1 degree C), fish must have become active enough to move up. So we headed upstream about a mile.

Mike and I joined forces this time, leaving Blumreich and Linsenman to "Bob" their way downstream. (Sorry.) I switched to a chartreuse egg fly when I saw two steelhead (?) ghost up to the edge of an empty salmon bed, then drop back into darker, slower water. I was curious not only about how the fish would react to the roe pattern, but how Mike would take it. He is into fishing traditional wets and Speys to the point where he will not even *tie* an egg fly, let alone fish one. But he is a live-and-let-live kind of guy, it turned out. In fact, he made some comment to the effect that with my bottom-ticking rig and his upper- to midwater-level Spey, we should soon find if any fish were in the mood.

One was. He hit Mike's Spey fly near the far bank and spit it out just about as quickly.

"That was an unweighted fly," Mike remarked. "It couldn't have been a foot down when he banged it."

"Is that typical in your rivers—the take on a shallow drift?"

"It happens a lot," he answered. "The Spey fly doesn't need to go deep if the water is, oh, 5 feet or less. You have the right color and silhouette, fish will come up to hit it."

I hefted Mike's 13-foot Gold'N West Spey rod once again as we stood in the shallows taking a break. "Man, this seems heavy, yet you fish it all day to the exclusion of the one-handed rod. Doesn't it wear you out?"

"Actually I think there is less effort involved. You probably noticed how I prop the butt against my hip during most of a drift, and the drift is longer, the mends bigger and therefore fewer."

"Okay, pretend I'm ambivalent. Sell me on the technique. What are other advantages?"

"I feel I have more control of the fly with the greater ease in mending. Let's see . . . you don't have to set as hard, you get more distance, especially with roll-casting, which is the most commonly used cast, and since backcasts aren't a factor, you can fish with your back tight to a bank or woodline. And once you hook a fish, you can't break it off."

"Maybe *you* can't," I had to say. "Any disadvantages?"

"Not so good in the wind. That's when I might go back to the one-handed rod, but that's rare. I'm pretty much in love with the whole tradition of Spey fishing and the feeling that I'm back to the roots of the sport."

About this time the two Bobs came slogging up the bank, fishless. I had failed to interest any fish in my egg fly offerings, despite switching to various washed-out salmon egg hues, and Mike's Spey flies drifted untouched also. Once again the four heads came together. Once again it was, "Let's move even farther up."

What light there was, it having been a consistently gray day, was rapidly fading. The last area we tested looked promising, so we resolved to put our remaining time to good use. Some late salmon could be seen drifting about, over the gravelly flats; maybe a steelhead or two would be mixed in. And as Blumreich declared, "The bite occurs twice in the morning, twice in the afternoon. Have faith in the solunar tables. We are due."

Then he promptly hooked a fish, about a 17-inch brook trout. Wow and rats. Where were those vaunted Chambers Creek steelhead?

Bob had worked his way over to where Blumreich was fishing, curious what the brookie had hit. I had done so a few minutes before, getting a close look at one of the guide's favorite nymphs, a Hex imitation featuring a strip of brown rabbit fur for that tantalizing wiggle that makes the bug so attractive to most salmonids.

Bob swam the nymph in the eddy at his feet and evidently liked what he saw. He handed his own rod to Blumreich at the latter's prompting and moved down to fish a likely run carrying our host's home-built 9-footer for a 7-weight. "It's a fairly soft rod," Blumreich had told me earlier, "like the old Sage." He markets these custom-built beauties and was close-mouthed about the blanks he uses.

Whatever he used, Bob immediately put it to the test. On maybe his third presentation, I saw him pick up in mid drift, much as if he'd hung a snag and was trying to free his rig and get it back on course. Then he got really serious, leaning back into that throbbing bend we'd seen so little of this promising day.

"Oh camera boy," he warbled.

"Yeah, yeah. Don't screw this up," I said, moving in his direction. "We can give our Wolverine pride a big boost by landing the only real fish of the day—even if you are using Badger gear."

Mike came splashing over, intoning some drivel about "Michigan lifters" displaying their low art, but we would have none of that. Bob

Mike Yarnot—a committed, traditional Spey angler

kept his sangfroid, the large buck cooperated, and Mike got to demonstrate a pretty fair tailing move. The fly was well back inside the 12-pound-plus male's jaw, but some quick work with the forceps, a couple more photos, and the fish was back in its element. It was a pleasing way to end a hard day on new waters.

"How did you like that Kevlar-core fly line?" Blumreich inquired of Bob. "Couldn't you feel every pebble, every grain of sand?"

"I don't recall," was the response. "I didn't get to complete more than two drifts before that fish took. Hey, nice tailing grab there, Mike, after six misses. Do you advocate that over beaching?"

"Yeah, how would you like *your* belly sandpapered?" was the succinct response. (The cotton net they usually carry had been left in the car.)

We had intended to fish again in the morning and spent some considerable time that evening tying flies and talking strategy. Morning greeted us with 2 inches of snow already on the ground, and flakes big as Wisconsin cheese wheels coming down hard.

"Adios, boys," we said upon looking out at the snowscape.

"Glad to see you have a little more sense than the average Michigander; drive carefully and come back in the spring."

We averred we likely would—if only to tell them that the snow quit right exactly as we crossed the state line into Michigan's Upper Peninsula. They probably wouldn't believe it. But it did. Right at the line.

TACTICAL SUMMARY

- Wisconsin rivers fish better on sunny days.
- Try darker flies first in these darker waters.
- Gray Polaroids work better when it's really bright; amber is the choice for other times; wear glasses of *some* kind for safety.
- Felt soles, while fine on gravel, can be treacherous on ice and snow. Consider lugs, cleats, or chains under these conditions.
- Sometimes you can spot fish better by looking for shadows—or what's *not* river, what doesn't belong.
- A cotton bag net enables you to land fish more quickly with less chance of injury.
- Don't be in too big a hurry to move to a new spot before thoroughly covering water you are presently on.
- Use flies with high-set hair wings in faster water—for better action. (Sparse ties rule.)
- Learn to mend for that "eating speed" and maintain contact with your fly.
- Make a drastic color change—or go a couple of sizes smaller before going to a bigger fly—to set up the "P.O.ed" hit.

RECOMMENDED TACKLE

- Mike favors a 13-foot Gold'N West Spey rod (by Mike Maxwell on Fisher blanks) with a 10-weight floating line. In one-handed rods, both Bob and Mike recommend 9- to 10-footers in weights 7 to 9, the Blumreich custom-built being top choice.

- Blumreich likes the Air-Flo line with Kevlar core.
- They advocate Heron reels with 150 yards of 20-pound backing.
- Mike gives the nod to Spey flies year round, varying sizes and colors depending on water conditions.
- When not using Speys, Blumreich will go with leeches in black, white, and lime in size 4, especially in spring. He also likes the Polar Shrimp, Glo-Bugs (try yellow, loop-dubbed for translucency), and Stone Fly and Hex nymphs in varied sizes as small as 16s.
- Both of these Wisconsin anglers like Maxima for leaders and tippets.

18

John Dembeck

Storm Fronts and Steelhead on the Oswego River

The drive from Michigan to Oswego is about 500 miles, and it took roughly 9 hours. The December sun was shining, traffic was light, gasoline prices had dropped, and there was a good selection of music on the radio. Our track record has caused us fatalistically to consider such phenomena (particularly clear skies) as bad omens. We need not have worried (weatherwise) about a break in tradition.

While Steve checked us into the Day's Inn in Oswego, I phoned John Dembeck and arranged to meet, ready to roll, at 7:30 next morning in the motel parking lot. The local weather forecaster suspected a change was in store, perhaps high winds and rain and much colder temperatures. More like steelhead conditions, we thought. She was right . . . in spades.

On the short drive from the motel to the launch site near Varick Dam, John talked about the Oswego River and its unique trophy fishing. Within a few hours' drive, he pointed out, East Coast and Midwest anglers can pursue very large salmonids that take flies readily, and one or more species are present in the river nearly year round. Salmon, steelhead, large brown trout, and lake trout enter the Oswego and other smaller tributaries to Lake Ontario in heavy concentrations from September through April.

Cohos and kings (and some Atlantics) dominate from September through November. Cohos range from 8 to 12 pounds, with kings sometimes pushing the 40-pound mark. The less common Atlantics run from 8 to 20 pounds. The lake-run browns enter the streams with the salmon and hold over through December. They feed heavily on salmon eggs and baitfish and are incredibly strong. The steelhead action lights up in October and carries well through April. John recommends November, December, February and April as the best fly-fishing months for the 8- to 20-pound wonders.

He explained that the steelhead would probably be looking for brown trout eggs in the Oswego, and we would start with small Glo-Bugs on 3X tippets and sink-tip lines. Alternatively, we would be ready with rods rigged with full-sinking lines, or shooting heads and large Clouser Minnows.

The Oswego River is an intimidating piece of water. Wide, deep, rocky, and fast, it gives one an impulse to don the life jacket even more securely and worry about fly presentation as a second priority. Do you like big rivers? This is bigger than the Madison. Do you like white water? The Oswego has an area, thankfully short, that will command your attention. John was wearing a full drysuit out of respect for this water, a safeguard that has served him well. The floundering, hypothermic anglers he rescued on a couple of past occasions were undoubtedly even more pleased that he was so geared.

He skillfully rowed the wooden drift boat across the river (no small task) where we disembarked and pulled upstream through some manageable current edges to a spot John wanted us to try with our Glo-Bugs. He dropped the anchor so that we held just off to the right of a smooth slick that formed a narrowing, downstream V in the confluence of two heavy, rocky runs.

"We are very close to the fish," John said. "Because the water is high and a little dirty, they won't spook. Cast quartering upstream at 45 to 50 degrees, enough distance so the entire sink tip stays in the water. Let the fly dead-drift until it is straight downstream, and watch for a soft twitch—any seemingly unnatural movement of the line or leader. These fish just inhale the fly and quickly spit it out; they do not take it hard or hit it in any sense of the term."

This rain, at about 34 degrees F (1 degree C), would not turn to soft snow, even in the high wind. It stayed as rain—wet, stinging, and numbing. "Does this miserable weather affect these fish and their willingness to take a fly?" asked Steve after 20 minutes with no visible action.

John asked him to cast a bit farther, then answered, "Not so much the steady stuff, but they are incredibly sensitive to even the slightest variation in weather and barometric pressure. Changes that we barely see or feel can have significant impact on their activity. Remember, they make their living out here every day. One or two degrees change in air or water temperature, an increase or decrease in cloud cover, a directional change in wind, a fluctuation in water volume—all of these can and do affect the fish. I've had some of my best fishing, spectacular is the fairest word to describe it, when a series of small fronts came through over a 12-hour period. Each time a new front hit us, the fish went wild."

The fact that John is a practicing fisheries biologist who, when he is not guiding, consults on the impact of hydro energy on aquatic life in the tributaries of Lake Ontario, gave special credence to the technical accuracy and relevance of his remarks.

We had no takes on the egg patterns and switched to Clouser Minnows in colors that would imitate baitfish. A slow, erratic retrieve would give the appearance that the phony gizzard shad had been injured at the dam or stunned by the cold water and was easy, disoriented prey.

We dropped downstream to the edge of a small, partially submerged island and got out to wade the heavy riverside run and a smaller bankside riffle. As if to prove John's point about the weather, the rain abated and the air seemed to warm ever so slightly. On Steve's second cast a steelhead smacked the Clouser and the dance began. "This fish has been in the river for awhile," John noted as Steve removed the hook and released the smallish male.

"He's not real dark," Bob observed.

"Steelhead just in from the lake are really bright," John said, whetting our appetites.

Steve had three more strikes, landing one bright fish of about 4 pounds, in the next 15 minutes. I had a heavy strike but could not set the hook. While I slogged to the boat in search of dry gloves, John borrowed my rod and cast into a run I had abandoned despite his suggestion I fish it more thoroughly. Predictably, on his second cast he hooked a 6-pounder that was downstream and into the backing in a heartbeat. "When you're good, you're good," I offered a few minutes later as, with just a trace of the I-told-you-so smile, he released the fish.

We hammered away for another 30 minutes, switching colors on the Clousers and trying other patterns including the gray and pearl Zonker, which John feels is the best copy for the gizzard shad, but the fish had gone into a holding pattern as a fresh batch of low rain clouds came through from the south.

We took a break for hot coffee and sandwiches back at the launch site, and John talked about his favorite fly patterns for this time of the year and why they work.

From Thanksgiving through the winter, baitfish imitations are the key to success on the big river, although small Glo-Bugs will still produce fish in the smaller streams. Clousers and Zonkers tied to imitate smelt and shad produce the biggest fish, and do so consistently. John suggested that visiting anglers bring Clousers in chartreuse and white, gray and white, dark brown and pale orange, orange and white, red and white, and blue and white. He also recommends Zonkers in gray with a pearl body, chartreuse with a chartreuse body, and orange with a gold body. "All the streamers should be large and weighted, size 2 and 4 on good needle-sharp hooks. A pattern I created to mimic a "baitfish hatch" is the Oswego Smelt. It is very effective on these big fish."

Steve asked if the steelhead in the Oswego River will take a dry fly, and John acknowledged that he is often asked that question. He said that he discourages customers from making the attempt because it takes considerable time to raise a fish with surface patterns and techniques. "It can be done, though. I've done it, and if you absolutely must try it and can deal with very long odds and failure, look for fresh, undisturbed fish in broken water. Use Bombers, wakers, any big 'waking' fly, and lots of patience. But it's more of a stunt; it's not a productive use of time."

The coffee, food, and sound technical discussion warmed and prepared us for another round with the big river. We knew the fish were there, and John felt that the big streamers would be effective on the remainder of the float.

We shoved off and drifted into the heavy flow. "Bad omens and driving rain are only significant if you are not catching fish. We are catching fish," Steve chirped as we moved down. "What kind of cover do these fish favor most? What should anglers look for?"

John moved us to the edge of a widening tail-out behind a deep, churning hole and dropped the anchor. "This is a good example. We're quite close to the bank because there is gravel here. Where there is gravel suitable for spawning, you will usually find fish. A lot of guys wade right through this spot to fish out farther where there are no fish. You know how that goes—people often think they should wade as deep as they can and cast as far as they can, but the truth is they've waded through the fish and spooked them. They're straining to cast 70 feet into barren water when a quiet approach and a 30-foot cast would have produced.

"This river has quite a bit of ledgerock, and ledgerock pools and runs look great to a novice, but they rarely hold fish. Trout are not comfortable over a flat, tabletop surface. They instinctively know they are visible to predators from above. They prefer and seek out mixed substrate—gravel, boulders, and rocks."

We drifted on. John moved us both to the front seat for the run through the white water, and once through, he positioned the boat about 40 feet from an old stone bridge piling well out into the mainstream. He advised us to work our streamers out on long reach casts, let them sink behind the piling, and retrieve with short, hard strips. I moved to the back of the boat and had just began to false cast when Steve grunted, "Fish."

"Big fish," John quickly added. Steve's 9½-foot, 9-weight graphite was straining in an extreme bend, and his reel was playing that oft-chronicled beautiful music. The fish stayed deep in the heavy current, but it had been seen right after the strike. It was an imposing brown that had no intention of wearing itself out with leaps or long runs.

Over the years I have had the pleasure of watching Steve fight scores of steelhead, salmon, and large browns on fly tackle, and he definitely knows the drill, but this fish was special. It afforded the opportunity to observe the effect of deft, technical coaching by a pro on fighting a fish in deep water from a drift boat.

Several minutes into the game, the fish was still fresh and holding deep. When Steve would pump, the trout would come up a bit, shake its head, and bore slowly and inexorably back down. John began a "halftime speech" worthy of Holtz or Paterno. "Big fish are usually lost in the first 10 seconds or at the net. We're past any concern about how well this trout is hooked, so let's concentrate on getting it to the net as quickly as we can. If you lift a heavy fish too high, head up, it panics and leverages by shaking its head and turning to gain more depth. Not the safest technique. But if you simply hold steady, you are not taxing the fish; it has gained an advantage; it has achieved a position that relieves the strain and irritation relative to the pressure from the angler. Maintain the bend in your rod, of course, but change angles on the fish. Make him work to get back to his position of relative comfort with minimal straight-up lift and the resultant head-shaking."

Steve moved the rod upstream and to the left about 45 degrees. The trout made a short run and settled back. Steve changed angles again and again, and each time the fish had to work to regain its position.

As the big trout tired slightly, John continued. "Keep your rod

*John Dembeck displays a trophy before release. The large net
is a big help on the Oswego River.*

very low to the water and try to lead the fish upstream; pump and
reel while holding that angle, and we should gain the leader. The
leader soon showed and John instructed Steve to pull the fish upstream without pumping or reeling and then to raise the rod when
John gave the word. "When the rod is raised this time, the fish will
turn to go downstream and should swim into the net." It took two
plays and a stellar long-arm net reach, but it worked. Thirty minutes
after the take, Steve and John worked the Clouser from the jaw of a
28-inch, 9-pound male brown trout. Hook-jawed, brightly spotted,
and unusually thick and muscular, it was photographed, kissed, and
released, but Steve looked the more weary. He didn't resume fishing
for quite a while. Instead, he sat and massaged his rod arm and shook
his aching wrist.

We changed color combinations on the Clousers as an experiment,
hoping to entice the steelhead we were really after. Steve had taken
Mr. Big on a yellow and dark brown, so while he rested and pon-
dered the benevolence of the trout gods, John tied on a chartreuse
and white, and I opted for red and white. Five casts later John had a
nice 3-pound female, and a minute later I landed one of about 4
pounds. They were both browns so we moved a bit, hoping for some
variety, but it was not to be.

"Since we'll be quitting soon, try every kind of erratic retrieve in the book," John suggested. "The steelhead will sometimes go for the offbeat when the traditional isn't doing it."

We persevered for a time, but the light was fading, the rain continued, and the last fish hooked was another brown, a beautiful female of about 5 pounds. While she wasn't the trophy steelhead hoped for, she certainly was a pleasant finale to a fish-filled day.

John loves fly-fishing for steelhead because, "It is technical and artistic; it combines science and aesthetics and tradition."

By the way, if his somewhat cryptic moniker "Two Dogs Outfitters" is a puzzle to you, run it by a friend who claims to know every joke . . .

TACTICAL SUMMARY

- The best time to fish for steelhead is under low-light conditions. If the sky is clear and sun bright, this obviously means at dawn or dusk. The best period for steelhead on a fly in John's area is from Thanksgiving to Christmas. The angling pressure is down and the fish are aggressive.
- Some of the hottest action can take place just before and during a thunder- or snowstorm.
- A series of small weather fronts will often keep fish active.
- Where possible, release fish in a side eddy or in moderate flow.
- Balanced leaders with tippets ranging from 1X to 4X are useful to turn over smaller flies and to create an effective drift under clear conditions.
- Maintain a respectful distance. Many anglers try to get too close to fish (particularly those they can see).
- When you first approach fish and reach your position, stand still for awhile before casting. When you do cast, keep your arm and rod motion to a minimum and the rod angle low.
- Avoid smooth, even bottom areas of sand, clay, and ledgerock. Look for a mixed rubble bottom, a combination of gravel, rocks, and boulders where fish are more likely to hold.
- Be careful not to stand in, wade through, or cast over holding water; fish the area close to you first.
- Look for side channels and moderate to small runs away from the main current flow.
- Attitude is one key to success. John asks that his clients come with an open mind. Some of his most successful trips are with beginners

and women. "They listen, and if they are not sure how to do something correctly, they ask questions."

RECOMMENDED TACKLE

- A basic outfit for fly-fishing the Oswego River and similar large, fast rivers is a 9- to 10-foot graphite rod for a 7-weight line with a quality (smooth drag) reel, 10-foot sink-tip line, and 150 yards of backing.
- For clear water, bright sun situations, John suggests a 9- to 10-foot rod for a 6-weight line.
- Throwing large weighted streamers for distance requires more muscle and a 9- or 9½-foot, 10-weight outfit.
- John recommends Loomis rods and Ross reels and favors Cortland lines and Umpqua leader material.
- His arsenal of flies features Glo-Bugs, Clousers, Zonkers, Comet variations and his personalized Lemon Drops, Cherry Blossoms, and Oswego Smelt.

19

Rick Kustich

Lake Ontario Trophies in New York Tributaries

Our idle, midriver discussion of fly choices was a welcome respite from hours of casting, but a sudden whoop and attendant commotion of leaping fish made Brian and me look downstream. It was perfect timing. Even though Bob was a good 100 yards below us, I could see as clearly as if right next to me, a huge mercurous form seemingly suspended in mid-leap, its iridescence framed beautifully against the gray sky and dark, dripping trees. Then its re-entry splash echoed back, then it was in the air again, and yet again. Bob and fish soon disappeared around a bend, but we could, minutes later, hear more splashes and muted exclamations from the beleaguered Bob.

"It hasn't released young Robert yet," I called to Brian Slavinski, a local angler.

"No. I hope he gets her into picture range," he answered. "That's one fine fish."

It was. With Rick Kustich's help, Bob had managed to beach his prize way down below us (we got to hear the whole story later with much gusto in the retell), then measure and photograph a 33-inch, 13-plus-pound pure silver female. It was the fish of the day, which meant that every one of the four of us had landed a fish of 32 inches or better. Not too shabby by steelhead standards anywhere on the planet, we decided.

How we came to be on this richly productive river in New York is interesting happenstance in itself, illustrative of the "small world" phenomenon one sees so much of in fly-fishing circles. Bob and I have always been voracious readers, and our love of literature extends, of course, to publications dealing with fly-fishing. Steelhead material in particular gets our attention, so when Bob saw the book *Fly Fishing The Great Lakes Tributaries* with its attractive cover photo of a fly-angler releasing a large, bright hen, he immediately bought it. In little more than 100 pages, we found that author Rick Kustich presents a wealth of accurate, easily digested information and instruction on fly-fishing, emphasis on Great Lakes salmonids. We read, we discussed, we liked.

So it was with some bemusement that Bob answered the phone one past winter day to hear, "Hi. Bob Linsenman? You don't know me. I live in New York, my name is Rick Kustich, and I hear you and a coauthor are working on a steelhead book."

Bob averred that he did, in fact, know Rick (through his book), but how did Rick know of us and our then barely started project?

That fraternal fly-fishing grapevine had been at work again. We had had dealings with Greg Lilly, formerly of The Winston Rod Company in Twin Bridges, Montana, and had mentioned our book plans. Rick's brother Jerry (an accomplished steelheader) also lives in Twin Bridges, worked with Greg, heard about and told Rick of our intentions . . . To make a lengthening story short, the phone conversation led to our meeting and working with one of the country's more knowledgeable steelhead fishermen/guide/writer/teacher/lecturers. We later touched base briefly with Rick at the Midwest Fly Fishing Exposition in Southfield, Michigan, in March and set up a mid-April trip to New York.

The 35-year-old Rick was born and still lives on Grand Island in the Niagara River. He and his wife Ann have an attractive home, made more attractive still by an extensive collection of fly-fishing and bowhunting paraphernalia, the pursuit of whitetails being Rick's second major sporting interest.

Along with his previously mentioned 1992 book, Rick has written articles for national magazines. He runs a small accounting business, gives slide presentations to varied groups, runs fly-fishing schools and tying classes, and still manages to fly-fish over 100 days a year— excluding outings with clients.

On our way to New York to fish with Rick, Bob and I reminisced about recent trips as we kilometered across southern Ontario and its plethora of doughnut shops. We also speculated on what kind of streams we might fish on arrival.

"I hope it isn't this one," Bob said as we crossed the immense Niagara River linking lakes Erie and Ontario. The sheer volume of water in the Niagara is staggering. It turned out we did not fish it, but we probably wouldn't have been disappointed if we had. "It's one of the best big-fish rivers in the lower 48," Rick told us, and he showed us some recent photos of 15-plus-pound steelhead taken from this water by wading fishermen, some caught in the gorge area we had observed with no little trepidation from the Rainbow Bridge. "Obviously you have to know where to wade," Rick cautioned, "but with care it can be done, and the rewards can be staggering."

Rick had decided that we would instead fish another Lake Ontario tributary farther east, Oak Orchard Creek. I recalled the name from his book as being one of the best rivers for a quality fly-fishing experience, and after viewing his slides of this and a couple of nearby rivers, Bob and I were both eager to see this new water.

Rick is no slouch as a photographer, we were to discover after "arm-twisting" him into running through a typical slide presentation. One focus of his program is to win converts to the sport by showing the diverse beauty of area rivers through the seasonal changes—the verdant spring greens, mellow autumn colors, stark whites of winter—pointing out that fish can be taken in one's choice of weather and scenery.

"What do you emphasize to these beginning steelheaders, then, since there is quite a diversity of water running into Lakes Erie and Ontario?" I asked.

"Obviously, it's important to know the timing of the runs. Make contacts and friends within fly shops, Trout Unlimited, and similar groups; then a phone call every now and then can help immensely if the normal run timing is out of sync. I also encourage people to learn two or three rivers very well. A lot of the tributaries here are spate rivers so rain has a big effect, but one may color up faster or clear more quickly than another, and it's good to know what shape one will be in as opposed to another. And if you get to a river and the water is high and discolored, if it's a river you know well, you can still fish effectively because you already have a handle on holding areas, and you should have learned where fish will go under high-water conditions."

"Looks like we'll get to test your local knowledge in the morning," I predicted. "It's supposed to get wet and grungy."

"Yeah, it'll be great. Especially if it stays warmish. We could get into some good fish." Rick's prognosis would prove true.

Bob asked if we should tie some special local patterns before sack time, even though we carry a good universal selection. We travel with a fair amount of tying material since it always seems a slight variation is the current hot item.

"Do you have the Frammus pattern?"

We didn't, so we all adjourned to Rick's basement tying bench and had at it. This fly is a good example of Rick's (and many steelhead fly anglers') philosophy of a good fly—it is simple to tie. (See the "egg-fly" dressings in chapter 4.) Lots of offerings are lost in the rocks and snags of steelhead haunts, so one gets a bit chary with the really pretty, more involved patterns. The use of egg colors in wet-fly-style attractor patterns is often effective in the area, we were advised.

"People who fish the Ontario watersheds don't seem to be into exact insect copies so much as you Wolverines," Rick said. "It's probably a combination of a greater abundance of natural food items in the richer Michigan tributaries than here, and the simple fact that the brighter stuff works extremely well locally—and is easy to tie." (We did not leave our Hex patterns and Stone Fly nymphs at his house when we left the next morning, but it turned out they got barely any water time).

"Really," he said, "you can pare things down to about six favorite patterns and just adjust colors and sizes to water conditions. You know as well as I do how much depends on presentation." Woolly Buggers, the Frammus, lots of Glo-Bug variations and the Salmon Flea were primary choices for our mid-April jaunt to Oak Orchard Creek.

We were up at 4 AM, on the road at 5 AM, and on the river as dawn broke on the chilly, overcast scene. Bob and Rick assembled 9½-foot graphite rods to handle 8-weight floating lines rigged with strike indicators near the butt section of 12-foot leaders tapered to low-diameter 2X and 1X. They both pinched on removable split shot 2 or 3 feet above the unweighted fly to get down at a good rate. Rick is a proponent of heavier tippets since we hoped to be dancing with big, fresh, less finicky fish, and we would be in fairly heavy water with lots of good-sized, abrasive rocks. "Sometimes light tippets are required, of course," he added, "but then a long fight is often required, which decreases the odds of a successful release."

We had parked off Park Avenue near the Waterport Dam, and as we readied for the 300-yard walk to a gravelly stretch Rick had in mind, he asked one of those feeling-out questions dealing with a sometimes controversial area with some steelheaders: "How do you feel about fishing to bedding fish?"

"That doesn't pose a moral problem for me," I replied, "but I don't usually spend a ton of time at it because fish exposed on beds have generally been so pestered it proves a waste of time. I'd rather fish adjacent runs or the darker holding water between the redds."

Bob concurred, adding, "When we fish to the spawners, we stay away from the females, and since we release fish anyway, it doesn't seem unfair. When you think about it, all steelhead are up to spawn. That nonbedding fish a guy catches may have been 5 minutes from going on the redd. It is tough to see that as more ethical. But if runs decline, I can see the day when we won't go near the redds."

Rick shared similar sentiments, preferring to avoid bedders, particularly where natural reproduction occurs. But he had wanted to check because he has fished with the occasional angler who, for whatever personal philosophy, was dead against it.

That issue resolved, we walked a point of land dividing the river into two channels for a short way below the dam. A few hardware- and bait-tossers were in evidence directly around the dam pool and its tail-out, but when we reached the confluence of the two channels and the divided river again became one broad expanse of water, no one else was around.

Oak Orchard Creek was a bit high and roily, but it was certainly wadable, with a pretty uniform depth of 1 to 3 feet; it had a predominantly gravel bottom with plenty of larger rocks to break current— and make angler ambulation touchy here and there. You could go with a fish, we were to discover, but not at a full gallop.

Unlike many of the Michigan rivers we were used to probing, this one was wide, ranging from 100 to 250 feet. Our backs were not so often up against the bankside, fly-grabbing vegetation. Hallelujah. Full backcasts were usually available, and often we were in midriver working bank-tight lies.

We began by fishing blind in a long, heavy riffle section. I hung at Rick's elbow to see what revelations local expertise would bring me. "I like to overpower the cast with this weighted setup," Rick explained. "See how this causes the fly and split shot to hit first and cut through the surface before the fly line lands." He demonstrated a neat tuck cast, adding a right-hand (upstream) reach to keep the line above the terminal rig and lessen drag for an optimum dead drift. A couple of well-timed mends brought him nicely through the heart of the holding water. As the fly swung below him, Rick held most of his fly line off the water and with rod tip pointed at the fly, let it swing directly below him until it was well off the main current. "As you have probably experienced, fish often take on the swing at the end of a drift. I've even had them hit egg patterns—just about everything—at that point."

Since I was rigged with optic running line, I used more of a tight-line technique. Keeping the rod tip high, I could run the small-diameter line through the water easily and be well attuned to the tapping of my weight on the rocks. Any hesitation, and a flip of the rod tip would set the hook . . . mostly into large, immovable rocks at first. Rivers may be unique, but snags are universally common, I was proving for the thousandth time. Then that slightly different hesitation, a hint of throb as I flip the rod tip, a lunge, a surface roll, and . . . he's gone. But at least I now knew they were around. Time to get really serious.

Bob did a similar quick-release after the fish ran a little farther and swirled for added drama. Then Rick hooked and quickly landed a darkish male of about 6 pounds. "He wasn't real dynamic, was he?" Rick admitted. "But don't worry. There are some electric fish in here. I hooked this guy right in that current seam (pointing). They like to hold in spots like that where they can expend less energy, yet be near faster water for security."

We snapped a couple of pictures, then resumed fishing. Bob walked upstream while Rick continued his methodical coverage of the initial area, slowly working downstream so as to drift and swing through every portion of that water.

So far pretty traditional stuff. But then occurred one of those anomalies that make one say, "Just when I thought I'd seen everything . . . "

I watched quizzically from a hundred yards away as Rick just stood, not casting, near the end of the riffle he had been covering. His head was cocked at a strange angle, and he simply continued the cigar store Indian routine. "Must've dozed off," I thought, and finally shrugged and turned away to resume my coverage of a likely run behind a current-breaking sweeper.

Maybe 10 minutes had passed when my reveries were interrupted by the smack of an airborne fish returning to his element at an off-kilter angle. Rick had come awake, and so had the bright male steelhead that had taken his Woolly Bugger and was now essaying to be rid of it.

"Darndest thing," he said as he cleaned his hands after releasing the 6-pound fish. "I'd been standing there for quite a while fishing the end of that stretch we started on, then I changed tippet and fly, more standing, and then I happened to glance down near my feet. A large female had moved into the eddy created by my legs and was settling in to do her thing. That's what I was watching for so long,

Rick Kustich (right) and Steve carefully remove the fly from a large buck.

and sure enough, pretty soon this buck showed up to join her, and I went to work—damned carefully, I should add, since I didn't dare move much." He had backstepped carefully for casting room and hooked up after only a few passes.

Some remarks passed re the unfair advantage anglers have who can pass for generic river flotsam or riprap. The possibilities of a line of waders made to resemble rocks or pilings received brief discussion also. I had to tell Rick how Bob already looked so much like a weathered snag that a kingfisher once lit on his leather hat. We decided it was time to get back to fishing . . . but I was all fired up to tell Bob about the new practical purpose he could be put to besides tying flies and netting fish for me. Let's see, he'd probably want a title. Current Diverter? Seam Creator? Maybe just Eddy? I'd let him decide.

Speaking of the latter, I had noticed him intently fishing the same location upstream for some time, and I thought I'd seen his rod bend on one occasion, so I waded up to him. He had indeed found some holding fish tight to the bank in an awkward position to cast to effectively.

"See what you can do. I've had a hit or two, but I'm so tight to the trees I can't seem to set properly," he groused.

I moved well up above the gravel, figuring I could keep low, cast toward midriver, and swing the fly in just above the fish. I had, after seeing Rick's last fish crunch a Woolly Bugger, switched from a Glo-Bug to a Black Leech with a chartreuse head.

As so often happens when you step in to relieve someone, you connect immediately. I had a solid take on the second swing. This fish had been out in the current well away from the visible fish, but he now made it his pressing business to rip over, visit, and emphatically scatter them before cartwheeling across and down the river in the general direction of Lake Ontario.

The fight was long, tough, and fruitful. Rick had time to set up his tripod on a nearby spit of land for some steady camera work; I got to test my new Heron reel with the silent drag (I missed the music, but the smoothness compensated); Bob got to show the locals that he is one mean net man.

"This is more typical of an Oak Orchard steelhead," Rick exclaimed as he taped the fish at 32 inches. "He has a good girth to him, too, and lots of muscle at around 12 pounds."

Ben Wright, the British golf commentator, might have enjoyed describing this steelhead: "One of the aggressive young lions, not afraid to sally out and attack the course, a strapping, brawny lad of a salmonid . . . " Since he wasn't around, I settled for "Good fish!" from Bob. If not Ben Wright, he was sincere.

Incidentally, before we let this steelhead swim away, we had removed not only my Egg-Sucking Leech, but a Silver Doctor a previous angler had lost in the corner of the fish's jaw not a half inch from my fly. This guy had definitely been on the prowl.

We broke for lunch and when we came out of the nearby cafe, the rain was picking up. It was around 3 PM, we were tired, and someone broached the notion of heading for home.

"This weather will likely activate more fish," Rick ventured. "And the faint-of-heart will be off the river," Bob added.

Minutes later at another access site we were gingerly working our way down a cable handrail back into the Oak Orchard Creek gorge. Our perseverance was rewarded. We were into active fish right away. Brian Slavinski, a local guide, fly-tier, and one of Rick's frequent fishing companions, had joined us, and he and Rick both landed large fish on egg patterns—but only after switching from orange to an Oregon cheese color. "It sure is strange how a seemingly minor change in color will get results, but it does," Brian remarked.

"Yeah, I've seen that with just about every pattern I use on steelhead," I said in agreement. "I even carry five colors of Hex imitations, and I never know which will be the fly of choice."

Bob had reinforced the color issue with his big fish described at the beginning of this New York adventure. "She just slammed a yellow Spey," he enthused as we fished the same lucky spot later in the day. "But I changed shades three times before she took."

We continued to cast, reaching, mending, and swinging in tandem as we chatted on. Then Bob tightened his line. "Fish," he flatly stated as he worked excess line back on his reel.

I quickly reeled in to get out of his way, but as I watched the action, something didn't look right. "Are you sure that's a steelhead?" I asked.

"Got to be. But maybe it's fouled. It is acting strangely."

"No, you've got it right in the mouth," I said minutes later as his tippet and its attached "fish" swung into the shallows right next to me.

"Well, what is it?"

"Can't tell for sure. Either a Midas or a Tuffy." I held up the 2-foot section of bent exhaust pipe with the yellow Spey firmly impaled in the opening of one end. "Should I release it now, or do you want pictures?"

"Put it back, quick, before other guys see it and want to fish here." The unflappable Bob took his lumps relatively cheerfully, and carrying his trophy (for proper disposal), we shortly joined Rick and Brian, compared notes, and decided to call it a day. Rick had a safety class to attend that evening as part of his guide qualification, so he was ready to go even though fish were active.

"Hey, we have a couple of spare minutes. Pull in here. I want you to meet a friend." He indicated a driveway that led to a combination home and fly shop. "The coffee will be on here."

"Look at all the goodies," was Bob's reaction as we entered the shop section. "What have you got that I'll just have to have?"

"Nothing," the owner deadpanned. "I love everything here too much. That's why I've priced it so high, so guys like you can't buy my stuff."

This set the tone for a few minutes of pleasant banter around a warm stove. If you are in the vicinity of Albion, New York, make it a point to stop here at the Oak Orchard Fly Shop. Jerry Senecal is a good source of current information as well as a delightful character.

Our travels have taken us all over the Great Lakes Basin, but this area of New York is already on the calendar for a return trip, not to "work"—just fish for the sheer fun of it.

TACTICAL SUMMARY

- In cold-water conditions (near 32 degrees F, or 1 degree C) fish the areas with less current flow.
- Deer-hunting seasons and holidays will open places usually crowded.
- If there is a slight temperature rise in cold weather, fish afternoons since it takes most of the day for the water to warm.
- Learn three or four rivers well.
- Crush down barbs, or use small-barbed or barbless hooks to facilitate release.
- Try "twanging" your line to move a sulky fish.
- Don't slide your hand much more than 6 inches above the rod handle. Too much leverage means less rod is being used, and rod-breaking possibilities increase.
- Keep your drag setting light and add tension manually if needed.
- This area has lots of ledgerock (especially Lake Erie streams) and fish hold tight to it. Look for fast current coming off a ledgerock edge.
- Under high/dirty water conditions, look for fish out of the main flow in clearer water.

RECOMMENDED TACKLE

- Rick advocates a 6- to 8-weight rod, between 9 and 10 feet; his personal preference is a 10-foot Sage RPL for a 7-weight line.
- He recommends click-drag reels with exposed outer spools for manually added drag. The Orvis Battenkill is a good reel for the price. He also likes the Lamson.
- He uses Maxima tippets for abrasion resistance, but also likes Orvis Superstrong for great strength relative to diameter.
- Chemically sharpened hooks with small barbs are his choice.
- Rick believes in keeping flies simple with plenty of color variations. Glo-Bugs in sizes 2 to 10, Frammus in sizes 4 to 12, Woolly Buggers in 2/0 to 10, Clouser Deep Minnows, and some dark nymph patterns in varied sizes can meet most situations.

PART III

THE WATER

The five inland seas named Superior, Michigan, Huron, Erie, and Ontario carry enough water to flood the continental United States to a depth of 10 feet. For many months of the year the surrounding region is covered with ice and snow. The ice, snowpack, and consistent midwestern rains continually refuel the springs and tributaries that feed the giant lakes.

Some of these rivers flow through huge, sand-capped aquifers and maintain relatively consistent flows of fresh, cool water throughout the year. Others, the spate rivers of the North Shore of Lake Superior, for example, will surge and swell to 5, even 10 times their midsummer levels with the rush of snowmelt or glut of heavy rains pounding through thinly soiled hillsides and rock-lined chasms.

Each lake can be divided into numerous regions, each with distinctive geologic characteristics, weather variables, and population densities. The combination of these and other factors, such as accessibility, which equates to angling pressure, produces a variety of environmental parameters for steelhead and unique fly-fishing experiences for anglers.

In the following pages we briefly describe some features and conditions you will encounter in selected regions, as best we could delineate them. Within each geographic area we present a selection of rivers that support good runs of steelhead and provide the opportunity for a memorable fly-fishing experience. Lastly, we offer slightly more detailed maps of 20 very productive streams throughout the basin—from the North Shore wilderness of Lake Superior to the south shore agricultural and industrial belt of Lake Ontario.

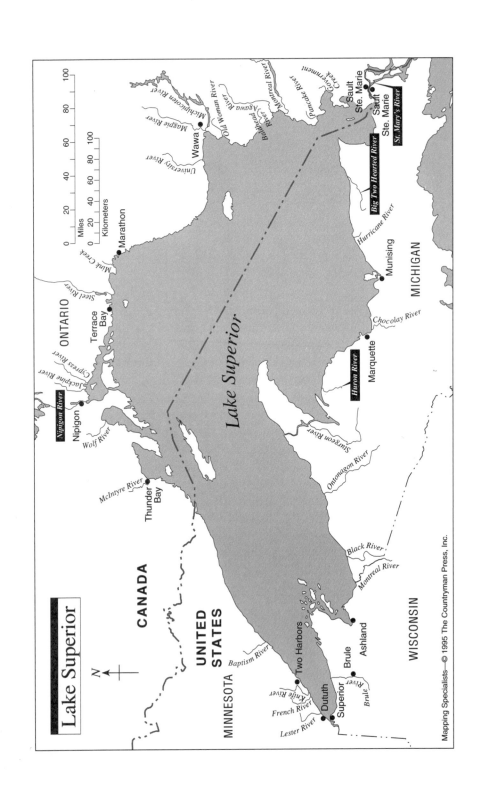

Lake Superior

Lake Superior

N

CANADA

UNITED STATES

MINNESTA

ONTARIO

MICHIGAN

WISCONSIN

Miles
Kilometers

100
80
60
40
20
0

100
80
60
40
20
0

Mint Creek
Marathon

Steel River

Terrace Bay

Cypress River

Jackpine River

Nipigon River
Nipigon

Wolf River

McIntyre River
Thunder Bay

Magpie River

University River

Michipicoten River

Old Woman River

Montreal River

Agawa River

Batchewana River

Pancake River

Government Creek

Sault Ste. Marie

Sault Ste. Marie

St. Mary's River

Big Two Hearted River

Hurricane River
Munising

Chocolay River

Marquette

Huron River

Sturgeon River

Ontonagon River

Black River

Montreal River

Ashland

Brule
Superior

Brule River

Duluth

French River

Lester River

Knife River

Baptism River

Two Harbors

Wawa

Lake Superior

Mapping Specialists—© 1995 The Countryman Press, Inc.

20
Lake Superior

NORTH SHORE

Writers often describe a river as giving the angler "the feeling of a true wilderness experience, even though one is near a bustling population center." In most riparian settings along Lake Superior's North Shore, this wilderness aura is not just a feeling—it is reality. Driving Highway 17, which hugs the rugged northern borders of the lake, you gaze out over vast expanses of mountainous, spruce-covered terrain with stark outcroppings of granite. Much of the time there is little sign of the hand of man; it is as intimidating as it is beautiful.

Off the highway—and there are not many secondary roads—things are really wild. Fishing with a companion is highly advisable, and it would be wise to let others know of your whereabouts.

We were told of a World War II prison camp in the upper North Shore area that had no escapees, even though it was minimally guarded. There was no road at the time, only an easily patrolled railroad track, and anyone who walked away overland soon came back, if they could, preferring the comparative joys of confinement to communing with tangled bush, raging rivers, bogs, wolves, bears, black flies, mosquitoes, "intemperate" weather, and all the various and assorted amenities offered to someone lost in the Ontario wilds.

By the way, don't neglect to buy staples like gas, food, and Canadian lager when the opportunity presents itself. It is often a *long* drive between supply depots, and while we seem to enjoy learning the hard way, there's no reason you have to.

The small streams the highway spans, which you can easily splash across in summer, look and sound like slightly downscaled Niagaras during spring runoff—just when steelhead are ascending. If a winter freeze hits early, which has been the case in recent years, these same streams can be throttled by ice, forcing the fall-run fish to seek a bigger, open tributary.

The gradients are steep, the streams generally very fast, and the natural obstructions formidable to fish and man. The steelhead are tough and streamlined to match their habitat, naturally adapted into the wild Lake Superior strain that Ontario fisheries people and concerned anglers are intent on maintaining. And nearly all these tributaries, under normal conditions, have good runs of these feisty fish.

So where do you start fishing, considering dozens upon dozens of beautiful spate streams and larger rivers to choose from?

Beginning at the St. Mary's River at the Soo (if you tire of beating up on fish there) and heading north on Highway 17, you would do well to sample Government Creek and the Pancake River north of Heyden, and any of several streams in the Batchawanna River area.

The Montreal, Agawa, and Baldhead Rivers are good choices as you head north toward Wawa. Once in the vicinity of this sizable

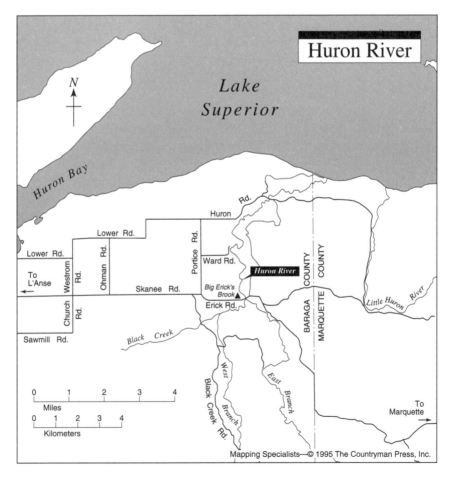

town and its sizable statue of a goose (Wawa means "goose" in the Ojibway tongue), the scenic Old Woman River and the larger, very productive Michipicoten River ought to be sampled (see chapter 6). The Magpie is a local favorite also, as is the nearby University River.

Up by Marathon you should like the looks of frothy little Mink Creek, or farther north, the Steel River, where we once again learned it's better to inquire about impassable barriers *before* trekking to the upper reaches of river . . .

The Cypress and Jackpine Rivers just southeast of Nipigon can be dynamite when conditions are decent. We've enjoyed considerable success fishing for steelhead on the former, and Bob has pictures of fall-run brook trout that make everyone sit up and take notice.

The Nipigon River (see map on p. 260) near the northernmost "peak" of Lake Superior is huge water but has great potential for true trophy fish. You will find a launch site in the town of Nipigon, and the river can be navigated from here by motorized boat for several kilometers up to Alexander's Dam. There is fine fishing along the way, and some particularly fruitful water above and below the Parmacheene train bridge by Clay Hill Creek, which is about halfway from Nipigon to the dam.

Another option is to take Highway 585 up the west side of the Nipigon River and hit some of the access points reachable from this road. There is some decent walk-in-and-wade water near Alexander, but you would be wise to engage a guide or consult a knowledgeable local so as to make the best use of your time.

As you turn southwest and head down from Nipigon toward the US, try out the Wolf River and the McIntyre River near Thunder Bay. Then buy a Minnesota trout stamp and sample the remaining cornucopia of North Shore steelhead streams.

Minnesota has had hatchery problems, and recent severe winters have also impacted rivers and fish returns in many of the 60 or so steelhead streams along this state's portion of Lake Superior's North Shore.

Fisheries personnel and various sportsmen's groups are working hard to assess problems and improve steelhead returns. Habitat improvement and allowance for increased spawning areas through "barrier alteration" are high on the list as the state works to rehabilitate wild steelhead stocks.

But the wandering, hardy Lake Superior steelhead still find the streams of the Gopher State. And even more so than in the Ontario watershed, the streams they choose, with a few exceptions, are short. The first impassable cascade or waterfall might be just a few yards from Lake Superior. The usually narrow, rocky streams sometimes come off the steep North Shore landscape at drop rates of several hundred feet in a 1-mile span. This is a picturesque and rugged fishery.

Good fly-fishing opportunities exist in most of these brief stretches, nonetheless. The Baptism, French, and Lester Rivers have long been popular selections.

The longer, many-branched Knife River has several stretches of good water for fly-anglers, particularly in its lower reaches and in the falls areas, and fish are free to run the many miles of this historic favorite.

SOUTH SHORE

The most westerly point of the Great Lakes is the tip of Superior at the Duluth, Minnesota/Superior, Wisconsin harbor. From this harbor eastward to Sault St. Marie, the southern shore undulates along a coast that is alternately gentle plain, dense primal forest, and abrupt, sometimes sheer, hillside and crag.

Iron and copper ore, white pine, and fiery maple were magnets to the early white settlers. Scandinavians, Welsh, Irish, and Italians were well represented in the settlements along the shore, in the huge mines, in the rolling forests and cedar swamps, and on the floating, heavily laden vessels of interlake commerce.

Early political structures of the region were more loosely bound than today. French and Scottish fur traders and explorers considered the area to be the "Northwest Territory." The Ottawa, Chippewa, Ojibway, Pottawatomi, and Sauk scarcely concerned themselves with such until the late 18th century, when the contest for control among the French, British, and upstart Americans (or Long Knives) reached deeply into their own lives. Later, when Michigan petitioned for statehood, the Upper Peninsula was granted to Michigan as recompense for that state relinquishing the remainder of its western holdings, which then included all of Wisconsin and a major chunk of Minnesota.

Some subliminal confusion is evident in the current era, particularly among citizens of the Upper Peninsula who stray westward to Duluth to shop for Christmas presents, and who wave Green Bay Packer banners on fall Sunday afternoons.

From Superior, Wisconsin, eastward along the coast to the Michi-

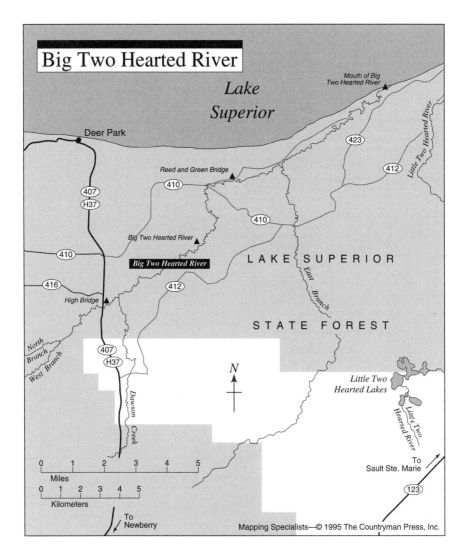

Big Two Hearted River

Lake
Superior

Mouth of Big
Two Hearted River

Deer Park

423

412

Little Two Hearted River

Reed and Green Bridge

410

407

H37

410

Big Two Hearted River

Big Two Hearted River

L A K E   S U P E R I O R

East Branch

410

416

412

High Bridge

North Branch

West Branch

S T A T E   F O R E S T

407

H37

Dawson Creek

N

*Little Two
Hearted Lakes*

Little Two Hearted River

0   1   2   3   4   5
Miles

0 1 2 3 4 5
Kilometers

To
Sault Ste. Marie

123

To
Newberry

Mapping Specialists—© 1995 The Countryman Press, Inc.

gan state line, several fertile rivers of exuberant character welcome steelhead on their upstream migrations.

The Nemadji River enters the big lake within the city limits of Superior and provides good to excellent steelhead angling well upstream, across the state line and into Minnesota. A short drive east on US 2 presents a cluster of worthy streams near Ammicon Falls State Park—the Ammicon, Middle, and Poplar Rivers.

Just a few miles farther east on US 2, the small village of Brule sits on the bank of its namesake river—arguably one of the state's best

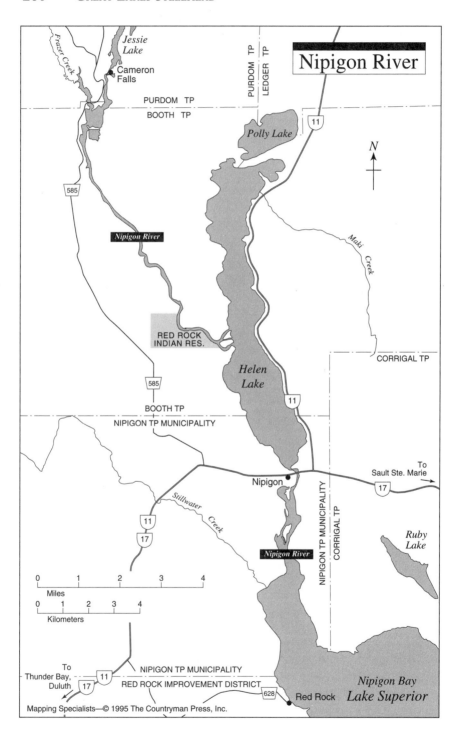

trout streams. The Brule (also known as the Bois Brule) has long been famous for its anadromous rainbows, with spring runs of heavy, mature fish and fall runs of aggressive silver rockets mixed with lake-dwelling, barrel-shaped browns up for the nuptials.

The Wisconsin Department of Natural Resources has developed a classification system for its trout rivers designed to protect and enhance wild, naturally reproducing populations, and the Brule fits into the very highest classification of quality water. This means special regulations. Be sure to consult the state's *Trout Fishing Regulations and Guide,* a detailed, professionally prepared, color-coded publication with *excellent* maps for the angler. Copies are free when you buy a license, or you can write to the address in appendix B.

As you continue east toward Michigan, many smaller rivers lure steelhead from the lake. You will be well rewarded if you are willing to probe and explore along the coast toward the Apostle Islands and the Red Cliff Indian Reservation and back down the small peninsula to Ashland.

From Ashland to Hurley and Ironwood the largest flows are the White and Bad Rivers, which join at Odanah on the Bad River Indian Reservation. Several small streams in the neighborhood of Marble Point also often hold fish.

The Montreal River forms the state line and from this point eastward, through the pristine splendor of Porcupine Mountains Wilderness State Park and the jagged thrust of the Keweenaw Peninsula, to the Huron Mountains north of Marquette, you have entered the playground of guide John Ramsay (see chapter 7). Much of this country is pure, formidable wilderness, and we suggest your expeditions will be more productive and comfortable with a guide's services.

Waterfalls, some truly magnificent, define the upstream limit for steelhead on many of these streams; the Black River and the Presque Isle are two notable examples. Farther east the steep land fall mitigates, and the Ontonagon and Firesteel Rivers present many miles of water accessible to steelhead.

The Sturgeon River in Houghton and Baraga Counties is usually reliable, and the Falls, Big Traverse, and Slate are among several lesser known but productive tributaries in the area.

From the handsome village of L'Anse north, east, and south to Marquette, the Silver, Huron, Salmon, Yellow Dog, Garlic, Dead, and Chocolay Rivers are highly regarded.

East of Munising and Grand Island Harbor the lakeshore rises vertically and pushes northward past Pictured Rocks National Lakeshore into a remote wilderness that features the Hurricane, Sucker, and Two Hearted rivers. The Two Hearted (also known as the *Big* Two Hearted) is reasonably accessible and supports healthy runs of steelhead as well as salmon, brown trout, and some coaster brookies (see map on p. 259).

Several small streams between Tahquamenon Bay and Sault Ste. Marie support steelhead, but this is largely a brush-busting and very chancy adventure, so whenever we are this close to Sault Ste. Marie we feel honor-bound to check on Dan Donarski and the state of affairs in the St. Mary's rapids.

From the Wisconsin state line to the international boundary with Ontario, the Michigan Department of Natural Resources lists 58 rivers that merit special regulations for steelhead. Add to this approximately 40 rivers in Wisconsin, and you will develop a fair picture and appreciation of the wealth of this magnificent shoreline.

21
Lake Huron

EASTERN SHORE

The second largest of the Great Lakes (23,010 square miles, 59,595 square kilometers) divides into two main sections at the point where the St. Mary's River splits to accommodate a series of islands and their attendant bays and channels. The North Channel, and subsequently Georgian Bay, begins at the upstream point of St. Joseph Island (Canada) and continues past Drummond Island (US), Cockburn Island (Canada), and onward east and south to Georgian Bay and straight south to Lake Huron.

The Province of Ontario holds all of the shoreline of the North Channel and Georgian Bay, and a major portion of Lake Huron. Its Ministry of Natural Resources, Fisheries Branch, manages the vitality of Huron's steelhead population with close scrutiny.

From the southern scape at Sarnia, past the agricultural wealth and tourist attractions of the Gray-Bruce area, up the rugged coast of Georgian Bay and the North Channel, to the heartland of the Ojibway Nation at Whitefish Island, the big lake teems with game fish.

Steelhead nose into bays, inlets, and river mouths throughout the year, but peak activity is in April, May, October, and November. These months find fish ascending the rivers in earnest. They push upcurrent in the slow, silt-edged flows of the farmlands as well as the churning flows of the North Country, where sandstone bedrock is still gradually rising after being freed from the crushing weight of the glaciers.

The countryside through which the tributaries flow is handsome and vast. Moose, bear, and wolves are the glamor species we think of most often in the context of wild country, and although present along Huron's northern shores, they are only a complement to the mergansers, eagles, and blue kingfishers; to the garter snakes and frogs that hide among the blue flag iris and joe-pye weed; to the beavers, minks, and otters that course the streambanks through cranberry, hawthorn,

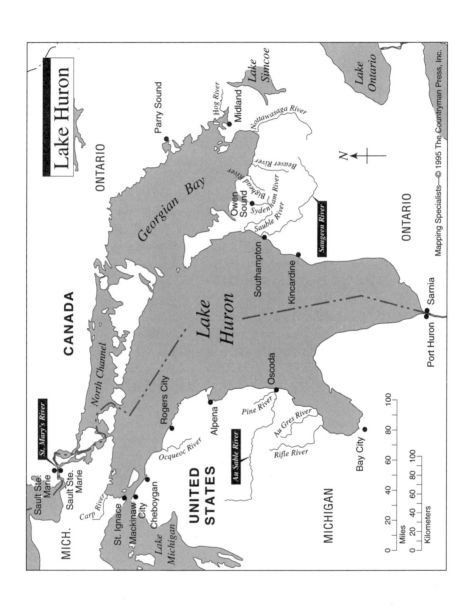

yarrow, pine, and balsam. It is beautiful, wild country.

A high percentage of tributaries throughout this wide expanse of land support steelhead populations, but consensus among top fly-anglers and fisheries management professionals is that the streams well suited to fly-fishing comprise a finite, explorable number.

The Gray-Bruce area of Ontario is but a short drive from Toronto and Detroit. It borders Lake Huron to the west and bulges into the shore of Georgian Bay to the north. The Bruce Peninsula continues the push northward, fingerlike, forming a narrow land spear into the lake. This is Bud Hoffman's (see chapter 12) home ground and he concurs with Les Stanfield, Ontario's senior project biologist for Great Lakes salmonids, that the rivers here are among the very best Lake Huron has to offer to fly-anglers in pursuit of steelhead.

Most famous among the region's streams is the Saugeen, which winds a serpentine course from Hanover west to Walkerton, then north by northwest through Paisley to its mouth at Southampton (see map on p. 267). In addition to steelhead, the Saugeen receives runs of king salmon and brown trout and its fertile reach is home to other game fish—including musky and smallmouth bass. Fish ladders, strategically placed to allow passage at dams, provide access to many miles of prime gravel, and steelhead have made the Saugeen a very productive venue.

Another river in the vicinity that hosts sizable runs is the Sauble, which flows north from Invermay to Sauble Falls very near the Chief's Point Indian Reserve and Sauble Falls Provincial Park a few miles north of Southampton.

To the east, across the isthmus of Gray-Bruce, the southern edge of Georgian Bay boasts five rivers with significant runs of very large steelhead. The Bighead, Beaver (see map on p. 268), Nottawasaga, Sydenham, and Pottawatomi Rivers are highly esteemed by knowledgeable Canadian fly-fishers, with the Beaver River near Thornbury and the upper reaches of the Nottawasaga being the most popular.

East toward Georgian Bay Islands National Park, Highway 400 from Toronto ends its northerly course near Victoria Harbor on Minnisaugwa Bay. This bay receives the flow of the Hog River and from the mouth to near the town of Coldwater, the Hog is a prime target for fly-anglers.

Manitoulin Island to the north, and the vast scape from Parry Sound to Algoma, hold rivers with substantial steelhead runs virtually unexplored by fly-fishers. You need to consider logistics and travel time in detail before an adventure into this part of Ontario, and an early phone call to the Fisheries Branch of the Ministry of Natural Resources could be very helpful.

WESTERN SHORE

At the very top of Lake Huron the St. Mary's River drains Lake Superior through a narrow isthmus, feeding trillions of gallons of cold, pure water past a paradise of islands inhabited by wolves, moose, otters, and eagles. The flow spreads east to Georgian Bay, west to the Straits of Mackinac, and south to the border towns of Port Huron and Sarnia, where a new constriction, the St. Clair River, forms current and feeds the lower lakes.

The western shore of Huron (Michigan's east coast) was once a favored and coveted territory of the Ottawa, Chippewa, Pottawatomi, Huron, and other tribes pressing their own ambitions as well as those of the British and French. These people recognized a very good thing when they saw it. The massacre of the British garrison at Fort Michillimackinac (Mackinaw City), the siege of Fort Detroit, Chief Pontiac's reign of terror, and the following War of 1812 moved matters toward the current political structure.

With the native peoples under control, energies turned to the more profitable and slightly less dangerous task of raping the land. By 1870 the sea of virgin white pine was under the ax, vessels of commerce were safe from attack, and fortunes were being made.

In 1876 a man named Fitzhugh walked down to the Au Sable River near Oscoda and released some rainbow trout hatched from eggs taken from the McCloud River in California. History was made that day—it was the first planting of rainbow trout (steelhead) in the Great Lakes.

From Sault Ste. Marie at the top of the lake to Port Huron at its southernmost point, the western shore of Huron is met by rivers, large and small, that sustain and nurture steelhead through their spawning rituals. The fisheries biologists for the Michigan Department of Natural Resources consider 24 of these streams to be significant enough to warrant either extended seasons or year-round opening to sport fishing for anadromous species. (See appendix B for more information on boundaries, dates, and special regulations.)

We have reverently praised the majestic St. Mary's River elsewhere in this book, and we refer the reader to chapters 8 and 9 on Dan Donarski and Karl Vogel for more information on the mystique of its

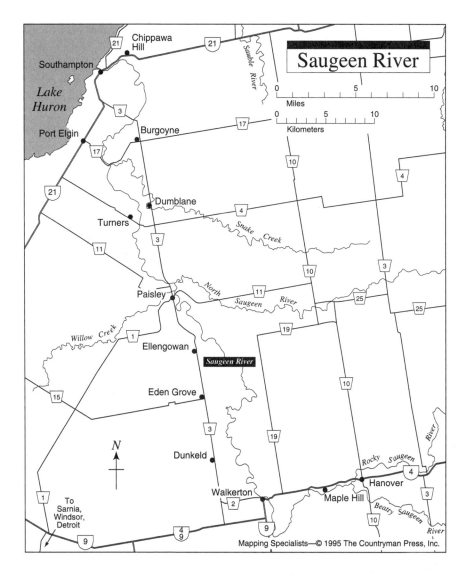

fishery as well as specific methods for angling success. We have also selected it as one of our favorite rivers, and therefore a map of the rapids is included in the following pages.

The St. Mary's rapids may only be fished from the Canadian border, and an Ontario fishing license is required. The short approach to the rapids is by footpath through a small park that supports geese, ducks, shorebirds, beavers, minks, otters, and other wildlife. On the 10-minute walk from the parking area you will likely encounter jog-

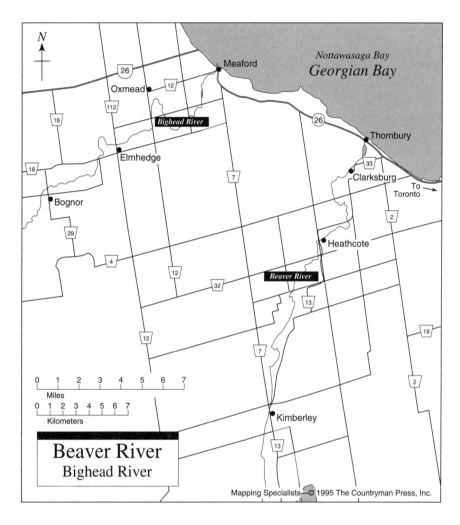

gers, bird watchers, people walking their dogs, perhaps an amorous couple, and, most likely, a few wader-clad anglers happy to give you a report or forecast.

Farther south, the big river widens into the breadth of Lake Huron, and just north of St. Ignace, Michigan, the Carp River enters from the west. This handsome stream is born near Trout Lake in the Upper Peninsula and meanders through forest and swamp on an easterly course for several miles before crossing I-75 and entering Huron quickly thereafter.

In its upper reaches the Carp is a good brook trout stream, but interest here is on the steelhead that seek the gravel pockets in the spring.

Proceeding south across the Straits to the Lower Peninsula, then east, and south again on US 23 along Michigan's east coast, you will encounter a few streams that enter Lake Huron between Mackinaw City and Cheboygan. The Cheboygan River, Green Creek, Maple River, Mill Creek, Ocqueoc River, and Trout River are some of the productive streams between Mackinaw City and Rogers City.

South of Rogers City past Alpena and on to Oscoda and the Au Sable River, the Swan River, Thunder Bay River, Devil's River, Black River, Pine River, and Van Etten Creek are among those tributaries with significant steelhead runs, according to DNR listings.

At Oscoda the Au Sable River meets Lake Huron after having been stayed by several major power-generating dams beginning in Mio. Foote Dam, the obstruction farthest downstream, is the upper boundary for steelhead and other anadromous species. (The map on p. 270 concentrates on this last free-flowing stretch between Foote Dam and Lake Huron.) This is big, deep, dark water for the most part, and only a few locations are suitable for walk-in, wading anglers. The fishing is excellent, however, and we urge you to consider a float trip with a qualified guide.

There are several more streams of merit along the southerly and

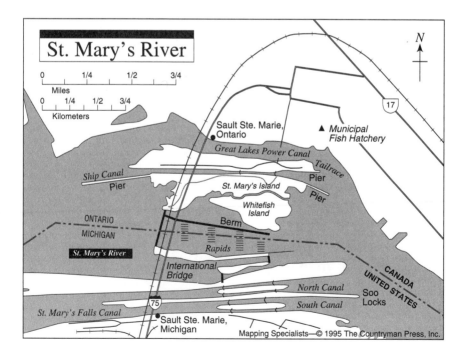

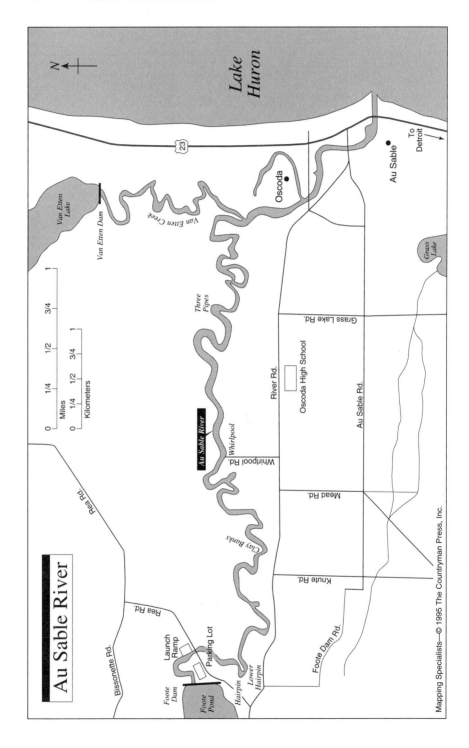

easterly route around Saginaw Bay and Port Huron, and the two most notable for fly-fishers are the Au Gres and Rifle Rivers. The best fishing on the Au Gres is usually on the East Branch downstream from MI 55 to the vicinity of Turtle Road in Iosco County. The Rifle River is most productive in the late spring, with sizable runs of 6- to 10-pound fish in close proximity to Rifle River Trail in southern Ogemaw County. Both rivers can cloud quickly with rapid snowmelt or rain, but are worth considerable attention, particularly during midweek.

In general, the tributaries to Lake Huron's western shore peak a week or two later than rivers that feed Lake Michigan. Lake Huron steelhead seem to be inordinately fond of small egg patterns, Egg-Sucking Leeches, multicolored Woolly Buggers, Jeff's Hex, and Sparrow nymphs.

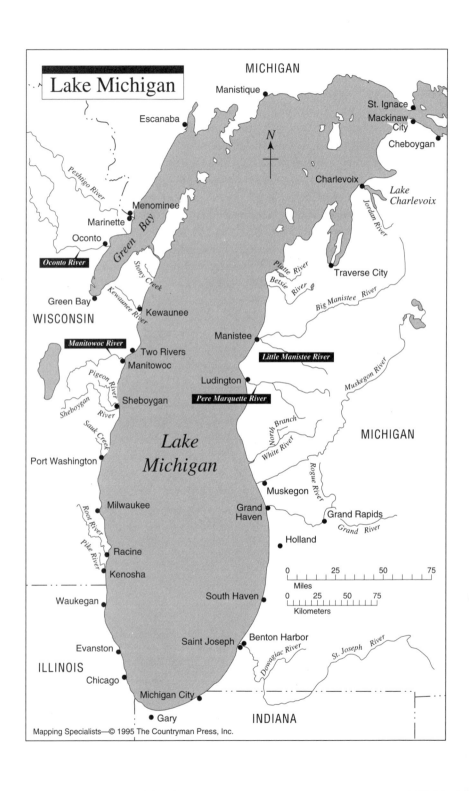

Lake Michigan

MICHIGAN
Manistique
Escanaba
St. Ignace
Mackinaw City
Cheboygan
N
Charlevoix
Lake Charlevoix
Peshtigo River
Menominee
Marinette
Green Bay
Oconto
Oconto River
Stony Creek
Platte River
Betsie River
Big Manistee River
Traverse City
Jordan River
Green Bay
WISCONSIN
Kewaunee River
Kewaunee
Manistee
Manitowoc River
Two Rivers
Manitowoc
Little Manistee River
Pigeon River
Ludington
Muskegon River
Sheboygan River
Sheboygan
Pere Marquette River
Sauk Creek
Lake Michigan
North Branch
White River
MICHIGAN
Port Washington
Rogue River
Root River
Milwaukee
Grand Haven
Muskegon
Grand Rapids
Grand River
Pike River
Racine
Holland
0   25   50   75
Miles
Kenosha
0   25   50   75
Kilometers
Waukegan
South Haven
Evanston
Saint Joseph
Benton Harbor
Dowagiac River
St. Joseph River
ILLINOIS
Chicago
Michigan City
Gary
INDIANA

Mapping Specialists—© 1995 The Countryman Press, Inc.

22
Lake Michigan

EAST SHORE

"National treasures" are the words sometimes applied to several of the more northerly rivers along Michigan's west coast. Most anglers have heard the names—the Pere Marquette, the Big Manistee, the Little Manistee, the Platte—of these crown jewels in the glittering array of beautiful water with which the state is blessed. They are the giant spring creeks of the Midwest, as rich in groundwater as any streams in North America. The steelhead, of course, find these clear, cold, stable, spring-fed waters most attractive and have used them for decades. Anglers are doubly blessed in that the forested environs through which they run rival many areas of the world for sheer natural beauty. And anglers come in droves.

But steelhead also find many other west coast Michigan streams worthy of attention. From the Amish farmland of the far southwest corner of the state, up through the vineyards of "Wine Country," on through the midstate temperate fruit belt and the storied northerly rivers flowing through vast tracts of state and federal forest, to the Sleeping Bear Dunes regions, clear up to the majestic Mackinac Bridge, the west coast of Michigan hosts wonderful runs of anadromous rainbow trout.

The huge St. Joseph River drainage, in the relatively unheralded southwest corner of the Lower Peninsula, is often overlooked. Since much of its flow is through Indiana as well as Michigan, both states have worked hard to maintain what is now one of the top steelhead rivers in the Great Lakes Basin. It is big water, best attacked by boat, but with a few wadable stretches.

A river of this magnitude has many tributaries. The short stretch of the Dowagiac River below the dam in North Niles is a wadable, highly touted flow, as is Pipestone Creek.

The traditional Lake Michigan strain of steelhead can be counted on to show up in the fall in the St. Joe and head for the gravel in spring,

273

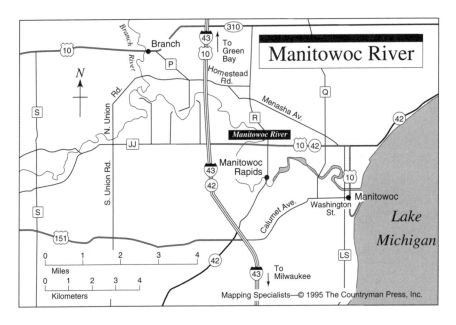

but in recent years this river has gained a reputation for its summer run. Skamania have been known to arrive in the first week of May, nearly causing a traffic jam with "normal" steelhead heading back down. The Skamania will also head up small, cooler tributaries.

A pamphlet called the "St. Joseph River Interstate Anadromous Fish Project" is available by calling or writing the Michigan DNR. It lists and maps access sites.

Just about every major river and/or small creek entering Lake Michigan will carry steelhead, but as you proceed up the coast from the St. Joe, probably the next real fly-fishing water would be the Rogue River, a major tributary to the huge Grand River. The small town of Rockford, Michigan, a few miles north of Grand Rapids, is a good place to start. From this point south to its confluence with the Grand, the Rogue River offers an abundance of wadable, classic steelhead water.

Moving farther north, you encounter the mighty Muskegon River, which, like the St. Joe to the south, has its wadable sections and a reputation as one of the state's best steelhead rivers. Try it between Crotan Dam and Newaygo. If it's not to your liking, it's only a short jaunt to the White River and its excellent tributary, the North Branch of the White River.

Other productive rivers near here, like the Pentwater and Stoney Creek, carry excellent runs in both spring and fall, but when this close, you *must* sample the Pere Marquette River (see map on p. 278 and chapters 13 and 14). The flies-only water from M-37 down to Gleason's Landing is unsurpassed. Most of it is easily waded under normal conditions, and access maps are readily available in fly shops in Baldwin, Michigan. Expect crowds, even in midweek, during peak times—but we have always found areas to fish in relative peace.

This river and its near neighbors the Big Manistee and the Little Manistee just a bit more to the north are as fine a triumvirate of blue-ribbon streams as exist within an hour of one another anywhere—period. Some sections of the Big Manistee can be waded below Tippy Dam (the upstream anadromous limit), but a drift boat makes more water available with fewer chancy bouts with the depths. A major feeder to the Big Manistee, Bear Creek, provides a smaller-water experience for fly-anglers. We like it just below the Coates Highway crossing north of the town of Brethren.

The Little Manistee (see map on p. 277) has for years maintained its reputation as one of Michigan's very finest steelhead rivers, and it is still one of the prime sources of fertilized eggs used to stock other waters. Unlike many rivers, it is not open year-round. This allows brood stock to congregate at the egg-taking weir below Six Mile Bridge.

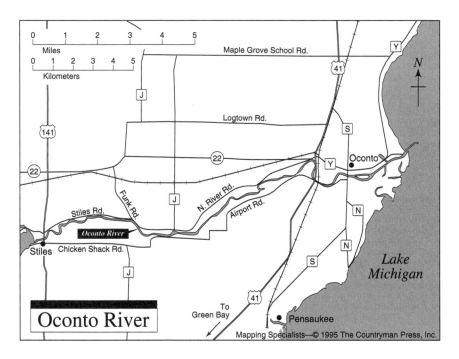

Oconto River

The gravel riffles and fast slicks are wadable for most of the stream's length, but be wary. Narrow chutes and sudden drops in gradient, particularly in one of the very best sections between Six Mile and Nine Mile Bridges, can get you in trouble in a hurry.

Johnson's Bridge has been the upstream limit for spring and late fall steelheading.

The Betsie River and the Platte River up in Benzie County are two more fine northwest Michigan steelhead rivers. Of these two, the Platte is a bit more challenging due to its shallow, ultraclear water. When fish are in, they are often visible to you, as you are to them. Approach and presentation are more critical here than in many rivers.

There are many more rivers before you get as far north as the Mackinac Bridge. One more deserving selective mention is Michigan's first National Scenic River, the Jordan. Before it empties into the South Arm of Lake Charlevoix, it runs through beautiful, rugged country and reputedly has one of the best water quality measures in the Lower Peninsula. Its lower reaches host sizable spring and fall steelhead runs.

WEST SHORE

The glaciers responsible for the formation of the Great Lakes also did a remarkable job creating spectacular landscapes in the state of Wisconsin. Limestone and sandstone formations in the Dells and other places around the state rival anything found in the West. Kettle moraines, lakes by the hundreds, marshes, swamps, forests, hills, prairies—the topography of the Dairy State has more variation than most people could ever imagine.

It also has dozens of rivers. The Fox-Wisconsin Waterway from Lake Michigan to the Mississippi River, traveled by Marquette and Joliet in the late 17th century, is just one of several famous water routes important to Wisconsin history. Many streams and rivers carry the names of Native American tribes and French explorers. But it is the Wisconsin rivers that carry present-day travelers like the Chambers Creek, Ganaraska, and Skamania strains that catch anglers' attention.

The steelhead rivers that flow into Lake Michigan from Wisconsin's east side are many and varied. Since the state plants heavily and wants a good return on investment, the Wisconsin Department of Natural Resources is working hard to restore quality to rivers degraded by the effects of human population, so that streams can better sustain

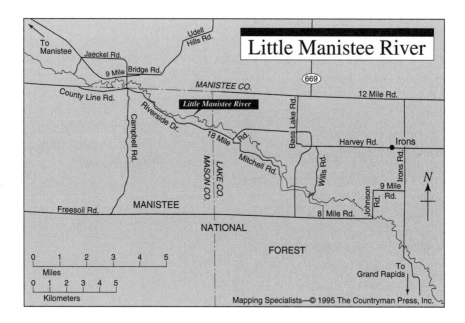

spawning migrations. Habitat management is a priority in making good streams better. The often turbid nature of many of these Lake Michigan tributaries is a consideration in fly colors and sizes (see Blumreich/Yarnot, chapter 17).

The state has a good attitude toward access to these improving waters. If a waterway is navigable, it is public. Navigability is determined by whether it can float a canoe part of the year—even if only during spring high-water time. Once on a navigable waterway, as long as you keep your feet wet, you are not trespassing.

Down in southern Wisconsin, almost at the Illinois border, the Pike River reaches the big lake near Kenosha and provides good fishing and wadable conditions. Not too far above, at Racine, flows the Root River. Fish can reach the Horlick Dam, but a weir has been installed midway between the dam and Lake Michigan. Check regulations for current special closures.

Farther up the coast between Milwaukee and Sheboygan lies Sauk Creek which empties at Port Washington. A power plant discharge can attract and hold large numbers of steelhead near the creek's lower end.

Midway up the lake is the Sheboygan River, running in at the town of Sheboygan. This is a very productive, fairly large (but wadable) river. Some of the better water flows through the large Kohler holdings, necessitating permission to reach many sections, but there is

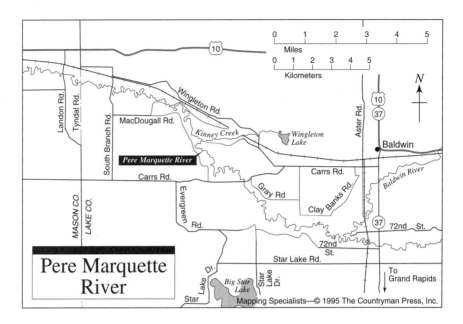

good water below Highway 43. And one is not too far from the Pigeon River north of Sheboygan. This stream has excellent water quality and the fishing can be amazing, according to one local expert.

The Manitowoc River (see map on p. 274) enters Lake Michigan at Manitowoc and is receiving high-priority treatment from the powers that be. There are more than 20 miles of fishable water before it reaches Clark Mills Dam. The river can be waded, but caution is advised. Slick cobblestones combined with fairly heavy flow can cause problems. However, the quality fly-fishing here warrants the effort.

The Kewaunee River is a very popular Lake Michigan tributary found at the base of the Door Peninsula. This is a brood-stock stream with a weir up from the mouth, testimony to the excellent steelhead runs it receives. It too provides quality opportunity for fly-anglers. Just a bit farther up the peninsula lies Stony Creek. Due to its smaller size and steep gradient, water levels can fluctuate, but when running right, it can be a delight.

The town of Oconto is situated about midway between the city of Green Bay and the Michigan border. Here the Oconto River (see map on p. 275) flows into Green Bay, giving the angler about 10 miles of eminently fishable water before the dam at Stiles. The guaranteed minimum flow from the dam makes for dependable water conditions. This Lake Michigan tributary is a favorite of many wading fly-fishermen.

The Peshtigo River near the Michigan/Wisconsin border gets good runs of fish, but it is big water and mostly fished at the dam, which can get pretty crowded.

Over the years the east coast of Wisconsin has been known mostly for its offshore fishery, but the streams mentioned here, and many, many others, provide rewarding, often overlooked steelhead-on-the-fly experiences.

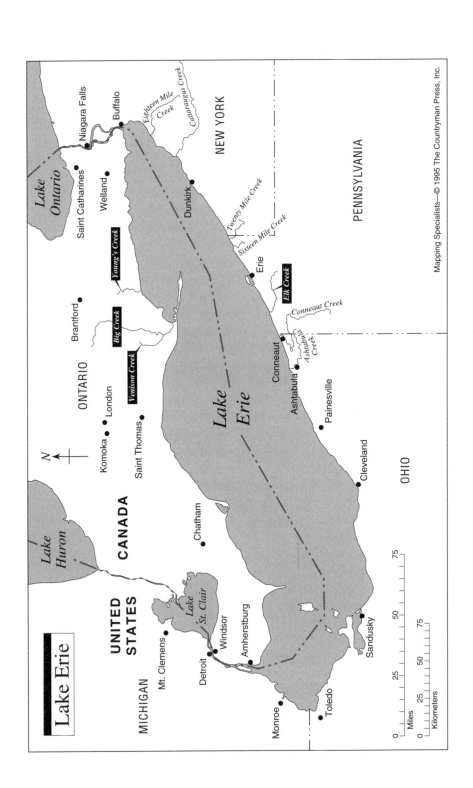

Lake Erie

Mapping Specialists—© 1995 The Countryman Press, Inc.

23

Lake Erie

NORTH SHORE

This part of extreme southern Canada played a vital role as a communication and supply route during one of the most intriguing and brutal periods of early North American history. The British forts at Michillimackinac and Detroit were at the remote, western edge of England's political influence and military control during the mid-18th century.

The Ottawa chieftain Mackinac and his vicious war chief Pontiac formed fluctuating alliances with the French and with Native American tribes from the Minnesota border to the Atlantic seaboard in order to purge Detroit and end British control.

Pontiac was a gifted orator, political organizer, and military strategist, as well as a propaganda/advertising specialist. His deserved (and nurtured) reputation as a bloodthirsty cannibal with a particular fondness for British steaks gave high interest and much urgency to the travel planning of couriers and supply detachments from Fort Niagara. Casual sightseeing was not on the itinerary.

The area today is bucolic. Rolling, gently sloping fields with windbreak wood lots, crops, chevrons of geese and ducks, and small agriculture-based villages will draw your eye.

The few streams suitable for steelhead on the north shore are restricted to the area known as the Norfolk Sand Plain. The streams in this region are freshened by groundwater seepage, so they retain relatively cold, stable flows. Unfortunately, sedimentation from intensive farming is a problem.

Approximately 140 kilometers southeast of London, Ontario, and 180 kilometers south of Kitchener, Long Point juts eastward into the lake like an outstretched talon. This elongated, narrow land spike is a provincial park and serves as southerly protectorate to Inner Bay, where Big Creek meets the lake near the town of Long Point Beach.

The folks involved in the Great Lakes Salmonids project for the

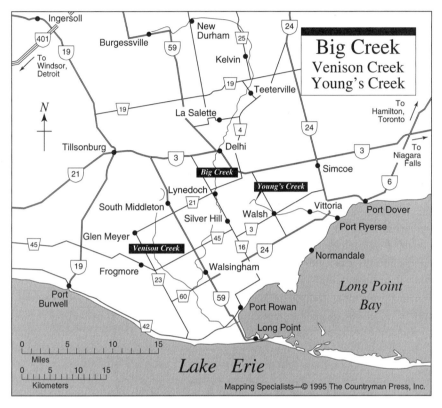

Ministry of Natural Resources indicate that Big Creek and neighboring Young's Creek at Normandale are the rivers best suited to fly-fishing for steelhead on the Canadian side of Lake Erie, and that fly patterns that produce on Georgian Bay and on Lake Ontario will catch fish here as well.

Big Creek is the best steelhead river in the area. The section of stream between Teeterville and Lynedoch is shallow enough for comfortable wading and fly-fishing, and the best area is in the vicinity of Delhi. Currently, the season extends until December 31 up to Delhi, but unless there has been substantial fall precipitation, most fish stay lower in the system, which is very slow and deep.

Venison Creek, a tributary to Lower Big Creek, is making a strong comeback after years of erosion problems, but is closed in the fall to protect spawning brown trout.

Young's Creek stays very cold and receives a small but reliable run of summer steelhead. It is small (10 to 15 feet wide) and heavily fished by local anglers in the spring.

Whiteman's Creek (a Grand River tributary) has hosted strong steelhead runs since the removal of a dam on the Grand River at Brantford in the 1980s. The lower reaches have an excellent gravel bottom and the stream seems to be turning into a steelhead "factory."

There is little if any natural reproduction by steelhead in the Lake Erie tributaries on either shore. This resource, to be sustained into the future, will apparently require continuation of managed, cooperative hatchery programs by bordering states and Ontario.

SOUTH SHORE

The proclamation that Lake Erie was dead proved premature. Sick yes, dead no. Industrial waste and urban effluent were tragic, and although it is stylish to lay blame on US manufacturing cities, it is more accurate to acknowledge international guilt in this particular crime of pollution.

The awakening and credit for subsequent efforts to clean and control waste must likewise be shared by the United States and Canada.

Today Erie is in better shape than when the Cuyahoga River caught fire, much better shape, and the resurgence of the lake's sport fishery is indicative of improving health. Walleye and perch, for which it had long been famous, have rebounded to near-record populations. Bass, pike, and panfish are plentiful in this, the shallowest of the Great Lakes. And steelhead, abetted by aggressive stocking programs, are making a significant impact on both sides of the border.

Ohio's shore has several rivers that receive steelhead runs in both spring and fall, and the fishing can be superb as long as water temperatures and flow levels are within tolerable levels. This is the southern edge of the steelhead's range in the Great Lakes, and streams can warm quickly, particularly under low-water conditions.

Streams of note include the Ashtabula and Conneaut in the extreme northeastern part of the state close to the Pennsylvania border. These flows are bedded by shale and rubble, and fish often lie next to the sparse cover afforded by underwater ledges.

The Elk, Walnut, Sixteen Mile, and Twenty Mile Creeks are popular steelhead rivers along Pennsylvania's short Lake Erie coastline, and local fly-rodders have been beneficiaries of very strong runs in recent years. Fall fishing can be sporadic, but is spectacular when favorable conditions prevail. Some Michigan anglers we know now favor repeated trips in November to Elk and Walnut Creeks over the

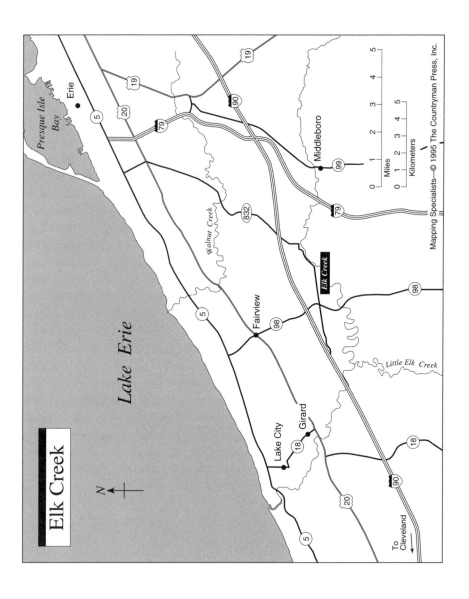

Elk Creek

backyard charms of the Pere Marquette and Au Sable.

New York's Lake Erie waterfront presents Cattaraugus Creek at Hanford Bay on the Erie County line, roughly midway between the Pennsylvania border and the city limits of Buffalo. This is a shale and ledgerock stream that receives heavy runs of eager, acrobatic fish. Guide Rick Kustich of Grand Island, New York (see chapter 19), fishes it regularly and holds it in high esteem.

Eighteen Mile Creek skirts the southern edge of the village of Hamburg about 10 miles south of Buffalo, New York. It then turns from its northerly course and flows westward the last few miles, crossing I-90, NY 20, the Conrail RR line, and NY 5 before meeting the lake near Highland-on-the-Lake.

This is a very popular river, in part due to its proximity to metropolitan Buffalo. In addition to the easy commute, it receives good numbers of steelhead in both spring and fall, and they are usually receptive to favorite regional patterns such as the Frammus, Salmon Flea, and Glo-Brite Egg as well as small, somber-hued nymphs and Woolly Buggers.

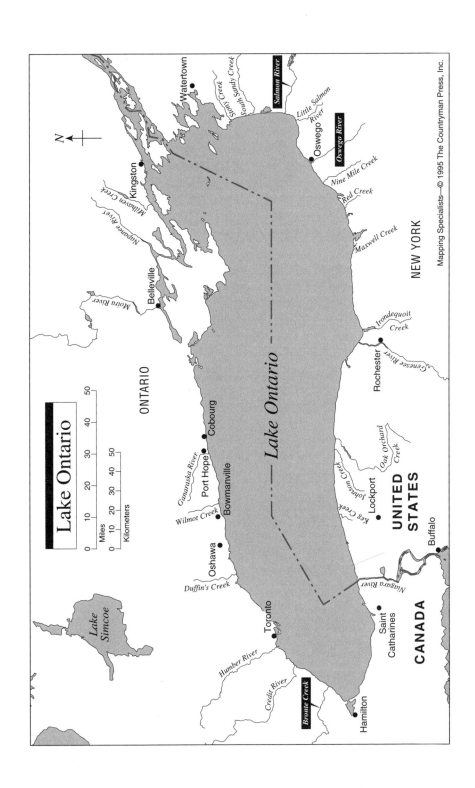

Lake Ontario

ONTARIO

NEW YORK

UNITED STATES

CANADA

Lake Simcoe

Lake Ontario

Miles
0   10   20   30   40   50

Kilometers
0   10   20   30   40   50

Watertown

Sandy Creek
South Sandy Creek
Salmon River
Little Salmon River
Oswego
Oswego River
Nine Mile Creek
Red Creek
Maxwell Creek

Kingston
Milhaven Creek
Napanee River

Belleville
Moira River

Irondequoit Creek
Rochester
Genesee River

Cobourg
Port Hope
Canaraska River
Bowmanville
Wilmot Creek

Oak Orchard Creek
Lockport
Johnson Creek
Keg Creek
Buffalo

Oshawa
Duffin's Creek

Toronto
Humber River
Credit River
Bronte Creek
Hamilton

Saint Catharines
Niagara River

N

Mapping Specialists—© 1995 The Countryman Press, Inc.

24
Lake Ontario

NORTH SHORE

Steelhead populations on the Canadian side of Lake Ontario are healthy and widely dispersed. From Niagara-on-the-Lake westward to Hamilton, then northeast to Toronto, and continuing east past Brighton to Kingston, the Ontario shore presents several popular rivers suited to fly-fishing.

The mighty Niagara River has runs of powerful fish and tempts more than a few adventurers to ply her majestic and terrifying flow with high-density sinking lines. North of Hamilton, Bronte Creek (see map on p. 289) intersects Highway 5 near the village of Tansley and crosses under Queen Elizabeth Highway just a few kilometers farther east before meeting the lake at Bronte Light. Although we have not fished it ourselves, we have heard from reliable sources that the Bronte and the Credit River, a short drive farther east toward Toronto, support strong runs of vigorous fish that take flies readily.

The Humber River and Duffin's Creek serve as counterpoint examples to the notion that steelhead fly-fishing is a wilderness experience. The Humber gathers its east branch near Woodbridge and its west branch at Weston, just a few kilometers from the skyscrapers and commerce of Toronto, one of the most energetic and sophisticated cities in the world. The Humber then flows through York to Humber Borg, providing first-class sport in an urban environment. Duffin Creek empties into the lake at Moore Point near Fairport on Toronto's east side. It too follows a populated course and produces reasonable sport close to suburbs and industry.

Wilmot Creek is just a short drive farther east past the town of Oshawa to near New Castle, where the stream crosses Highway 401 a short distance east of Bondhead. Highways 35/115 and 2, as well as the Canadian Pacific, cross Wilmot Creek farther upstream.

Ministry of Natural Resources fisheries personnel rate Wilmot Creek near the top of the list of streams that afford the best opportunities for fly-anglers.

The Ganaraska River, which feeds Lake Ontario at Port Hope, is generally regarded as one of the finest fisheries on the Canadian side of the lake. Anglers and fisheries biologists alike give it high marks, and the future of steelhead in this system seems secure.

The best fly-fishing opportunities on the Ganaraska are in the western sector of Northumberland County, and many fly-rodders take advantage of fishing the stream mouth area between the Canadian National Railway and Lake Ontario. There is a fish sanctuary, which is closed to angling all year, on that stretch of the Ganaraska River downstream from Highway 401 to a point 40 meters (131 feet) south of Corbett Dam.

At Belleville on the Bay of Quinte, the Moira River receives substantial late fall and spring runs. Several villages along Highway 37 are very near or on the stream bank and afford current, local knowledge to the visitor. At present the Moira River is a dedicated fish sanctuary through the month of April and the first week of May. Be sure to check current regulations.

The Napanee River comes into play about 20 kilometers farther east at the town of Napanee on Highway 2. This stream, as well as Milhaven Creek another 10 kilometers eastward, offers several stretches well suited to fly-fishing. Both have good populations of spring and fall fish, but be sure to review the most recent Ontario sport fishing regulations for extended seasons or specific sections closed to protect spawning activity.

From Niagara to Toronto, this Canadian shoreline is heavily populated and industrialized, yet its government and sporting citizenry have combined to develop and safeguard an outstanding fishery for the lake-dwelling rainbows. The fish are for the most part sizable, hearty, and aggressive, and take flies readily.

Leaving the eastern suburbs of Toronto and heading toward the end of the lake and the beginning of the Saint Lawrence River at Kingston, the roadside vistas change to small towns and rolling farmlands with wooded stream valleys. More and more forest becomes evident east of Brighton and on toward Kingston, but this area is still in Canada's high-population corridor.

The Fisheries Branch of the Ministry of Natural Resources for the Province of Ontario employs dedicated salmonid specialists, who oversee current developments through various research projects. They are critical to the long-range, continued success story of Lake Ontario's steelhead and should be cheered for their work so far.

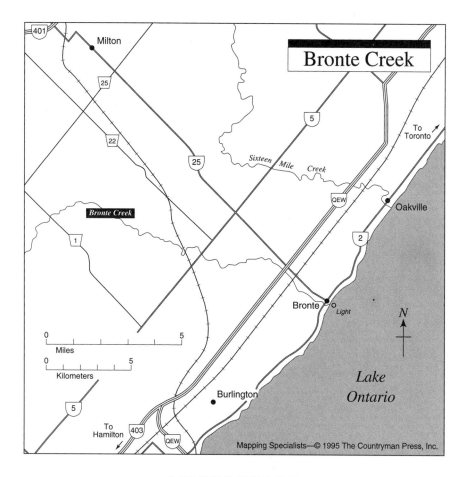

SOUTH SHORE

Some of our more traveled fishing associates, those who have "been around the basin" more than a time or two, rate New York close to Michigan as the best state for quality steelhead fly-fishing excursions. If our trips east to chase Lake Ontario steelhead are any barometer, this is an understatement. We have in recent years taken more fish from tributaries of this, the smallest of the Great Lakes, than just about anywhere else. And the steelhead here run large, as the state record of close to 27 pounds attests.

The Lake Ontario plain of western New York State is an attractive mix of hills, valleys, farms, swamps, and extensive fruit orchards. Like most state and provincial areas bordering a Great Lake, the New York landscape along Lake Ontario benefits climatically from this very deep (500 to 800 feet) lake. It rarely freezes in the winter except near shore, and surface water temperatures are warmer than average air temperatures, hence the moderating effect.

"Honest, Bob, I read it in an encyclopedia once. Temperate climate near the lake. We have nothing to worry about." This as we raced southwest out of the Oswego environs one December day (after a very successful winter steelhead foray with John Dembeck), a full-blown "blue northern" of a snowstorm dogging our 70-mph tracks, pretty much covering them to considerable depth.

This part of New York State worried us with its reputation for healthy snowfalls, but a local had assured us, "It's a bum rap. Just like some people say we got reckless, surly taxi drivers over in the big city."

If the steelheading stays as good as it has been, a little snow is but a minor concern, especially when the chance for trophy fish is a distinct possibility. Rick Kustich, a local guide/writer/angler, is high on the area's potential. He rates the lower Niagara River (below Niagara

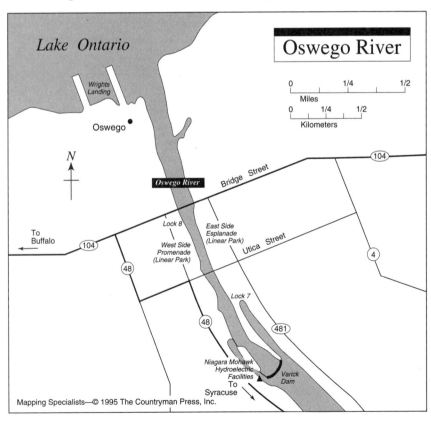

Mapping Specialists—© 1995 The Countryman Press, Inc.

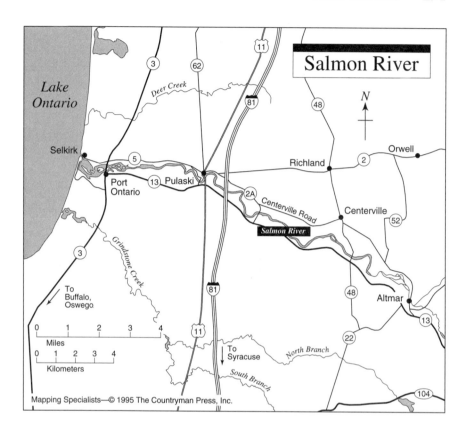

Falls, thank you) as "probably the best big-fish river in the Great Lakes, if not the entire lower 48 states." Wading is tough unless you know the water well. This river is probably best fished from a boat.

Moving east from Niagara Falls, you will find several good streams for fly-anglers. Keg Creek and Johnson Creek have potential for decent runs of Lake Ontario steelhead. An exceptionally good tributary is Oak Orchard Creek near Waterport (see Kustich, chapter 19). It is wadable, scenic, and one of those places you can walk away from with a pleasantly aching arm after a multifish day.

Traveling ever eastward toward Irondequoit and Rochester, New York, you cross a couple more decent flows. Sandy Creek and the Genesee River have good reputations, and Irondequoit Creek by the town of the same name is known to be kind to fly-fishermen.

As you near the eastern end of Lake Ontario and a couple of the most famous rivers in this country, you could stop and sample any of several smaller creeks in the area. The Maxwell, Red, and Nine Mile

Creeks are noted producers for the steelheader. But you are now in the neighborhood of the famed Oswego River (see map on p. 290), thought by many to have the best steelhead fishing in the state for the relatively short flow accessible to these fish. The approximately 3 miles of river up to Varick Dam is big water, ideally fished from a drift boat, but bank fishing is a viable alternative, particularly near the dam. Depending on time of year, chinook and coho salmon, lake trout, and *big* brown trout can interfere with the fly you are drifting for steelhead. Pesky things. If you don't mind being in the environs of a city, this river provides spectacular fly-fishing.

A note: There are special regulations from the Varick Street Dam down to the Utica State Bridge and are subject to change. Consult your up-to-date New York State Fishing Regulations and Guide carefully.

Many streams in this eastern area reportedly receive runs of purely wild steelhead along with strays from the plantings of other states, but New York relies heavily on its own fish plantings in Lake Ontario. One of its primary sources for brood stock is the nationally recognized Salmon River (see map on p. 291), which runs through the town of Pulaski. The Salmon River Hatchery in Altmar has in itself become something of a tourist draw, providing tours where visitors can view fish entering the hatchery, the egg-taking process, and fish-tagging.

But this extensive flowage (open up to the Route 52 Bridge) is best known for its consistent runs of salmonids, of which the steelhead run is a major part. Its fame has resulted in pressure at hot spots like Douglaston Salmon Run, the Black Hole, Trestle Pool, Schoolhouse Pool, and other fish-holding spots. (We have seen books that advertise aerial photos of every pool on the river.) But there is a wide variety of fishable, classic fly water up and down the river. There is even a short stretch of fly-fishing-only water, with rumors of more in the future.

The Salmon River receives a sizable run of chinooks and cohos beginning in September, so egg patterns and techniques one would use anywhere for fall steelhead coming up after the salmon are effective here. Spring spawners also provide excellent action for fly-anglers.

Again, special regulations make it prudent to check rules carefully regarding what can be done when and where on the Salmon River.

Other streams in this vicinity, while not as well known, can be most productive. South Sandy Creek, Stony Creek, and the Little Salmon River are some of the favorites.

Appendix A
Suggested Reading

BOOKS

Combs, Trey, *Steelhead Fly Fishing*, Lyons & Burford, New York, New York, 1991.

Giessuebel, Rich, *Good Fishing in Lake Ontario and Its Tributaries*, 2nd edition, The Countryman Press, Woodstock, Vermont, 1995.

Helsie, H. Kent, *Steelhead Fly Tying Guide*, Frank Amato Publications, Portland, Oregon, 1994.

Humphrey, Jim and Bill Shogren, *Wisconsin and Minnesota Trout Streams: A Fly-Angler's Guide*, The Countryman Press, Woodstock, Vermont, 1995.

Kustich, Rick, *Fly Fishing the Great Lakes Tributaries*, West River Publishing Company, Grand Island, New York, 1992.

Kustich, Rick, *River Journal—Salmon River*, Frank Amato Publications, Portland, Oregon, 1995.

Linsenman, Bob and Steve Nevala, *Michigan Trout Streams: A Fly-Angler's Guide*, The Countryman Press, Woodstock, Vermont, 1993.

Meyer, Deke, *Advanced Fly Fishing for Steelhead*, Frank Amato Publications, Portland, Oregon, 1992.

Richards, Carl, *Prey*, Lyons & Burford, New York, New York, 1995.

Richards, Carl and Doug Swisher, *Fly Fishing Strategies*, Lyons & Burford, New York, New York, 1976.

Richards, Carl and Doug Swisher, *Emergers*, Lyons & Burford, New York, New York, 1991.

Stewart, Dick and Farrow Allen, *Flies for Steelhead*, Northland Press, Intervale, New Hampshire, 1992.

Stinson, Bill, *Fly Rod Steelhead*, Frank Amato Publications, Portland, Oregon, 1982.

Supinski, Matthew, *River Journal—Pere Marquette*, Frank Amato Publications, Portland, Oregon, 1994.

PERIODICALS

American Angler, various dates, Abenaki Publications, Bennington, Vermont.

Fly Fisherman, various dates, Cowles Magazines, Inc., Harrisburg, Pennsylvania.

Fly Rod & Reel, various dates, Down East Enterprise, Inc., Camden, Maine.

Flyfishing, various dates, Frank Amato Publications, Portland, Oregon.

Midwest Fly Fishing, various dates, Midwest Fly Fishing, Inc., Minneapolis, Minnesota.

Wild Steelhead & Atlantic Salmon, Wild Steelhead & Atlantic Salmon, Inc., Mill Creek, Washington.

Appendix B
Information Sources

Here are the addresses and phone numbers for Great Lakes state and provincial Natural Resources headquarters. These primary sources can also provide regional addresses and phone numbers near areas you wish to fish.

Illinois Department of
    Conservation
605 State Office Building
Springfield, IL 62706
(217) 782-6384

Indiana Department of Natural
    Resources
608 State Office Building
Indianapolis, IN 46204
(317) 232-4020

Michigan Department of
    Natural Resources
PO Box 30028
Lansing, MI 48909
(517) 373-1280

Minnesota Department of
    Natural Resources
Box 12 DNR Building
500 Lafayette Road
St. Paul, MN 55155
(612) 296-3325

New York Department of
    Environmental Conservation
Bureau of Fisheries
Room 518
50 Wolf Road
Albany, NY 12233
(518) 457-3946

Ohio Department of Natural
    Resources
Fountain Square
Columbus, OH 43224
(614) 466-7313

Ontario Ministry of Natural
    Resources
Fisheries Branch
Queenspark, Toronto M7A1W3
(416) 965-4251

Pennsylvania State Game
    Commission
Box 1567
Harrisburg, PA 17120
(717) 787-3633

Wisconsin Department of
Natural Resources
Box 7921
Madison, WI 53707
(608) 266-2621

ADDITIONAL SOURCES OF INFORMATION

Institute for Fisheries Research
Michigan Department of
Natural Resources
212 Museums Annex Building
Ann Arbor, MI 48109
(313) 663-3554

Fisheries Region 7
Department of Environmental
Conservation
615 Erie Boulevard West
Syracuse, NY 13204-2400
(315) 426-7422

Fisheries Region 8
Department of Environmental
Conservation
6274 East Avon-Lima Road
Avon, NY 14414-9519
(716) 226-2466

Fish Management—Lake
Superior
Wisconsin Department of
Natural Resources
1325 Tower Avenue
Superior, WI 54880
(715) 392-7988

Lake Superior Salmonid
Management Unit
Ontario Ministry of Natural
Resources
435 James Street South
Suite 221
Thunder Bay, Ontario P7E 6E3
(807) 475-1231

Great Lakes Salmonid Project
Ontario Ministry of Natural
Resources
RR 4
Picton, Ontario K0K 2T0
(905) 832-7109

Sault Ste. Marie Sport Fishing
Development
PO Box 580
Sault Ste. Marie, Ontario
P6A 5N1
(705) 759-5446

Appendix C
Fly Shops and Featured Guides

The following is a selective list of fly shops in the Great Lakes Basin that carry specialized equipment and flies for area steelhead anglers and can also provide guide service information.

ILLINOIS

Orvis Chicago
142 East Ontario
Chicago, IL 60611
(312) 440-0662

On The Fly
3628 Sage Drive
Rockford, IL 61114
(815) 877-0090

Fly & Field
560 Crescent Boulevard
Glen Ellyn, IL 60137
(708) 858-7844 (Chicago area)

Riverside Sports
26 North Bennett Street
Geneva, IL 60134
(708) 232-7047 (Chicago area)

INDIANA

Jorgensens
6226 Covington Road
Fort Wayne, IN 46804
(219) 432-5519

MICHIGAN

Angling Outfitters
3207 Stadium Drive
Kalamazoo, MI 49008
(616) 372-0922

Backcast Fly Shop
1675 Benzie Highway
Benzonia, MI 49616
(616) 882-5222

Ed's Sport Shop
712 Michigan Avenue (M 37)
PO Box 487
Baldwin, MI 49304
(616) 745-4974

The Troutsman
4386 US 31 North
Traverse City, MI 49686
(616) 938-3474

RAM-Z Outfitters
M-37, Caledonia Plaza
Caledonia, MI 49316
(616) 891-9858

Streamside Orvis
4400 Grand Traverse Village
Williamsburg, MI 49690
(616) 938-5337

Johnson's Pere Marquette
  Lodge
Route 1, Box 1290
Baldwin, MI 49304
(616) 745-3972

Thornapple Orvis Shop
Thornapple Village
PO Box 133
Ada, MI 49301
(616) 676-0177

The Fly Factory
PO Box 709
Grayling, MI 49738
(616) 348-5844

Great Lakes Fly Fishing Co.
2775 10 Mile Road
Rockford, MI 49341
(800) 303-0567

Nordic Sports
218 West Bay Street
East Tawas, MI 48730
(517) 362-2001

Hexagon Rod & Fly Shop
2973 Midland Road
Bay City, MI 48706
(517) 686-6212

The Fly Shop at Frank's
MI 13
Linwood, MI 48634
(517) 697-5341

M. Chance Fly Fishing
  Specialties
5100 Marsh Road
Okemos, MI 48864
(517) 349-6696

Paint Creek Outfitters
203 East University
Rochester, MI 48307
(801) 650-0440

Riverbend Sport Shop
29229 Northwestern Highway
Southfield, MI 48034
(313) 350-8484

MacGregor's Outdoors
803 North Main Street
Ann Arbor, MI 48104
(313) 761-9200
(Southeast MI area)

The Woolly Bugger
32715 Grand River
Farmington, MI 48336
(313) 477-8116

Geake & Son, Inc.
23510 Woodward Avenue
Ferndale, MI 48220
(313) 542-0498

Lindquist's Outdoor Sports
131 West Washington
Marquette, MI 49855
(906) 228-6380

Little Forks Outfitters
143 East Main Street
Midland, MI 48640
(517) 832-4100

MINNESOTA

Rodcraft
6451 Lyndale Avenue South
Richfield, MN 55423
(612) 869-7151
(Twin Cities area)

Burger Brothers
98th Street and Lyndale
Bloomington, MN 55401
(612) 884-8842

The Fly Angler
7500 University Avenue
  Northeast
Minneapolis, MN 55432
(612) 572-0717

The Outdoor Company
600 East Superior Street
Duluth, MN 55802
(218) 722-8450

NEW YORK

Whitaker's Sport Store
7700 Rome Road
Pulaski, NY 13142
(315) 298-6162

Two Dogs Outfitters
PO Box 895
Oswego, NY 13126
(315) 564-6366

The Troutfitter
2735 Erie Boulevard East
Syracuse, NY 13224
(315) 446-2047

Carl Coleman's Fly Shop
4786 Ridge Road West
Spencerport, NY 14559
(716) 352-4775
(Rochester area)

Oak Orchard Fly Shop
1584 Oak Orchard Road
(Route 98)
Albion, NY 14411
(716) 682-4546
(Rochester area)

Reed's Fly Shop
5655 Main Street
Williamsville, NY 14221
(716) 631-5131 (Buffalo area)

The Urban Angler
118 East 25th Street
New York, NY 10010
(212) 979-7600

OHIO

Angler's Mail
6497 Pearl Road
Parma Heights, OH 44130
(216) 884-7476
(Cleveland area)

Dame Juliana
1261 Grandview
Columbus, OH 43212
(614) 488-4844

Woolly Bugger
4550 Kerry Road
Columbus, OH 43220
(614) 459-1333

ONTARIO

Lambef Rod & Tackle
55 Main Street East
Lambef, Ontario NOL 1S0
(519) 652-5598 (London area)

Natural Sports
1572 Victoria Street North
Kitchener, Ontario N2B 3ES
(519) 749-1620

Grand River Troutfitters
790 Tower Street South
Fergus, Ontario NIM 2R3
(519) 787-4359 (Kitchener area)

Angling Specialties
2104 Highway 7
Unit 15
Concord, Ontario L4K 2S9
(416) 660-9707 (Toronto area)

J & S Tackle
137 Goodrich Street
Port Elgin, Ontario N0H 2C1
(519) 832-2827
(Lake Huron area)

Outdoor Store
16 Bruce Street North
Unit 3
Thornbury, Ontario NOH 2PO
(519) 599-6344
(Georgian Bay area)

Watson's Tackle
125 B 14th Street West
Owen Sound, Ontario N4K
  3X6

(519) 371-0090
(Georgian Bay area)

River's Edge Fly Shop
RR # 13, Site 13, Box 13
Thunder Bay, Ontario P7B 5E4
(807) 983-2484

D & R Sport
485 Memorial Avenue
Thunder Bay, Ontario P7B 346
(807) 345-3323

PENNSYLVANIA

The Outdoor Store
Main Street
Volant, PA 16156
(412) 533-3212
(Northwestern PA)

South Hills Rod & Reel
3227 West Liberty Avenue
Pittsburgh, PA 15216
(412) 344-8888

International Anglers
503 Freeport Road
Pittsburgh, PA 15215
(800) 782-4222

Fishing Creek Outfitters
Fairmont Springs
Benton, PA 17814
(800) 548-0093
(Williamsport area)

Tulpehocken Creek Outfitters
2229 Penn Avenue
West Lawn, PA 19609
(610) 678-1899 (Reading area)

AA Pro Shop
Hickory Run Road
RD #1
Whitehaven, PA 18661
(800) 443-8119
(Wilkes-Barre area)

Anglers Pro Shop
2204 Old Bethlehem Pike
Souderton, PA 18964
(215) 721-4909
(Philadelphia area)

Cold Spring Anglers
419 East High Street
Carlisle, PA 17013
(717) 245-2646
(Harrisburg area)

WISCONSIN

The Fly Shop at Bob's
    Bait & Tackle
1504 Velp Avenue
Green Bay, WI 54303
(414) 499-4737

Brule River Classics
6008 South State Road 27
Brule, WI 54820
(715) 372-8153

Fly Fishing Chalet
2491 Highway 92
PO Box 14
Mt. Horeb, WI 53572
(608) 437-5465
(West Central Wisconsin)

The Fly Fishers
8601 West Greenfield

West Allis, WI 53214
(414) 259-8100
(Milwaukee area)

FEATURED GUIDES

Bob Blumreich
1221 Clark
Janesville, WI 53545
(608) 756-2184

John Dembeck
PO Box 895
Oswego, NY 13126
(315) 564-6366

Eric DiCarlo
Box 1620
Wawa, Ontario POS 1K0
(705) 856-2802

Dan Donarski
1116 East Portage Avenue
Sault Ste. Marie, MI 49783
(906) 632-7443

Jac Ford
2030 South Thomas Road
Saginaw, MI 48609
(517) 781-0997

Bud Hoffman
RR 4
Markdale, Ontario N0C 1H0
(519) 986-2351

John Hunter
1193 Plains Road
Leslie, MI 49251
(517) 589-9401

John Kluesing
RR 2, Box 2545
Baldwin, MI 49304
(616) 745-3792

Rick Kustich
895 Legion Drive
Grand Island, NY 14072
(716) 773-2543

Jerry Pytlik
2973 Midland Road
Bay City, MI 48706
(517) 686-6212

John Ramsay
N15414 Black River Road
Ironwood, MI 49938
(906) 932-4038

Ray Schmidt
PO Box 211
918 Seaman Road

Wellston, MI 49689
(616) 848-4191

John Skrobot
712 Harbor Street
Oscoda, MI 48750
(517) 739-4982

Scott Smith
150 Egan Place
Thunder Bay, Ontario P7A 2Y1
(807) 344-8279

Mike Yarnot
3722 South 17th Street
Milwaukee, WI 53221
(414) 672-0043

Karl Vogel
RR #2
Goulais River, Ontario P0S 1E0
(705) 649-3313

Index

Also from The Countryman Press and Backcountry Publications

The Countryman Press and Backcountry Publications, long known for their fine books on the outdoors, offer a range of practical and readable manuals on fish and fishing.

Bass Flies, Dick Stewart, $12.95
Building Classic Salmon Flies, Ron Alcott, $35.00 (hardcover)
Fishing Small Streams with a Fly Rod, Charles Meck, $15.00
Fishing Vermont's Streams and Lakes, Peter F. Cammann, $13.00
Flies in the Water, Fish in the Air, Jim Arnosky, $10.00
Fly-Fishing with Children: A Guide for Parents, Philip Brunquell, $19.00 (hardcover), $13.00 (paper)
Fly-Tying Tips, Second Edition (revised), Dick Stewart, $11.95
Good Fishing in the Adirondacks, Edited by Dennis Aprill, Updated Edition, $15.00
Good Fishing in the Catskills, Jim Capossela, with others, Second Edition (revised), $15.00
Good Fishing in Lake Ontario and Its Tributaries, Rich Giessuebel, Second Edition (revised), $15.00
Good Fishing in Western New York, Edited by C. Scott Sampson, $15.00
Ice Fishing: A Complete Guide...Basic to Advanced, Jim Capossela, $15.00
Michigan Trout Streams: A Fly-Angler's Guide, Bob Linsenman and Steve Nevala, $17.00
Pennsylvania Trout Streams and Their Hatches, Second Edition (revised and expanded), Charles Meck, $18.00
Trout Streams of Southern Appalachia: Fly-Casting in Georgia, Kentucky, North Carolina, South Carolina and Tennessee, Jimmy Jacobs, $17.00
Ultralight Spin-Fishing: A Practical Guide for Freshwater and Saltwater Anglers, Peter F. Cammann, $12.00
Universal Fly Tying Guide, Second Edition (revised) Dick Stewart, $12.95
Virginia Trout Streams, Harry Slone, $15.00
Wisconsin and Minnesota Trout Streams: A Fly-Angler's Guide, Jim Humphrey & Bill Shogren, $17.00

We publish many guides to canoeing, hiking, walking, bicycling, and ski touring in New England, the Mid-Atlantic states, and the Midwest. Our books are available through bookstores, or they may be ordered directly from the publisher. Please add $5.00 shipping and handling per order. VT residents please add 5% sales tax. VISA/Mastercard accepted. To order, or for a complete catalog, please contact: The Countryman Press, PO Box 175AP, Woodstock, VT 05091-0175 • 800/245-4151.